Serve and Learn

Implementing and Evaluating Service-Learning in Middle and High Schools

Serve and Learn

Implementing and Evaluating Service-Learning in Middle and High Schools

Florence Fay Pritchard
Salisbury University

George I. Whitehead, III
Salisbury University

LAWRENCE ERLBAUM ASSOCIATES, PUBLISHERS
2004   Mahwah, New Jersey   London

Senior Acquisitions Editor:	Naomi Silverman
Assistant Editor:	Erica Kica
Cover Design:	Kathryn Houghtaling Lacey
Textbook Production Manager:	Paul Smolenski
Text and Cover Printer:	Sheridan Books, Inc.

Camera ready copy for this book was provided by the authors.

Copyright © 2004 by Lawrence Erlbaum Associates, Inc.

All rights reserved. No part of this book may be reproduced in any form, by photostat, microform, retrieval system, or any other means, without prior written permission of the publisher.

Lawrence Erlbaum Associates, Inc., Publishers
10 Industrial Avenue
Mahwah, New Jersey 07430

Library of Congress Cataloging-in-Publication Data

Pritchard, Florence Fay, 1936–
   Serve and learn : implementing and evaluating service-learning in middle and high schools / Florence F. Pritchard, George I. Whitehead.
      p. cm.
Includes bibliographical references and index.
ISBN 0-8058-4420-1 (casebound : alk. paper)
ISBN 0-8058-4421-X (pbk. : alk. paper)
1. Student service—United States. 2. Education, Secondary—United States—Curricula. I. Whitehead, George I. II. Title.
LC220.5.P75   2004
361.3'7—dc22   2003049522
                                                                                                             CIP

Books published by Lawrence Erlbaum Associates are printed on acid-free paper, and their bindings are chosen for strength and durability.

Printed in the United States of America
10 9 8 7 6 5 4 3 2 1

Contents

Preface   xi

Section One: Foundations for Service-Learning

Chapter I: A Collaborative Model for Service-Learning   1
   Service as a Fundamental Human Value   1
   Service as an Element in Education   2
   Defining Service-Learning   2
   Why Use Service-Learning?   4
      Service-Learning Can Enhance Intellectual Development   5
      Service-Learning Can Increase Academic Achievement   7
      Service-LearningCan Strengthen Citizenship Education   8
      Service-Learning Can Accelerate School Reform   9
   A Model for Using Service-Learning   10
      Experiential Learning   10
      Social-Process Learning   11
      The Collaborative Service-Learning Model   12
   Using the Collaborative Service-Learning Model   13
   In Conclusion   14
   Activities for Increasing Understanding   14

Chapter II: Designs for Service-Learning Projects
In Middle and High Schools   17
   Chapter Focus   18
   Designs Emerging from Contemporary Practice   18
      Service-Learning as an In-Class Approach   18
      Service-Learning as a One-Day Event   21
      Service-Learning as Prototype Project   23
      Service Learning as a Recurring Curriculum Component   25
      Service-Learning as a Cross-Disciplinary Program   28
   Selecting a Service-Learning Project Design   30
      Teachers' Experience Levels   30
      Students' Service-Learning Competencies   31
      Available Resources   31
      Match Between Service Needed and Students' Curriculum   32
      Time Needed for Planning and Implementing Designs   33
   Putting it All Together   34
   In Conclusion   36
   Activities for Increasing Understanding   36

Chapter III: Preparing to Use Service-Learning   37
   Chapter Focus   38
   Service-Learning Readiness Factors   38
     Instructional Management Skills   38
     Students' Service-Learning Competencies   46
     Integrating Student Service-Learning Competency Profiles   50
   Service-Learning Support Networks   51
   Putting it All Together   53
   In Conclusion   54
   Activities for Increasing Understanding   55

Section Two: Designing Service-Learning Projects Using The Collaborative Service-Learning Model

Chapter IV: Committing to a Service-Learning Project   57
   Chapter Focus   58
   Community Needs and Issues   58
     Gathering Needs and Issues Information
     in High Resource Situations   59
     Gathering Needs and Issues Information
     in Moderate Resource Situations   60
     Gathering Needs and Issues Information
     in Low Resource Situations   61
   Connecting Students' Academic Goals to Service   61
   Students' Capacities and Interests   64
     Direct Service   65
     Indirect Service   65
     Advocacy   66
   Putting It All Together in a Service-Learning Project Commitment   67
     An Example of Collaborative Commitment
        to a Service-Learning Project   68
   In Conclusion   70
   Activities for Increasing Understanding   70

Chapter V: Setting Goals in a Student Outcomes Plan   71
   Chapter Focus   72
   Assembling Key Players   72
     Clients to be Served   72
     Parents   73
     School Administrators   73
     Community Members   73
   The Initial Meeting: Focusing on Outcomes   75
     Task One: Identifying Student Outcome Expectations   76
     Task Two: Specifying Indicators of Outcome Expectations   78

Task Three: Selecting Strategies to Measure Indicators   82
Task Four: Assigning Responsibilities   84
Accomplishing Outcomes Planning at the Initial Meeting   88
Student Outcomes Planning and Service-Learning Support Networks   89
   Example One: Awareness Support Network   89
   Example Two: Planning Support Network   91
   Example Three: Resources Support Network   92
   Looking Forward to Measurement Strategy Selection and Design   94
Measuring Indicators of Other Constituents' Outcomes   94
   Example One: One-Day Event Plan   94
   Example Two: Prototype Plan   95
   Example Three: Cross-Disciplinary Project Plan   95
In Conclusion   96
Activities for Increasing Understanding   96

Chapter VI: Linking Service and Learning
With Reflective Learning Experiences   97
   Chapter Focus   98
   Using Student Outcomes Plans to State Goals and Objectives   98
   Reflective Learning Experiences   99
      Learning Activities That Focus Students on Relevant Experience   100
      Learning Activities that Engage Students in Reflection   107
      Learning Activities that Help Students Construct New Concepts   110
   Sharing Instructional Responsibilities   114
      Two Ways to Share Instructional Reponsibilities   115
   In Conclusion   117
   Activities for Increasing Understanding   117

Chapter VII: Evaluating Projects and Celebrating Growth   119
   Chapter Focus   120
   Developing Service-Learning Evaluation Plans   120
      The Student Outcomes Component of an Evaluation Plan   121
      The Project Impact Component of an Evaluation Plan   123
      The Project Team Self-Evaluation
      Component in an Evaluation Plan   124
      An Example of an Evaluation Plan   125
   Implementing Service-Learning Evaluation Plans   129
   Analyzing and Interpreting Evaluation Information
      With Inductive Thinking   129
      Using Inductive Thinking With Partners   130
      Expressing Results of Inductive Thinking as Value Judgments   130
   Celebrating New Learnings and Perspectives   133
      Example One: Culminating Activity   134
      Example Two: Strategy   134

Developing and Implementing Culminating Activities   135
Developing and Implementing Dissemination Strategies   136
In Conclusion   140
Activities for Increasing Understanding   140

Section Three: Resources for Service-Learning Projects

Chapter VIII: Strategies for Encouraging Commitment to Projects   141
   Chapter Focus   142
   Analyzing a Community of Interest   142
      Mapping   143
      Working With Fact Sheets   143
      Exploring Communities' Needs Services   144
   Gathering Needs and Issues Information   145
      Finding Service-Learning Success Stories   146
      Contacting Umbrella Agencies   148
      Formal Needs Assessment   149
   Motivating Potential Community Partners   151
      Class Introductions   151
      Resource Group Descriptions   153
      Class Directories   153
   Selecting Strategies for Use   154
   In Conclusion   154
   Activities for Increasing Understanding   156

Chapter IX: Strategies for Measuring Student Outcomes   157
   Chapter Focus   158
   A Framework for Student Outcomes Measurement   158
   Criterion-Referenced Strategies for Measuring Academic and
      Problem-Solving Outcome Indicators   159
      State Standards Tests   159
      Teacher-Developed Criterion-Referenced Tests   161
      Collection and Use of Criterion-Referenced, Contructed-Response
         Test Data   169
   Observational Strategies for Measuring Service Outcome Indicators   170
      Rating Scales   171
      Anecdotal Observation   173
   Self-Report Strategies for Measuring Personal Growth Indicators   174
      Surveys   175
      Interviews   179
      Focus Groups   182
      Experience Analysis   186
   In Conclusion   189
   Activities for Increasing Understanding   190

Chapter X: Strategies for Designing Reflective Learning Experiences   191
   Chapter Focus   192
   Stating Instructional Goals and Objectives   192
   Selecting Activities for Reflective Learning Experiences   193
      Focusing Activities   194
      Reflection Activities   203
      Conceptualizing Activities   207
   Using Journals to Integrate Reflective Learning   212
   Sharing Responsibility for Reflection and Conceptualizing Activities   212
   In Conclusion   213
   Activities for Increasing Understanding   213

Chapter XI: Strategies for Evaluating Projects
   and Celebrating Growth   215
   Chapter Focus   216
   Team Members' Responsibilities for Evaluation Planning   216
      Identifying Instruments Used to Collect Evaluation Information   219
      Collecting Feedback About Project Impact   219
      Collecting Project Team Self-Evaluation Information   221
      Developing Guides for Instrument Use   222
   Using Inductive Thinking as an Analytical and Interpretive Tool   227
      The Nature and Use of Inductive Thinking Steps   229
      Practicing Inductive Thinking   230
      Stating Generalizations   231
      Using Generalizations to Judge Project Worth   232
   Celebrating Service-Learning   233
      Two Dimensions of Celebration   233
   In Conclusion   241
   Activities for Increasing Understanding   241

Chapter XII: Additional Resources for Service-Learning   243
   Chapter Focus   244
   Additional Human Resources   244
      Same-Subject-Area Teachers   245
      Other Subject-Area Teachers   245
      Teachers with Service-Learning Experience   246
      School Administrators   246
      School Workers   247
      Parents   247
      School and School System Resource Staff   248
      Higher Education Faculty   249
      Community Contacts   249
   Internet Resources for Service-Learning   250

Conflict Resolution Resources for Service-Learning 252
   Scanning for Conflict 253
   Using Problem Solving to Resolve Conflicts 256
   Involving a Conflict-Resolution Mediator 258
In Conclusion 259
A Final Word 260
Activities for Increasing Understanding 260

References 263

Author Index 269

Subject Index 271

Preface

Several years ago, we had the opportunity to teach a course in the foundations and use of service-learning for teachers in grades K-12. As we prepared for the class, we found many articles and books on aspects of service-learning, but no one book that brought the wealth of emerging knowledge about this method together into a text for teachers—one that grounds the method in learning theory and suggests guidelines for its use in today's classrooms and communities. Our intent was to fill that void.

As we worked on the book over the last several years, we began to realize that the potential of service-learning is even greater than we had at first understood. And as our understanding deepened, our single global purpose became three specific purposes. The first of these is to provide a framework grounded in theory and best professional practice that middle- and high-school teachers, their students and community partners can use to design, implement and evaluate service-learning projects that address authentic community needs. The second purpose is to demonstrate ways collaborative service-learning can enhance students' intellectual development, promote their academic achievement, strengthen their citizenship skills and accelerate the kinds of educational accountability and reform initiatives emphasized in the national educational standards movement, and the 2002 No Child Left Behind Act. The third purpose is to suggest ways schools and their community partners can channel the energy for service released in the United States by the September 11, 2001 World Trade Center catastrophe into activities, projects and programs that help transform the lives of students and those they work with and contribute to the development of strong, diverse communities.

We believe that many individuals and groups will find the book useful. Among these are teachers and students who want to learn about the potential of service-learning and try it with community partners in simple exploratory ways, as well as teams of teachers, students and community partners already committed to service-learning projects. We expect the book to be useful to teacher educators who are introducing service-learning to pre-professional students and education interns and who are guiding graduate students in in-depth study of service-learning. Instructional supervisors and other school administrators who wish to create a climate for service-learning in their schools and communities or to enrich service-learning initiatives already underway should also find the book helpful. Finally, we believe there is much here for community agencies interested in collaborating with the schools on service-learning initiatives, and for school-community service-learning advisory groups and councils that seek to extend and strengthen their service-learning activities and networks.

Overview

The book is organized in three sections that present service-learning along a theoretical to practical continuum. Section One lays foundations for the method by proposing in its first chapter a collaborative model for service-learning. In this model, reflection integrates commitment to shared purposes, planning, team work, consultation and culminating activity in ways that transform academic study and service experience into learning. Chapter II proposes five designs for service-learning projects that are based in current professional practice and make it possible for teachers, students and partners with varying levels of experience and resources to develop service-learning projects appropriate for their situations. Chapter III describes teacher leadership skills, student competencies and resource support networks that influence the implementation of collaborative service-learning projects.

Section Two explicates the collaborative service-learning model and explains in Chapters IV through VII the four sets of processes that teams use to commit to a project, cooperatively determine students' project outcomes and ways to measure them, develop learning activities to help students achieve outcomes, then evaluate their projects and celebrate growth.

Section Three provides resources for carrying out the collaborative model. The first four chapters here parallel the four chapters of the second section by providing specific strategies teachers and their students can use with each phase in the model. Chapter VIII suggests ways teachers and students can identify community partners and enter into service-learning project commitments with them as a team. Chapter IX explains how teams can develop instruments for measuring agreed-upon student outcomes, and Chapter X explains how teams design reflective-learning experiences that help students conceptually link their classroom study and service. Chapter XI proposes a service-learning project evaluation model, demonstrates it use and offers strategies service-learning project teams can use to celebrate project outcomes. The final chapter in the book identifies an array of additional resources available to service-learning teams and offers strategies for resolving conflicts that may arise as teams work together.

As this book has evolved, we have worked to give it what we believe are five distinctive features. *Serve and Learn*

- provides what may be, as of this writing, the only comprehensive guide to implementing, evaluating and celebrating service-learning in today's middle- and high schools;
- emphasizes and explicates a collaborative approach to service-learning in which teachers, students and community partners team together to advance learning and meet genuine community needs;

- demonstrates how service-learning teams use key elements of standards-based education, multiple intelligences theory and cooperative learning to guide project development, implementation, evaluation and celebration;
- offers optional designs for service-learning projects that are suitable for use by interns and beginning teachers as well as by experienced and master teachers, and that can be used in a developmental sequence by school and community partners to build from small, individual projects toward school, system- and community-wide projects;
- includes end-of-chapter activities that help those who use the book as a text practice the model and its strategies and create their own service-learning projects.

The evolution of *Serve and Learn* has convinced us that collaborative service-learning can contribute to the advance of education and community building in two ways: first, we believe that this approach can help revitalize the connections between the schools and society; and second, we believe that collaborative service-learning has the power to transform the perspectives and the values and attitudes of all who join it—teachers, students, parents, community partners, school personnel and community members.

Just as we have collaborated in the writing of this book, so too have we collaborated with many in bringing it to birth, and we wish to thank and acknowledge them. Our editor, Naomi Silverman, has shown consistent and unwavering confidence in our abilities to write the book and inspired us to give it our best. Our reviewers, Jeffrey Anderson of Seattle University and Shelly H. Billig of the RMC Research Corporation have examined and re-examined our drafts with care, then made us listen to theory, best practice and good sense, and thereby helped us reach out to all within our intended audience. Paul Smolenski and Erica Kica have guided us with calm and good cheer through the maze of production and kept the light at the end of the tunnel burning. And we deeply thank our spouses, Douglas and Barbara, who have read and questioned, critiqued and suggested, and above all, stood with us every step of the way.

—Florence Pritchard
—George Whitehead

Chapter I: A Collaborative Model for Service-Learning

> "Every function in the child's cultural development appears twice: first, on the social level, and later, on the individual level; first, between people (interpsychological) and then inside the child (intrapsychological). This applies equally to voluntary attention, to logical memory, and to the formation of concepts. All the higher functions originate as actual relationships between individuals."
>
> ~ Lev Vygotsky

Service as a Fundamental Human Value

Human beings provide service in nearly every culture in every corner of the earth. One would be hard pressed to find a group of people who do not commit at some time and in some way to assisting one another. Why is this so? Why does a helping ethic persist in both the best and worst of human living situations? It is likely that our motivations to serve were born in the initial, parent-child experiences of our species. We can speculate that as the first human parents struggled to ensure the survival of their offspring they laid down the template for service. As parents and children came to feel affection and loyalty to one another, loving and caring became an essential feature of their shared situation.

Service is fundamental to our own United States culture. All around us we see that service ranging from direct care-giving through developmental nurture to civic participation and social problem-solving is an integral part of the social fabric. Service functions as a structuring element in religion, imbues the goals and activities of health, education and social welfare agencies, provides the dynamic for cultural and environmental preservation, and motivates individuals to engage in political leadership. We speak of people who work in these service fields as members of the "helping professions," and hold to the belief that although they are paid for their work, they do not work for pay, but rather seek to help their fellow human beings toward self-actualization.

Service as an Element in Education

In light of the importance of service to our society, it is not surprising that schools—universities and colleges, elementary, middle and high schools—increasingly include student service in their programs. Many of these institutions encourage students to perform service in their communities, and some are taking the concept of service to a new level. They are exploring a creative new perspective on service that is uniquely consistent with their educative missions, an approach that has come to be known as service-learning.

Defining Service-Learning

The essential features of contemporary service-learning first appear in the 1993 National and Community Service Trust Act. That act characterizes service-learning as an educational experience

- under which students learn and develop through active participation in thoughtfully organized service experiences that meet actual community needs and that are coordinated in collaboration with school and community;
- that is integrated into the students' academic curriculum or provides structured time for the students to think, talk, or write about what they did and saw during the actual service activity;
- that provides students with opportunities to use newly acquired skills and knowledge in real-life situations in their own communities; and
- that enhances what is taught in school by extending students' learning beyond the classroom and into the community and helps to foster the development of a sense of caring for others.

(Schine, 1997, p. 188)

The Compact for Learning and Citizenship (CLC; 2001), a project of the Education Commission of the States, amplifies the Trust Act definition of service-learning by discriminating it from community service.

> Service-learning ... has documented benefits that extend well beyond what is normally termed "community service." It combines service to the community with in-depth student learning in a way that can benefit students, schools and community members.

> An effective service-learning project is carefully planned by educators and meets an authentic need in the community. In addition, there are continuous links between classroom instruction and the actual service as it progresses. The service project involves activities that students themselves help plan in collaboration with school and community members. In addition, students have decision making and problem-solving capabilities within the project to foster a sense of ownership. A crucial component of the learning process is structured time to allow students to reflect upon their service experiences. The primary difference between community service and service-learning, then, is the latter's ongoing connection to the curriculum and the education setting itself. (p. 6)

Taken together, these two definitions identify four fundamentals of service-learning:

- Students provide service to meet authentic needs.
- Service links through deliberate planning to the subject matter students are studying and the skills and knowledge they are developing in school.
- Students reflect on the service they provide.
- Service-learning is coordinated in collaboration with the community.

Additionally, the two definitions make clear that service-learning involves both social and psychological elements. It is a teaching and learning method that can aid students' growth as community members and contributors, and as individuals. The Trust Act definition speaks of service-learning as a method that "helps foster the development of a sense of caring for others," and the CLC definition makes clear that within service-learning, students have opportunities to exercise decision-making and problem-solving skills. Finally, the two definitions reveal an evolution of expectations for student involvement in service-learning. The Trust Act definition speaks of their "active participation," and their use of school skills in the community. The CLC definition calls for student involvement in collaboratively planning service activities and developing a sense of project ownership.

In 2002, the National Commission on Service-Learning chaired by Senator John Glenn published *Learning In Deed: The Power of Service-Learning for American Schools*. The executive summary of this report explains what the Commission means by service-learning. First, the summary discriminates service-learning from volunteerism and various forms of community service. (Implementing Quality Service Learning Section, para. 2).

School-based service-learning is not . . .

- a volunteer or community service program with no ties to academics.
- an add-on to the existing curriculum.

- logging a certain number of service hours in order to graduate.
- one-sided—benefiting either the students or the community.
- compensatory service assigned as a form of punishment by the courts or school administrators.
- only for high school and college students.

Next, the summary defines service-learning as "a teaching learning approach that integrates community service with academic studies to enrich learning, teach civic responsibility and strengthen communities" (The Promise of Service-Learning, para. 8). The summary then operationalizes this definition by emphasizing that "service-learning is effective only when students address real unmet needs or issues in a community and when young people are actively involved in decision-making at all levels of the process" (Implementing Quality Service-Learning, para. 2). These National Commission attributes of service-learning can be integrated in the following comprehensive definition:

Service-learning is a teaching and learning approach that integrates community service with academic studies to enrich learning, teach civic responsibility and strengthen communities. It engages students in addressing real unmet needs or issues in a community and actively involves them in decision-making at all levels of the process.

This comprehensive definition includes the core concepts in the Trust Act and CLC definitions of service-learning as well as the central thrust of the many definitions used across the country today. It also provides the foundation for this book's proposals for the use of service-learning by middle- and high-school teachers, their students and community partners.

Why Use Service-Learning?

Among the many benefits that service-learning practitioners across the country identify, four in particular help demonstrate the method's value. The first is its power to enhance students' cognitive development—their intellectual capacities. Learning theory makes clear that the kinds of experience-based activities in which students engage when they use service-learning can stimulate the development of their capacities for thought. A second benefit is service-learning's potential to increase student's academic achievement. Research suggests that students who learn as they serve may be more motivated to learn and may perform better in their academic subjects. A third benefit of service-learning is its potential for strengthening students' citizenship education, their sense of community responsibility and their abilities to participate as citizens. Service-learning's imperative that students and community partners work together to address real issues *is* education for democracy, and research again suggests that it helps students understand and enact civic values. A fourth benefit of service-learning is its potential for accelerating school reform. Service-learning can transform the processes of schooling so that students build knowledge, skill and understanding through active problem-solving rather than through passive information consumption and imitative learning. A more detailed look at these four benefits of service-learning helps build the case for its use.

Service-Learning Can Enhance Intellectual Development

Service-learning has the potential to increase students' capacities for thought because it is a form of constructivist learning. Students who engage in collaborative problem-solving have opportunities to construct understanding from their experiences, and according to lead theorists of intellectual development Jean Piaget (1896-1980), Lev Vygotsky (1896-1934), and Jerome Bruner (1915-), this process of constructing understanding results in the elaboration and strengthening of the mental structures that make thought possible.

Piaget's theory of intellectual development (1936, 1955, 1975) asserts that children's interaction with the world activates their nascent intelligence and persistently transforms that intelligence into higher-order, abstract thinking. Essentially, children's experience stimulates their minds to construct increasingly complex, mental structures that organize their perceptions. These structures become tools that make it possible for children to take in, interpret and understand more experience and by abstractly relating the resulting structures to one another, to create new ideas that are independent of experience.

Piaget suggests that infants organize their perceptions of objects using an innate, non-verbal form of thought to compare things and their features and to organize their conclusions in non-verbal cognitive structures. While children are doing this work, adults provide them with word labels for what they see, touch and do. Soon, children imitate these words, attach them to their experiences and to relevant cognitive structures in their own minds. They then use these words to express—first to themselves and ultimately to others—the relationships within and between their mental structures. In this way language makes expressive thought possible. Once children can use language to abstractly express their understandings of the world, they have full intellectual capacity; they can reason hypothetically, test their hypotheses and further develop cognitive structures.

Russian psychologist Lev Vygotsky (1987b) critiques Piaget's theory of intellectual development and concludes that rather than being a process of increasing abstraction, intellectual development relies on continual, mentor-guided analysis of experience. Language is essential here, as well, but in a way different from that proposed by Piaget. In Vygotsky's view, children meet their initial physical needs by using oral, social speech which they learn from their caregivers. Gradually children internalize social speech to "inner speech" which they use to think. Once they have synthesized language and thought, they can guide themselves through their environment in child-like and pre-logical ways. To develop and use mature, rational thought, however, they must be led by mentoring adults in solving problems.

Vygotsky observed that with collaboration, direction, or some kind of help, children are always able to do more and solve more difficult tasks than they can on their own. He proposes that this is because each child has a "zone of proximal development" (ZPD) that consists of the gap between what the child is presently capable of doing and what the child is ultimately capable of doing. For Vygotsky the existence of the ZPD signifies that intellectual development does not unfold automatically in response to the child's interaction with things in the world. Rather, it unfolds as a result of social interaction. When children can use speech to talk with adults such as teachers about the world and how it works, they mentally stretch to new knowledge and understanding. Thus, dialogic interaction develops children's maturing functions and thereby stimulates their intellectual growth. "This," says Vygotsky, "is the significance of instruction for development." Moreover, "development based on collaboration and imitation is the source of all the specifically human characteristics of consciousness that develop in the child" (p. 210).

Bruner (1962) accepts Vygotsky's and Piaget's premises that experience and mentoring social interaction stimulate the growth of cognitive structures, and adds that it is discovery learning that brings these elements together to maximize intellectual growth. Children, he asserts, are intrinsically motivated to construct meaning from their experiences (to grow intellectually) because they gain pleasure from satisfying their curiosity, developing competence and working reciprocally with others to solve problems. Educators who use discovery-learning situations powerfully elicit these intrinsic motivations and thereby stimulate children's intellectual development.

> Emphasis on discovery in learning has precisely the effect on the learner of leading him to be a constructionist, to organize what he is encountering in a manner not only designed to discover regularity and relatedness, but also to avoid the kind of information drift that fails to keep account of the uses to which information might have to be put. Emphasis on discovery, indeed, helps the child to learn the varieties of problem solving, of transforming information for better use, helps him to learn how to go about the very task of learning. (p. 87)

Further, Bruner (1966) asserts, as children grow intellectually, their progress is characterized by "benchmarks" such as the following:

- increasing independence of response from the immediate nature of the stimulus.
- increasing capacity to say to oneself and others, by means of words or symbols, what one has done or what one will do.
- increasing capacities to deal with several alternatives simultaneously, to tend to several sequences during the same period

of time and to allocate time and attention in a manner appropriate to these multiple demands. (pp. 5-6)

The connections between these propositions from constructivist learning theory and service-learning are readily apparent. Service-learning engages students in interacting with the world and thus helps them build new cognitive structures in accord with Piaget's general view of intellectual development. It involves students in collaborative work with teachers, peers and community members, and thus engages them in the dialogic social interaction identified by Vygotsky as crucial to intellectual maturation. Finally, in Bruner's terms, service-learning elicits students' intrinsic motivation as it enlivens their curiosity about what service to provide and how to provide it, their desire for competence as they plan for and provide service, and their sense of reciprocity as they work throughout with community partners and each other.

Service-Learning Can Increase Academic Achievement

In "The Impacts of Service-Learning on Youth, Schools and Communities: Research on K-12 School-Based Service-Learning, 1990-1999," Billig (1999, 2000a) analyzes over 25 published studies of the use of service-learning that documented results and showed positive outcomes. As she points out, "The research in the field has not caught up with the certainty and passion that educators feel for service-learning. What is available, though, begins to build a case for the impacts that practitioners believe to be true." (1999, p. 1) Billig organizes findings of analyzed studies into areas of positive impact, two of which relate directly to the power of service-learning to strengthen academic achievement. In the areas of "The Impact on Student Academic Learning" and "The Impact on Schools," (2000, pp. 661-2) she finds the following:

- Service-learning helps students acquire academic skills and knowledge.
- Students who participate in service-learning are more engaged in their studies and more motivated to learn.
- Service-learning is associated with increased student attendance.
- Service-learning results in greater mutual respect of teachers and students.
- Service-learning improves the overall school climate.

Billig (2000b) conducted follow-up analysis of 16 additional studies of service-learning in middle and high schools during her term as director of the Kellogg Foundation's Learning In Deed website. This analysis provides increased evidence of service-learning's positive impact on middle- and high-school students' academic growth as evidenced by their improved grades in math, science and social studies and their grade point averages. (Melchoir & Bailis, 2002, Morgan, 1998, Santmire, Giraud & Grosskopf, 1999)

Billig's research suggests that teachers across the curriculum can engage students in service-learning with confidence that it has the potential to positively affect students' academic outcomes. This research also invites the speculation that positive trends may be related to service-learning's requisite link between service and the academic curriculum, and its earlier discussed potential for activating students' constructivist knowledge building and thereby their capacities to derive meaning from their academic studies.

Service-Learning Can Strengthen Citizenship Education

In "Citizenship and Service-Learning in K-12 Schools," the RMC Research Corporation (2002) proposes that service-learning is a promising method for use within a two–fold, contemporary vision of citizenship education. Service-learning can help students develop a sense of the common good and their responsibility to contribute to it, and service-learning can help students develop the knowledge, skills and dispositions they need to participate in democratic institutions (pp. 5-9). Billig's findings (2000a, pp. 660-1) support this promise.

- Service-learning has a positive effect on the personal development of public school youth.
- Students who participate in service-learning are less likely to engage in "risk" behaviors.
- Service-learning has a positive effect on students' interpersonal development and the ability to relate to culturally diverse groups.
- Service-learning helps to develop students' sense of civic and social responsibility and their citizenship skills.
- Service-learning provides opportunities for students to become active, positive contributors to society.

These findings suggest the possibility that when used over time, service-learning can encourage students to progress developmentally in their citizenship education. In this view, service-learning's potential for helping students become self-aware and self-respecting individuals can lead them to a genuine respect for others and increase their skills and abilities for relating to culturally diverse groups. As they internalize multiculturalism as an element in democracy, students are more likely to develop a rich conception of communities and to extend their sense of civic and social responsibility beyond their own primary groups to the larger society. This in turn can open their eyes to increased opportunities to contribute to the common good and to participate in the range of social institutions that make it possible.

From the perspective of best professional practice, service-learning is consistent with the definition of Democratic Learning, articulated by the League of Professional Schools (2003). This University of Georgia sponsored school-improvement network envisions schools as "communities that prepare students for a democratic society," (Vision for the Future, para. 1) and defines democratic learning in terms of five principles congruent with service-learning (Democratic Learning: Logic Model):

- Students and teachers working together to make students' learning a contribution to their community
- Students working actively with problems, ideas, materials, and people as they learn skills and content
- Students being assessed according to high degrees of academic objectives learned and contributions to a larger community
- Students demonstrating their learning in public settings and receiving public feedback
- Students having escalating degrees of choice, as individuals and as groups, within the parameters provided by the teacher

Taken together, these research findings and principles of democratic learning build a strong case for service-learning as a teaching-learning method that can help students develop personal and interpersonal values they need to contribute to the achievement of the common good. They also suggest that service-learning can help students practice and develop skills they will need to participate in democratic institutions, and begin while they are in school to play contributing roles in their communities.

Service-Learning Can Accelerate School Reform

Comprehensive School Reform (CSR) is a federal initiative included in the No Child Left Behind Act of 2002. This initiative offers incentives to schools to create and carry out reform programs that involve the school, parents and the community in designing and delivering teaching and learning approaches that are grounded in research and proven practice. Pearson's (2002) survey of 28 CSR school reform models that "represent the general field of school reform" finds that "significant common ground exists between service-learning advocates and education reformers" (p. 11). Key service-learning elements that school reformers found supportive of their efforts are summarized as follows.

- Teachers use a variety of learning materials.
- Students are provided opportunities to apply knowledge and skills to real-life situations and problems.
- Alternative assessments such as portfolios, presentations and rubrics are used.

- Time is provided for student reflection in journal entries and classroom dialogue.
- Instructional methods include project-based learning, interdisciplinary team teaching and experiential learning.
- Flexible time arrangements such as block-scheduling are used.
- Curriculum addresses specific local community needs.
- Students play a role in planning curricular activities.

On the basis of these and other findings, Pearson concludes that "Service-learning is a powerful tool for reaching both the academic and social objectives of education. It has the potential to reinvigorate the education reform movement by encouraging the creation of a caring community of students to improve the school's culture and positively impact our world." (p. 114).

From the perspectives, then, of students' own intellectual development, their academic achievement and development of dispositions, knowledge and skill essential for citizenship, and from the perspectives of the school and the community, service-learning has much to offer. As Billig (1999) states, "Educators are drawn to service-learning because they believe it produces important educational results for students, schools and communities" (p. 1).

A Model for Using Service-Learning

Awareness of the wide-ranging benefits that can flow from service-learning is a critical first step for those interested in its use. It is not enough, however, to make service-learning happen. Beginning teachers, experienced teachers and even master teachers who plan to use service-learning need a model process that can guide them toward achieving the benefits that service-learning promises. Such a model can be derived from the work of experiential-learning and social-process-learning theorists. The following discussion draws upon this work to propose a collaborative service-learning model.

Experiential Learning

Service-learning has long been viewed as a form of experiential learning, and its practitioners frequently use David Kolb's (1984) Experiential Learning Model as a conceptual framework for developing and implementing service-learning curricula. Kolb's model integrates Kurt Lewin's (1890-1947) action research process, Jean Piaget's (1896-1980) dynamics of assimilation and accommodation and John Dewey's (1859-1952) concepts of reflection and action to propose that when learners reflect upon and analyze real experience, they can form new concepts, test them and use them for future productive action. Kolb schematically visualizes his theory of experiential learning in the following manner.

Figure 1.1 Kolb's Experiential Learning Model

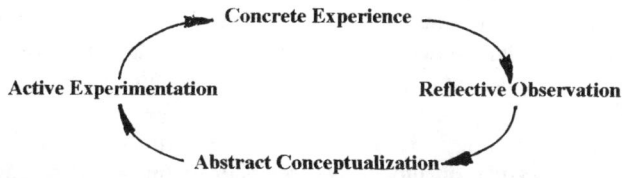

The experiential learning process that Kolb's model describes makes eminent good sense as well as being based on widely accepted theories of learning. Its core premise—that reflection transforms experience into new and usable understanding—also lies at the heart of service-learning. Clearly, service is experience, and when students reflect on service itself and on the relationships between service and their academic study, they gain new understanding, skills and values. The Kolb model however, does not explicitly address the central role of students' interaction among themselves and with mentoring others in the service-to-learning transformation. A contemporary model for service-learning needs elements that address the collaborative social processes essential to learning from experience in addition to the Kolb elements of experience itself, reflection, conceptualization and experimentation.

Social-Process Learning

Herbert Thelen's Group Investigation Model (1972), which centers on the social dimensions of learning from experience and calls for student collaborative problem-solving and decision-making, provides essential additional elements for a contemporary model of service-learning. Thelen's model is also based upon the work of Dewey and Lewin, but it builds upon these theorists' propositions about the social aspects of learning from experience as well as their propositions about the cognitive aspects of such learning. Thelen builds on Dewey's foundational idea that the process of learning "occurs in a social context in which students have cooperative interchanges with their fellow students and in a school whose structure and operation embodies the principles of democratic society. Students' interest in the subjects they study is stimulated by giving them a reasonable measure of responsibility for influencing and directing their work in school" (Sharan & Sharan, 1992, p. 2). To this Thelen adds Dewey's propositions that schools can encourage students' reflective thinking by confronting them with issues to resolve and engaging them in a disciplined search for answers.

Thelen integrated Dewey's ideas with propositions about the effects of working in groups developed by Kurt Lewin, widely recognized as the founder of social psychology. Lewin (1947a, 1947b) proposed that when people work in a group to accomplish a task, the way the group is organized and functions affects what members do and the overall group outcome. He believed work groups can markedly increase their effectiveness by analyzing their function, then democratically reshaping that function toward improved task completion. Thelen "forged the link" (Sharan & Sharan, p. 7) between Dewey's and Lewin's ideas. He proposed that students who work in groups to solve real problems learn academically, and they also learn democratic and scientific problem-solving skills.

In *Models of Teaching* (2000) Joyce and Weil with Calhoun characterize Thelen's Group Investigation model as a member of the social-processes family—a model grounded in cooperative learning and organized to build learning communities. Figure 1.2 shows Thelen's conception of the social processes in group investigation. In his approach, students work individually and collaboratively (cells 1-6) to identify, commit to, plan solutions for and solve a real, academically grounded problem. As they work, students integrate their own personal knowledge and the knowledge accessible to them from the resources and activities of schooling (rows 1 and 2) to move toward solving the original problem or issue they confront. In Thelen's view, teachers can sequence group investigation activities according to the cell numbers shown, but may also move from activity to activity in accord with the logic of their disciplines and students' learning and psychological needs and without attention to sequence.

Figure 1. 2 Thelen's Group Investigation Model

Social Organization ▶ Knowledge ▼	Individual Alone	Small group, psyche-group or team	Formal assembly (whole class)
Personal Knowledge	Cell 1 Confrontation, Involvement	Cell 2 Clarification of own thoughts and feelings	Cell 3 Commitment to shared purposes, plan investigations
Traditional Knowledge	Cell 4 Individual Investigations	Cell 5 Team work, team consultation	Cell 6 Consummatory activity, reflexive dialogue

(From *The Classroom Society* by Herbert A. Thelen, London: John Wiley & Sons: Copyright 1981. p. 147. Reprinted by permission. All rights reserved.)

The Collaborative Service-Learning Model

With its basis in social collaboration and cooperation, Thelen's model contributes key elements to a contemporary model for service-learning. Specifically, the group investigation elements of involvement, commitment to shared purposes, planning, teamwork, team consultation, reflexive dialogue and consummatory activity can be combined with Kolb's central dynamic of conceptualizing from reflecting on experience to generate such a model. The schematic in Figure 1.3 shows this integration as a Collaborative Service-Learning Model that addresses both the cognitive and social dimensions of service-learning and relies upon collaborative problem-solving and decision-making in each of its phases.

Figure 1.3 A Collaborative Service-Learning Model for Use in Middle Schools and High Schools

Figure 1.3 represents a four-phase, collaborative service-learning process that involves both students and their community partners. The process begins as these constituents link service needs to students' academic goals and their capacities to provide service in a service-learning commitment. Commitment leads to the formation of a school-community project team that cooperatively develops a service-learning outcomes plan. Next, the team designs learning experiences that guide student's class work and their service toward reflective understanding of their communities, their school work and themselves. The team then celebrates these new learnings and enriched perspectives by evaluating its project to identify and share ways in which participants have grown.[1]

Using the Collaborative Service-Learning Model

Teachers use the Collaborative-Service-learning Model to design and implement service-learning in the following way. A teacher, a group of students

---

[1] Several higher education advocates of service-learning also offer or call for service-learning models that account for social processes. Whitfield (1999) advocates problem-based learning as a model. Here "the student's role is to actively search, question and engage in constructing meaning and relating it to the problem, the service, and the academic material in the course" and "participate in every step of the group problem-solving process" (p. 108). Cone and Harris (1996) draw on theoretical concepts from Bruner and Vygotsky to advocate a "lens" model "to capture both the individual psychological nature and the socio-cultural nature of service-learning" (p. 33). Wolfson and Willinsky (1998) work from their analysis of situated learning as rooted in the work of Vygotsky to advise that service-learning models must address the particular challenges that collaborative contexts pose for transfer of learning—the processes "by which students reflecting on their experience are able to ensure that what is learned in one setting can be applied to another" (p. 27).

and a community partner identify a service need and enter into a service-learning commitment. These constituents form a service-learning project team. The team develops a service-learning student outcomes plan that identifies the desired project outcomes for students and strategies for measuring student achievement of those outcomes. Next, the team develops and implements reflective-learning experiences that help students achieve the outcomes. Finally, the team evaluates their project in terms of students' outcomes, feedback from project participants and team self-evaluation. They then share evaluation results.

When teachers, students and community partners design, implement and evaluate service-learning in this collaborative way, they create the conditions that enable students to grow intellectually and progress academically as they simultaneously develop decision-making and problem-solving skills. And as students engage in collaborative service-learning they develop a sense of their community and their roles as community members by working with their schools and communities to identify, plan, provide and reflect upon authentic service that relates to their studies.

In Conclusion

Schools recognize the importance of linking the fundamental human activity of service with students' classroom learnings. Increasingly they look to service-learning as a way to do this and define this method as one in which students grow academically, intellectually and as productive citizens by working with their schools and communities to plan, provide and reflect upon academically linked service that meets authentic needs. Theory and research indicate that service-learning can nurture students' intellectual development, academic achievement and civic education and can invigorate school reform. A Collaborative Service-Learning Model that enacts core principles of experiential and social-process learning theory offers a new conceptual framework for implementing service-learning in today's middle schools and high schools.

Activities for Increasing Understanding

1. In a paper of no more than 500 words, state and justify your own position on the proposition that the impetus to serve arises from the initial, parent-child relationship. If you disagree with this proposition, offer your own alternate explanation of why people serve. Provide justifications in reasoning and personal observations for the position you take.
2. Create a symbolic representation of the summary service-learning definition presented in this chapter. Select an image for each element in the definition and arrange the images in an overall schematic that represents the definition.

3. Describe in no more than 50 words each, three specific instances of student community-based activity that is not service-learning. Be prepared to use these in a discussion group in which group members determine which of the features of your instances make them non-examples of service-learning.
4. Locate and read the full text of any two studies of service-learning that were carried out in the past two years and found positive impact of the method—one that relates to service-learning impact on student academic learning and one that relates to any other impact in which you are interested. For each study you review, suggest one or more strengths and weaknesses and one or more implications for further investigation that you (not the studies' authors) see.
5. Read Joyce and Weil with Calhoun (2000) on the Group Investigation Model, then think back over your own teaching or learning experiences to find an instance in which you were involved in a group investigation approach or something reasonably similar to it. Describe this instance in no more than 100 words, and list 3-5 advantages and disadvantages you perceive to be associated with it. Consider these positive and negative features from the perspective of teachers, students, school administrators and others who were involved.
6. Use the Internet to explore constructivist learning theory and list as propositions three new understandings that you gain about this field.

Chapter II: Designs for Service-Learning Projects in Middle and High Schools

Tony Achmed grips the podium, looks out over the crowd of teachers at the August, county-wide teachers' meeting that opens each school year. The lights are down. He can't see faces, but in the high-school stage spotlights, they can sure see him—maybe see the pulse in his throat, his nervous swallow.

"I'm here to report to you on two things: the service-learning conference I attended last month and a little about how I use service-learning." Tony nods toward the superintendent of schools in the front row. "The boss seems to think more of us might want to get involved in it."

The audience laugh warms. Tony's hands relax. He leans forward and begins.

"So," says a tall, sharp-featured teacher who stands quickly as Tony concludes and asks for questions. "Will there be some kind of central-office structure to coordinate all this?"

"I hope so, eventually—maybe a coordinating office, a school/community advisory board. There are models in the handout I've put in the foyer. But we can begin on our own with principal support, help from each other and community partners, and some parents. Then, maybe the boss" again the nod to the superintendent, "will build on what we've started."

The superintendent stands, holds up a hand in a wave and makes his way toward the podium.

Chapter Focus

The purpose of this chapter is to describe five designs that middle- and high-school teachers, students and community-partner teams can use as frameworks for service-learning projects. These designs can help teams develop projects that involve the key elements of collaborative service-learning even though teachers' experience and students' maturity vary, community partners have a range of needs, and service-learning resources are limited or extensive. The chapter begins by describing the designs, providing examples of them and showing how each incorporates commitment, cooperative outcomes planning, reflective-learning and celebration of growth. It then identifies and discusses variables that a service-learning team can usefully consider when selecting a design for its own, unique service-learning project.

Designs Emerging from Contemporary Practice

Across the country, middle- and high-school use of service-learning provides examples of ways to infuse service-learning in a variety of teaching/learning situations. Billig has suggested (personal communication, August 11, 2002) that these activities tend to these be organized as approaches, events, curriculums and programs. Formalizing these organizations in five designs useful for curriculum development provides frameworks that service-learning project teams can use to develop their own, situation-specific projects. The designs include 1) in-class approaches, 2) one-day events, 3) prototype projects, 4) recurring curriculum components and 5) cross-disciplinary programs. The following describes these five professional-practice-based designs for service learning and provides examples of their use by collaborative service-learning teams. The descriptions and examples are not intended as step-by-step formulas for service-learning projects. Rather, they provide thumbnail sketches of ways people who want to use collaborative service-learning in a range of situations shape their efforts. Teacher, student and community-partner teams that want to use one of these designs to create and carry out their own collaborative service-learning projects can turn for more detailed assistance to the two other sections in this book. Section Two provides in-depth discussions of the four steps in collaborative service-learning, and Section Three describes specific strategies for implementing each of these steps.

Service-Learning as an In-Class Approach

The in-class approach design for service-learning is particularly useful when student teachers and beginning teachers are working with students who need a fair amount of structure by virtue of their chronological age and/or self-direction skills. These relatively inexperienced teachers may be working in schools and school systems that are only becoming aware of service-learning or may be in systems that have committed to the method and designated many resources to it. They may be working with community partners that have relatively straightforward needs or complex and multifaceted needs. By using in-class designs to team with their students and community partners, student teachers and beginning teachers can learn about service-learning and help their students begin to understand how to commit to service with community partners, share outcomes planning and engage in reflective learning, evaluation and celebration.

The in-class approach design often begins with a student teacher or a teacher and students meeting with a community partner to identify a community issue or need as a problem that students can help solve. The teacher then develops a two- to three- day lesson set in which students address the issue or need using knowledge and skills they are currently learning. Students and teacher work through the lesson set in their classroom to produce one or more products which helps solve the original problem and which they and/or their teacher deliver to appropriate community recipients. The example below demonstrates how a service-learning approach can work.

An Example of the In-Class Approach Design

At the suggestion of her cooperating teacher, a pre-professional intern teaching in fifth grade invites a representative from the State Office of Fish and Wildlife to speak to students as part of their work on a social studies standard on environmental protection. The speaker explains that a large part of his office's work is public education—convincing people to protect the environment so that fish and animals can thrive. He asks students to share the importance of environmental protection with their friends and neighbors in every way they can.

The intern has explored service-learning as part of her methods course. She also knows that her cooperating teacher and principal have attended a district-wide session on service-learning, are interested in the method, and would support her small-scale use of it during her internship. She designs a two-day lesson set in which she links her students' work in language arts to their social studies standard on environmental protection. She begins by having students read and discuss the enlivening use of metaphors in a poem that celebrates the ways children can work together to protect the earth. She then has students identify earth protection strategies they would like to encourage friends, family and community members to use—recycling, stopping litter, preserving water resources, and so forth. She and students also reflect on why people are often not careful about environmental protection and discuss ways to convince them to be more careful. Students agree that people need reminders. They also agree with their intern teacher's proposal that they ask the manager of a local supermarket if they could send such reminders in the form of poems and pictures on shopping bags that are distributed to customers. The manager agrees and provides the class with enough large, brown paper bags for each student.

The intern now asks students to write four-line poems that encourage community members to practice environmental protection strategies. Each poem is to contain at least one metaphor. In small groups, students draw pictures that symbolize their preservation strategies on the bags, write their poems beneath the pictures and consult with one another as they work. The intern asks students to suggest why it is important for them to use correct spelling, punctuation and capitalization in their poems and how they can help each other do this. Later, she grades poems for these mechanics and the presence of metaphors. When the bags are finished and returned to the supermarket, the intern and her students reflect in small groups and as a class on specific new learning they gained and on shopping bags as a communication channel. They speculate, too, on how grocery chains' use of bags for public service information helps the community and the grocery chains.

When students take their state-standards-based tests several weeks later, the intern and her cooperating teacher compare their scores on items related to the environmental protection standard with the previous year's student scores on the same items. They find that the class' average scores on these items are higher than those of last years. They discuss this with students who agree that while they cannot conclude that their service-learning project alone made the difference, they can celebrate the fact that it was an effective approach to learning and one they enjoyed.

Analyzing the Example

This small, in-class project permits an inexperienced intern teacher to address an academic standard by using a service-learning approach that shapes the service students provide in terms of their academic objectives. It also permits her to carry out her project with young students for whose safety and classroom management she is responsible and to do this in a situation that has few resources specifically allocated for service-learning. Finally, she is able to help her students respond in a simple, academically linked way to a community need that has many dimensions. While the intern's approach does not follow the collaborative service-learning model in a lock-step fashion, it does include the model's elements. Students develop a commitment to respond to a genuine request from a community agency. Students and intern together decide what the project's outcomes will be and reflect together on ways to effectively achieve those outcomes. They also reflect on methods of community communication they may not have thought of before and become newly aware of a community strength. They evaluate their project as a learning method and celebrate its efficacy.

Teachers in situations similar to that of the intern—with fairly limited teaching experience, young students, diffuse community needs and few resources—can use simple approaches like hers to relate service to academic learning through shared commitment, planning, reflection and evaluation. At the same time, teachers who are experienced and working with more mature students, who have access to rich, service-learning support networks and specific service requests from community agencies can use the approach initially to explore service-learning. They can begin with projects like the one in the intern example and use them to learn the basics of academically based service-learning curriculum design and the commitment, planning, reflection and celebration essential to collaborative service-learning.

Service-Learning as a One-Day Event

Teachers who are in the early stages of their profession have a good sense of its complexities. They may want to explore service-learning with their students, but in a way that uses in-place procedures and existing support structures. Whether these teachers find themselves in school systems that are just developing awareness of service-learning or in systems that have institutionalized the method, they can use a one-day event which is framed as a cooperative venture with a community partner and provides all a solid introduction to service-learning. These one-day events can be linked to national service-learning initiatives such as Make a Difference Day and Youth Service Day or to activities sponsored by community agencies. By developing projects related to such events, teachers, their students and a community partner can develop understanding of how to collaboratively commit to service, cooperatively plan project outcomes, reflect on connections between service and learning and celebrate growth.

Community agencies frequently design one-day events to increase resources for implementing their missions. Planners of events such as community health fairs, everybody-read, non-smoking and drug-awareness campaigns conceive these ventures as cooperative efforts and actively seek a wide range of participants to assist with everything from organization and publicity to the set-up and hosting of booths, displays and demonstrations. Agencies are usually enthusiastic about sharing their event needs with students, and an interested group of students can almost always assist agencies in ways that meaningfully link authentic service to classroom learning. Moreover, students can do much of the preparatory work for an event in their classroom, and when it is time to go to the event site, this can be arranged as a field trip with parents helping as supervisors. Taken together, the factors of ready collaboration, good potential linkages with academics, opportunities for parents to help, and controllable movement of students to a service site make the one-day service-learning event an excellent place for beginning and moderately experienced teachers help their students identify and work with a community partner to test the service-learning waters. The following provides an example of such a one-day service-learning event.

An Example of a One-Day Event Design

A tenth-grade health teacher who has taught for three years is working with his students on personal health standards. He teaches in a school system that is planning for service-learning and encouraging teachers to explore the method. The teacher invites a physician affiliated with the local unit of the American Cancer Society to explain to his class how smoking damages the body and people's health. Students reflect with the speaker on personal responsibility for health. The speaker asks students to assist her in informing community members of the dangers of smoking by distributing the Cancer Society's stop smoking brochures at an upcoming Community Wellness Day. Students agree and the speaker arranges for a booth. Students decide to make posters and form teams to talk with people who come by the booth about the benefits of not smoking. Each team prepares its own persuasive mini-presentation for the booth using a variety of media. The teacher arranges attendance at the fair as a class field trip. The school system provides a bus for the trip, and teacher and students enlists three parents in the project. One is a nurse, and offers to come to the class and provide technical assistance as students make preparations for their booths. Teams e-mail outlines of their presentation to the physician, who critiques them and makes suggestions for improving them. The teacher sets up a rotation so that every student group has the opportunity to host the class booth and also assigns all students the learning task of evaluating the accuracy and effectiveness of their own and other booths' presentations in terms of what they have learned about wellness in class.

After the event, students, teacher, parents and the physician evaluate the effectiveness of their own and others' presentations. They reflect on the role of wellness in community development, discuss their perceptions of the major cause of and reasons for health problems in the general population and complete a survey on their perceptions of the benefits of learning through service. The teacher compares his students' performance on personal health awareness items on the state standards test with those of other tenth-graders in the school system. Students contact the local paper about their project and its outcomes, and the paper writes a feature article about it that includes pictures as well as quotes from the physician, parents, student and teacher involved.

Analyzing the Example

In this example a beginning-stage teacher in a school system that is in the planning stage with respect to service-learning uses in-place community structures and school system policies on field trips to involve students in providing service—public health information—related to what they are learning. Students, who are, themselves, reasonably mature, propose the project in response to a request from a community agency representative. They commit to help the agency implement its own service mission, and they work with its representative to establish, reach, reflect upon and evaluate specific outcomes. Their project ties directly back to their health curriculum, yet leads them to consider broader public issues of the community in which they live and communities in general.

While this project takes place within a school system where few resources are assigned to service-learning, it is successful because the teacher is at ease with the curriculum, students are able to move into the community with appropriate supervision, and the community partner can contribute personal resources that help students relate their learning to a specific agency need. Given a team with the same general capacities, this one-day event project could also easily take place within a school system actively planning to use service-learning or in one with an established service-learning program. In any of these resource situations, a one-day event can introduce teacher, students, community agencies and parents to service-learning in ways that emphasize focused commitment, careful planning, reflective conceptualization and celebration of students' academically based community contributions.

Service-Learning as Prototype Project

A prototype project is a full-scale implementation of collaborative service-learning that provides a model for others to follow. The prototype design often appeals to experienced teachers, principals and instructional supervisors as a way to demonstrate how to use service-learning over the course of an academic marking period, semester or year. Because it is full-scale and offered as a defining example, a prototype visibly incorporates 1) strategies for obtaining commitment from all service-learning constituents, 2) cooperative outcomes planning, 3) reflective learning sequences that link service and classroom study and 4) evaluation of outcomes and celebration of growth. Prototypes often take shape as reformulations of existing instructional units that teachers have customarily presented through classroom-based methods and wish to renew and reinvigorate through use of service-learning. Because they are full-scale prototypes, they require long-term planning—certainly initiated at the beginning of the school year in which they are to take place, and perhaps initiated as early as the year before implementation. This long-term planning, in and of itself, offers satisfying opportunities for all involved to accomplish the collaborative decision-making and problem-solving goals of service-learning. Following is an example of a prototype service-learning project.

An Example of a Prototype Project Design

At the beginning of the school year, a high-school American history teacher alerts her students to a written request from their town's governing council for assistance with the town's centennial project which will take place in the spring. Students express interest and the teacher suggests that participation might be a way to address her own and her supervisor's interest in incorporating service-learning in the school system's American History curriculum. She, the supervisor and students invite a centennial project representative to discuss possibilities related to their history standard "understanding historical contexts." As a result of the discussion, students suggest that they create a town history based on academic reference materials, and accounts from community ethnic and interest groups and linked to events, trends and issues in American History. Students, teacher, the centennial project representative and the instructional supervisor for history agree to work as a team to plan and implement the project.

The team decides they want the project to help students 1) increase their knowledge of their community's history and 2) strengthen their abilities to interact productively with diverse community groups. To accomplish these outcomes, students will develop an outline of their town's history framed in the context of American history, will learn how their town's constituent ethnic and interest groups played roles in their town's history and will determine how to include this information in an historical document for the whole town. The team writes a project proposal which students present as a service-learning prototype to a joint meeting of centennial committee and school system representatives. They apply to both entities for support for planning time, evaluation assistance, transportation and other necessities. The committee and school system approve the project and agree to share costs.

Students create their town history outline. The centennial committee representative on the project team then sets up a meeting of students and representatives of the town's ethnic and interest groups. Students explain their project to all and with project team help, assign themselves in pairs to various groups as information gatherers. Students meet with their assigned groups over a six-week period, in which they review the class's historical outline with group members and gather information from them about ways the groups interface with the outline. Students now work in class with their teacher for several weeks to develop their document, fleshing out their basic outline with information from their groups as well as from their continuing study of American History. When they have completed a basic draft, they and their project team reflect on their findings and on the processes they used to interact with their ethnic and interest groups and to gather relevant historical information. They present their final product—an illustrated history of the community—to the town council at the centennial celebration opening. Afterward in their classroom, students complete essay tests in which they explain how events in their own town reflect and exemplify particular aspects of the history they have studied. They speculate in a panel discussion with all team members on how historical forces have shaped their town's current social, economic and value structure and what similar forces will affect the town as history moves forward. They also complete a survey about the effects of service-learning on their knowledge of their community, its diversity and their own commitment to future service. When all is complete, they present a project report and evaluation to their school system.

Analyzing the Example

The school system where this example takes place is in the service-learning planning stage. The teacher and supervisor are experienced and are familiar with service-learning, and the students are mature enough to function with reasonable independence in their community. Their community partner needs a complex service, one that will necessitate students' directly gathering information from diverse groups. Teacher, students, supervisor, and the community representative work as a team to integrate these variables in a well-defined, service-learning prototype design that links service to academic standards and can help the school system move toward institutionalization of service-learning as it simultaneously engages students in community building. As students help the team design and implement the project, they make commitments, share in planning, reflect to learn and evaluate their work in ways that deepen their understanding of history and their community. They help the project demonstrate how to use collaboration with community partners as a method for providing service and achieving academic standards.

Service-Learning as a Recurring Curriculum Component

When school systems are ready and able to provide resources for service-learning, school faculties, principals and instructional supervisors are often interested in making service-learning a recurring component in a subject-area curriculum. Here, by common agreement, a service-learning segment is incorporated into the yearly syllabus of a subject area, and teachers and students know that they will design and engage in a multi-class service-learning project as part of their work in that subject area. Supervisors or service-learning coordinators usually work with the subject-area teachers and students to help them create evaluation plans for their project. Identification of which subject area will house the service-learning segment each year is part of the school's overall long-range planning—often a function of the school's general advisory committee. Once a subject area has been selected, teachers, instructional supervisors in the area and representative students work with administrator, school advisory committee members, and identified community partners to select a service need for the year that links to the standards in the area. Together, this team designs a comprehensive service-learning project in which all students in the subject area can participate in ways appropriate to their own interests and maturity and to their teachers' experience.

An Example of a Recurring Curriculum Component Design

The faculty and principal at Mountain Meadow Middle School have designated eighth-grade language arts as the subject area that will include a service-learning component. Each year, an eighth-grade team of language-arts teachers and representative students from each class works with the schools' advisory committee to identify three possible service-learning initiatives for the year. These initiatives are community-service needs that community agency representatives who serve on the school advisory committee regularly bring to the committee. All eighth-graders vote on which of the three initiatives will become the focus for the year's project, and the agency whose need is selected sends several representatives to be part of the eighth-grade language-arts team that will now become the project team. The team plans the project over a one-month period by identifying three desired outcomes related to eighth-grade English standards and to service goals for students. For each outcome they list a range of activity ideas that teachers and students in individual classes can develop into reflective learning sequences that will help students achieve the outcome.

Last year, eighth-graders in language arts elected to focus on equipping a children's reading corner for a branch of the county library that had just opened and needed community support for its programs. The team for this project connected it to the National Council of English standards that students use writing for learning, enjoyment, persuasion and the exchange of information, and use a variety of technological and information resources, and to the service goal that students understand that effective service brings recipients and providers together in a mutual effort. The team listed over 25 activity ideas that individual language-arts classes might use to develop reflective learning experiences. Examples of these included the following:

1. write letters, articles, video scripts, computer presentations explaining the need for a reading corner and requesting donations,
2. write stories and poems to include in the reading corner collection,
3. write brochures, fliers and fact sheets to communicate about library services,
4. plan, implement and summarize interviews with parents and their youngsters to learn about reading interests and needs,
5. create and implement oral reading and discussion programs with youngsters,
6. help youngsters plan and implement ways to support the reading corner,
7. assist with check-out, shelving and other library services.

At this point, each language-arts class invited a parent representative and a library representative from their own media center or the county library to join their classroom teams. Each classroom team selected several activities they believed would help their students achieve both particular class objectives and the overall eighth-grade project outcomes. Each team integrated its activities in a class-specific project. Individual class teams wrote up their projects making sure that each activity they planned to use was accompanied by reflection that included either their teacher, their class's helping parent, or a worker at the library and wherever possible, young library users. In each class, students concluded their projects by writing essays about the benefits of mutuality in service. They agreed that their essays should reflect the state framework for expository writing, include direct quotes from people they have worked with during the project, and evidence use of grammar, punctuation and spelling rules that the class had covered. Later in the year, the language-arts supervisor assembled information about eighth-graders' performance on the state writing test and compared this with county averages.

All language-arts classes came together for a culminating fair in which they displayed representations of their class projects and attended small-group discussions—led by students themselves, teachers, parents and library personnel—of ways their projects helped them use information resources, write for multiple purposes, understand the meaning of service and make a difference in their community.

Analyzing the Example

In this example, an overarching curriculum-component design provides a framework for individual class projects that teachers with varying levels of experience can design cooperatively with students and community representatives. Individual class teams can adjust their projects to students' academic objectives and maturity by varying the type, number and complexity of activities they elect to use from the lists suggested by the comprehensive team. In spite of the variation possible, however, all projects implement the core elements of collaborative service-learning. They involve students in making commitment to address a genuine community need, determining ways they can best achieve desired student outcomes, creating and using reflective learning and celebrating progress and growth.

It is clear that implementing this design requires in-place structures that regularly involve school personnel, students and community partners in identifying genuine service needs that can link to academic curriculum. While it can involve interns, beginning and experienced teachers at the classroom level, master teachers will probably be most effective as leaders in the design of overarching grade-level projects. It should be noted, too, that individual class iterations of overarching projects are themselves collaborative. They create small project teams that involve students and already committed community partners in outcomes planning, reflective learning, and celebrating growth.

Service-Learning as a Cross-Disciplinary Program

This design also depends upon an institutionalized support network for service-learning, high-level planning by master teachers, and mature students, and integral participation of community partners. Typically an entire school implements a cross-disciplinary program and involves teachers and students in most, if not all, subject areas in a comprehensive service-learning collaboration with the community. Project planning is done at the school level under the leadership of a coordinating team that consists of teacher and student representatives from the various subject areas, administrators, parents, representatives of participating community agencies and other community members. Once a master plan is developed, individual schools and teachers develop their own plans to achieve project goals through reflective learning. Planning may take one or even two years and guidance from a skilled planner is essential. The final plan involves participants in playing a range of roles throughout the program and consists of elements such as a mission-based goal statement, a project overview, outcome objectives, reflective learning experiences, evaluation plans and scheduling and dissemination components. An example of a cross-disciplinary service-learning program is described below.

An Example of a Cross Disciplinary Design

Gulf View Middle School concludes each academic year with a school-wide interdisciplinary service-learning project designed by teachers, administrators, students, parents and community members to exemplify the school's agreed-upon mission which appears on its banner as "Learning for Personal Growth and Productive Citizenship." At the beginning of each year, the school's service-learning advisory council which is made up of representatives from each constituency meets with the Gulf View Regional Interagency Council to learn about service needs in the community and to broadly outline a year-end project.

Recently the project focused on the challenges created by the state's management of water flow from the state reservoir system through the Wacahatchee River to the Gulf of Mexico. For three years preceding the project, press reports about seemingly random and ecologically damaging water releases had cast the state as a villain in water management. After discussions with state representatives, the Interagency Council proposed a project to develop informed student understanding of the need to manage water flow and the decision-making processes used by the state to do this, then to share this understanding in a variety of ways throughout the community. Science, mathematics, social studies, language arts, music and art teachers all worked with their students to develop units that helped students use local, state and national standards-related academic skills and knowledge, research and data collection to accomplish project purposes.

Students listened to speakers from the water management agency, visited dam sites, attended public hearings on water management and did research. They then worked in small and large groups to create graphs, tables, charts, posters, pamphlets, videos, poems, plays, songs and so forth to express their understanding. They disseminated their information through a wide array of community communication channels such as newspapers, TV, businesses and community meetings. Throughout, they reflected with teachers and community members on their experiences and insights they were gaining. At the end of the program, students demonstrated academic progress on classroom and state standards tests of skills they used in the project and knowledge of the water management agency's decision tree and related procedures. They assessed their service contributions by asking a sample of recipients of their information to provide them with feedback about the value of their products and by asking community agencies to judge their products' content accuracy. They also completed self-assessments of their perspectives on community issues and their orientations toward the benefits of service and the responsibilities of citizens. Every student participant received a letter of commendation from the state's governor.

Analyzing the Example

This is a grand design and clearly could only take place in settings where service-learning resource networks are fully developed and institutionalized. Master planning requires master teachers with abundant general knowledge, community awareness and leadership skills. It requires school administrators and supervisors who support and facilitate service-learning. It also requires mature students ready to work collaboratively with adults on a "big picture," and community partners committed to young people's education as a key strategy for accomplishing their own agency missions. As with the curriculum-component design, however, it offers a wealth of opportunities for teachers with varying experience and students addressing different objectives at different maturity levels.

In spite of its complexity, the cross-disciplinary design is not a "pie-in-the-sky" or dream design. Cross-disciplinary programs like the one in this example are emerging across the country. The Wisconsin Department of Public Instruction, the Boston Public Schools and the Vermont Commission on National Service to name but a few, have developed comprehensive, cross-disciplinary service-learning programs. Teachers who find themselves in rich service-learning resource networks and want to initiate similar projects can learn about these and other broadly scoped programs by using the National Service Learning Clearinghouse at http://www.servicelearning.org.

Selecting a Service-Learning Project Design

When teachers, students and community partners develop and implement service-learning projects, their overall success will depend in great measure on selection of project designs appropriate to their combined situations. Teams can characterize their situations and use this understanding in design selection by thinking about five situation-descriptive variables. These variables include 1) teachers' experience level, 2) students' maturity, 3) available resources, 4) the match between the service the community partner needs and the students' curriculum, and 5) time required to implement the designs. The following provides a brief discussion of these variables, then summarizes them in an array that suggest ways teams can relate them to the five designs for service-learning projects.

Teachers' Experience Levels

A teacher's experience level contributes to successful service-learning in two important ways. At the most basic level, the longer a teacher has taught, the more familiar that teacher is with the routines of schooling, the curriculum and the management of students. Teachers who are in the initial stages of understanding and balancing these factors will have neither the time nor energy to engage in service-learning projects that have too many working parts. They will want to select simple designs, usually an approach or a one-day event. On the other hand, teachers who handle routines, curriculum and management smoothly because they are experienced, are likely to have the professional scope necessary to engage in a new teaching method that has its own complexities.

A second aspect of a teacher's experience level is management skill. From the beginning of their professional education, teachers work to become classroom managers. As they enter the classroom, they hone and use instructional management skills both intuitively and deliberately to help their students learn in many ways. As teachers become more experienced, as they work with other teachers, parents, school administrators and support personnel, they have many opportunities to strengthen the particular management skills essential to guiding service-learning project teams. Because beginning teachers' management skills are still developing, they are more likely to be successful leading small service-learning projects in which they plan and implement simple approaches or one-day events with teams comprised of their students and two or three other adults. As teachers become experienced and master teachers, they are usually ready to lead larger teams in carrying out more extensive projects. Teachers who would like to develop a sense of their own management skills for service-learning will find more detailed discussion of these skills in Chapter III: Preparing to Use Service -Learning.

Students' Service-Learning Competencies

Student's service-learning compentencies relate to their chronological age and their psychological and social competence and dictate the range of service-learning experiences open to them. Younger students cannot move unsupervised into the community. On the other hand, many high-school students drive, have part-time jobs and are able to go alone to community agencies and service sites. Thus teachers and teams have to select service-learning designs in terms of students' age-related abilities to come and go in the school and community. Additionally, students need to be sufficiently mature psychologically and socially to commit to service, engage in outcomes planning and reflective learning with people who are not their classroom teachers and to evaluate with others the service-learning projects they carry out. Specifically, to succeed in service-learning, students need to develop a concept of service, exercise self-management, cooperative-learning and information-gathering skills, work with authority figures and work with people whose cultures are different from their own.

Where students are reasonably mature in these areas, teachers and teams often help all participants become familiar with service-learning through one-day events, then move to more complex prototypes, continuing curriculum or cross-disciplinary designs. As teams use these designs to lay out specific projects, they can bear in mind ways in which students need to grow and use these understandings to shape particular service-learning activities as opportunities for growth. For instance, in the one-day-event example, the planning team can help students improve self-management skills by having them set up the schedule for bus transport, adult supervision and booth presentations. Or, in the centennial history example, the team can use a range of reflection activities to help students explore how the lives of members of community ethnic groups are different and similar to their own. Where students are less mature, a teacher can encourage their overall psychological and social maturation by engaging them in a service-learning approach that emphasizes reflection on developing shared commitment, student involvement in outcomes planning, the role of reflection in learning through service and the merits of project evaluation. Teachers and teams interested in determining students' maturity levels will also find more detailed discussion of ways to do this in Chapter III.

Available Resources

Teachers and the teams they work with can use the approach and one-day-event designs to become familiar with service-learning in situations where their school system are aware of the method but provide few if any resources for its use. As school systems and communities move into planning for the use of service-learning, they often make special funds available and teams find that prototype designs are not only possible as service-learning vehicles for students, but help school systems, themselves, determine the essentials needed for system-wide use of the method. As schools systems and communities institutionalize service-learning as a continuing initiative and commit resources to its implementation on a regular basis, teams can implement curriculum component and cross-disciplinary designs. Chapter III describes the features of these three levels of service-learning resources and helps teachers and teams profile available resources in their own systems and use this information to select project designs.

Match Between Service Needed and Students' Curriculum

On some occasions, a community agency needs a service that smoothly dovetails with what students are studying. For instance, a family services center might need people to help clients fill out income-tax forms, and students in a math-for-daily-living class at the local high school might have just learned how to fill out these forms. The center and the class could team to develop a simple, prototype project in which students directly help families fill out forms. As the team develops its project, there is no need to answer the often very difficult question, "How can the service needed be linked to what students are studying?" Students are learning the skills needed to provide the service and if they are appropriately mature, they can deliver the service through direct, face-to-face interactions with recipients.

When a community need does not relate as clearly to what students are learning, teachers, students and potential community partners can find connections by exploring possibilities for students' indirect service—their support to service delivery—or use of advocacy—convincing others to support service delivery. To explore indirect service and advocacy possibilities, teacher, students and potential partner can make two lists. One consists of the standard and related skills students are working on and the other consists of the support activities the community partner sees as essential to meeting its need. Analysis of possible matches in the two lists usually leads to ideas about how students can use what they are learning to provide service indirectly or as advocates. An example shows how this process can work.

A county agricultural office is mounting a program to encourage area residents to reduce use of chemical pesticides. The program director contacts area high-school science departments and offers certified teachers opportunities to teach in a series of evening, neighborhood seminars. A teacher and students in a tenth-grade biology class who are working on an "understanding ecological systems" standard see service-learning possibilities and invite the agricultural office program director to consider possibilities with them. This nascent service-learning team comes up with the following lists.

Standard-Related Skills	Support and Advocacy Needs
1. Identify natural elements and life forms in an ecology 2. Diagram relationships among elements and life forms in an ecology 3. Recognizes threats to an ecology's balance 4. Propose solutions for stabilizing a threatened ecology	1. Publicize seminars 2. Find certified teachers 3. Prepare instructional materials 4. Present seminars 5. Evaluate sessions

A first look at the list makes clear to all that students can use advocacy and their growing understanding of ecological systems to prepare a wide range of targeted materials that will help publicize the seminars and recruit teachers. Further discussion suggests that students can provide indirect service by helping to determine the contents of and prepare instructional packets and evaluation forms for use by seminar participants, and in some cases, can serve on site as aides to teachers who present the seminars. Teacher, student and the representative commit to a prototype design.

This example points to what may be the most challenging, yet ultimately rewarding aspect of developing a service-learning design, one that connects learning and service while engaging students in both with integrity. In its section on Implementing Quality Service Learning, the Executive Summary of Learning In Deed (2000) states "As the hyphenated name implies, service-learning consists of two equally important components, and effective service-learning requires that both elements be of high quality" (para. 2). Those planning service-learning projects can achieve this quality by taking time to think together through a range of service and learning possibilities for students. This activity, in itself, helps teachers, students and a potential community partner better understand each others' perspectives and missions and build a bridge that "integrates community service with academic study to enrich learning, teach civic responsibility and strengthen communities."

Time Needed for Planning and Implementing Designs

Examples of the five designs presented in this chapter make clear that the more complex a service-learning design is, the longer it will take to plan, implement and evaluate. Near the end of this chapter, Table 2.1 uses planning/teaching units—the typical 45-50 minute periods that teachers have for planning instruction and for delivering that instruction in the classroom—to show how time demands increase across designs. Teachers and project teams who consider these time demands in their design selection process need to bear three related ideas in mind. First, the time necessary for successful collaborative planning of a service-learning project—whatever its design—is likely to be equal to or exceed the time necessary for actually implementing the project. Second, flexibility will be essential to finding sufficient time for project planning and implementation. Examples of this flexibility include block scheduling, use of after-school time, and use of technologies such as e-mail to conduct electronic meetings and stitch team members' individual bits of time into a project time net. Third, while it is very possible for teams to develop projects around the service-learning approach and one-day-event designs within teachers' and students' normal planning and instruction time allowances, it is unlikely that teams can create and implement prototype, curriculum-component and cross-disciplinary projects without extra time resources. This means that teachers, particularly, may need compensated summer-workshop time or released time from regular responsibilities so that they can carry out planning for projects that use these more complex designs.

Putting It All Together

Teachers, students and community partners increase their chances for project success by selecting service-learning project designs appropriate to their own situations. To help them make their selections, Table 2.1 arrays the five designs and characterizes them in terms of their fit with teachers' experience levels and students' maturity levels, estimates of the time needed to plan and implement each design, the resource-level necessary to plan and implement each and the types of service connections each design seems to best facilitate. The figure derives from the authors' experience in implementing service-learning and teaching teachers to use the method, and from their general experience in curriculum and program development. It represents guidelines rather than rules, and teachers and their service-learning teams can use the figure's information as starting points upon which to build their own, unique and creative service-learning projects.

Table 2.1 shows that while the five designs differ in format, they share common core dynamics. Each engenders school-community collaborations that have the potential for deepening students' academic learning and understanding of their communities in ways that classroom instruction alone cannot always do. Each offers students opportunities to develop problem-solving and decision-making skills through collaborative commitment to service, outcomes planning, reflective learning, and evaluation and celebration of growth. Each helps students begin early engagement as citizen participants in community building and development.

Table 2.1 also suggests that in addition to providing types of frameworks for service-learning that are suitable to a range of school and community situations, the five designs can function as phases in the evolution of service-learning within a school system from simple to more complex implementation.

Table 2.1 Characteristics of Five Designs for Implementing Service-Learning (S-L) in Middle and High Schools

Design	Teacher Experience Level	Student Maturity Level	Planning Time	Implementation Time	Resource Support Level	Service Possible	Special Considerations
In-Class Approach	Pre-professional Beginning	Well suited to young students or students with relatively high structure needs	2-3 planning periods.	2-3 class periods.	Low. System aware of S-L but not using the method.	Indirect Advocacy	Centers on teacher control as it introduces S-L elements in the classroom with cooperation from community partners.
One-Day Event	Beginning	Useful with students of any age who have moderate to low structure needs	5-8 planning periods spaced over 2-3 weeks	1 week of regular class periods plus 1 full day on site.	Low. System aware of S-L but not using the method.	Indirect Advocacy	Helps students and community partners use school system structures to implement S-L elements in class and on site.
Prototype	Experienced, Master	Most useful with older students who can function autonomously	Once-weekly planning periods spaced over 6 months-1 year	Double or triple periods, once or twice weekly for 3-6 weeks	Moderate. System plans eventual use of SL	Direct Indirect Advocacy	Uses S-L elements in class and on site. Usually involves adjustment of student schedules and formal evaluator.
Continuing Curriculum Component	Experienced, Master	Provides opportunities for students of varying ages with varying needs for structure	Once-weekly planning periods spaced over 6 months- 1 year	Double or triple periods, once or twice weekly for 4-9 weeks	High. S-L institutionalized in system via continuing initiatives, structures and resources	Direct Indirect Advocacy	Joins school advisory committee, grade-level/subject-area teachers, students and community partners in annual S-L projects. Involves adjustment of student schedules, formal evaluator.
Cross-Disciplinary Program	All Levels	Provides opportunities for students of varying ages with varying needs for structure	Once-weekly planning periods spaced over 1 year	Double or triple periods, once or twice weekly for 9 weeks	High. S-L institutionalized in system via continuing initiatives, structures and resources	Direct Indirect Advocacy	Joins coordinating council, grade level/subject area teams, students and community partners in school-wide S-L projects. Involves adjustment of student schedules, formal evaluator.

Schools and school systems can use the designs in sequence to gradually yet systematically implement service-learning in a progressive process that helps service-learning become a "central strategy for teaching and learning in our schools."[1]

In Conclusion

Enthusiasm for the use of service-learning in middle and high schools is mounting, and across the country more and more schools are providing students opportunities to link genuine service to their academic studies. This activity is generating a variety of designs for service learning projects that range from simple, in-class approaches to broadly scoped cross-disciplinary programs, designs that can be used by pre-professional and beginning teachers as well as those who are very experienced and their administrative partners. Each of the designs helps users commit to service-learning, identify desired student outcomes of service-learning, transform service experience to learning through reflection, and celebrate new knowledge and understandings. The designs can be used independently within classrooms, schools and school systems or in sequence over time as stages in a service-learning capacity-building process.

Activities for Increasing Understanding

1. Use journal readings, the Internet and inquiry about service-learning activity in your own school system to identify and summarize three examples of service-learning implementation.
2. Characterize each of your examples in terms of the design it is most similar to among the five described here in Chapter II. Where an example does not appear to represent one of the designs here, explain your view of its design and depict the design in terms of the column headers in Table 2.1.
3. Speculate on what your three examples as a group seem to imply about service-learning implementation in general and for you in particular.
4. Present the results of your work and thought for activities 1-3 above in a paper of no more than 500 words.
5. Begin thinking about which design you might use to implement service-learning in terms of your own experience and interests. Make notes to record your preliminary thinking and save these for later use.

---

[1] U. S. Senator John Glenn in his cover letter for "Learning In Deed: The Power of Service-Learning for American Schools, A Report From the National Commission on Service Learning." 2002.

Chapter III:
Preparing to Use Service-Learning

"*More iced tea?*" *The waitress holds the dripping pitcher over their glasses.*

"*No thanks,*" *Jeri smiles, slides a ten-dollar bill toward her younger sister Kalisha, pushes back her chair as the waitress retreats.* "*That's for my share. I've got to see people at the museum about our class service-learning project next spring.*"

"*Sure wish I could try service-learning,*" *Kalisha replies.* "*But it must take a lot of preparation and real skill to manage kids out in the community. My kids are seventh graders—not seniors like yours, and I'm so new at teaching. Logistics must be tough enough in high school, probably just too much in middle school. And would my kids really see learning connections between English and community service, not see it as just a way to get out of class?*"

Jeri pauses, intrigued. "*I know you Kal. You're great with those kids, and I bet you'd find ways to make connections. You can use service-learning in almost any subject. You'd have to adjust your project for students' ages, but the basics ought to apply. We could kick it around if you're interested.*" *She grins invitation.* "*It'd give us a chance for another great lunch.*"

"*Hey! I'm always up for that. Let's set a date.*" *Kalisha fishes in her cavernous shoulder bag for her wallet with its pocket calendar.*

Chapter Focus

The conversation described in the opening scenario endorses what teachers across the country are coming to recognize, that service-learning can work in middle schools as well as high schools, and that teachers across the disciplines can use service-learning with students who range in ability, maturity and motivation. What the scenario only hints at, however, is the ways intern teachers, beginning teachers and experienced teachers can prepare to use service-learning. The purpose of this chapter is to explain how all these teachers can use techniques and strategies already within their professional repertoires to determine their own and their students' readiness to undertake service-learning. This in turn prepares them to commit with a community partner to a service-learning relationship.

Service-Learning Readiness Factors

Teachers can determine their own and their students' readiness to join with community partners in a service-learning relationship by gathering information about three factors that work together to make service-learning possible. These include teacher instructional management skills, student service-learning competencies, and resource support networks. By reflecting on the ways they manage the teaching and learning process, their students' capacities to function with increasing independence, and the constellation of resources available to support service-learning, teachers can prepare to commit to the method and use it confidently. They can also use the information they gather when the time comes to collaboratively select a service-learning project design with students and community partners and to shape the service-learning activities students will use within the design. The following describes these three factors and ways teachers can profile them.

Instructional Management Skills

Teachers are instructional managers and effective teachers use management skills both intuitively and deliberately to help their students learn. Teachers who elect to use service-learning will use these same management skills beyond their classrooms as they help students, administrators, parents and others work with community partners to design and implement service-learning projects. As teachers prepare to team with these constituents, it is helpful for them to become consciously aware of the particular management skills they can use to facilitate the commitment, outcomes planning, reflective learning and evaluation of growth in which successful service-learning teams engage.

In *Developing Management Skills*, Whetten and Cameron (2002) identify generic skills that are important for success in management settings. In their role as instructional managers, successful teachers use many of these skills to support teaching and learning in their classrooms. With respect to service-learning, teachers who confidently use five of the skills are likely to be most successful. These key skills are: motivating others, team building, supportive communication, analytical and creative problem-solving, and time management. Teachers who can consistently use these skills in their classrooms are likely to be ready to form and lead service-learning project teams comprised of students, parents, community partners and others. The following describes these five instructional management skills as they transfer to service-learning and suggests ways teachers can become aware of their own effective use of them.

Motivating Others

Teachers are well versed in educational psychology's extensive motivation knowledge-base. Accordingly, they use an array of motivation strategies to engage their students in learning activities that can result in their cognitive, psychomotor, and affective development. When teachers want to apply their understanding of motivation in the classroom to service-learning, it is helpful to group the many available motivation strategies into three categories: attraction strategies, intrinsic-reward strategies and extrinsic-reward strategies. Attraction strategies motivate service-learning participants by capturing their attention and interest either positively or negatively. Intrinsic-reward strategies motivate by offering participants opportunities to grow or gain intra- and interpersonally, and extrinsic reward strategies motivate them by offering material benefit for their performance of desired actions. Teachers who engage in service-learning can use these three types of strategies to initiate, support and sustain service-learning projects and can help project participants use them in the same way. For example, a teacher and her students may attract partners and participants to join a project by calling attention to community opportunities that can be enhanced or inequities that can be addressed by service-learning. Or students may immerse themselves in service-learning activities that have been shaped by a teacher and community partner in ways that reward intrinsically by challenging students to use their unique abilities and interests and offer them opportunities to develop confidence and self-esteem. Or a potential community partner may become involved in a project because students' service can bring real material resources to bear on the needs of the partner's clientele. Further, the partner may encourage students' persistence through challenging aspects of their service by awarding participation certificates.

Motivation strategies based on attraction and intrinsic reward are most consistently effective over the long term, and extrinsic reward strategies work best when they are used to build competencies that can eventually promote intrinsic rewards. In other words, people tend to move toward what interests them and helps them live according to their values, and they seek material benefits that enhance their opportunities to pursue their interests and values. This suggests that teachers who want to use motivation strategies as part of instructional management—whether in the classroom or on a service learning team—need good command of attraction and intrinsic reward strategies and need to use meaningful extrinsic reward strategies as backup. The easiest way for teachers to assess the degree to which they do this is to analyze several of their lesson plans over a period of a month or so. They look at each element in each lesson plan and ask two questions: "What motivating strategy is associated either explicitly or implicitly with this element?" and "To which category of motivators does this strategy belong?" When elements have been analyzed, teachers then turn attention to the extrinsic motivation strategies they have found themselves using in each lesson plan and ask a third question: "How are these extrinsic motivators supporting or leading to intrinsic rewards for students?" Teachers conclude this analysis by determining the degree to which they plan lessons that can attract students to learning by appealing to their interests and special capacities, reward students intrinsically for engaging in learning activities and use appropriate extrinsic rewards to help them grow as competent persons. Where teachers find that their tendency in the use of motivation is toward the use of a variety of intrinsic reward strategies, they will be in a good position to help their students and other service-learning project team members engage in learning through service as a source of intrinsic satisfaction.

Team Building

Teachers who engage in service-learning build teams made up of students, administrators, parents, community partners and others. These people have different perspectives and abilities, yet when they commit to service-learning, they must work together to develop and implement projects through which students make genuine service contributions and learn academically. These teams must also be able to accept and use the "messy" aspects of service-learning—the unpredictable and unexpected events that are bound to happen in any service-learning project. They must be able to use creative and critical thinking to find learning opportunities for students and themselves in these experiences. And as teachers help teams come together to do these things, they must build themselves into the teams, both as managers and members. They must find ways to function within project teams that enable them to keep students on track toward accomplishing the goals and objectives of a service-learning project while at the same time sharing responsibility for teaching and learning with other team members. Fortunately, many teachers develop the skills they need for service-learning team building by using what Cohen, Lotan, Whitcomb, Balderrama, Cossey and Swanson (1994) define as "complex instruction" in their classrooms with their students.

In complex instruction, teachers share responsibility for teaching and learning with their students. They assign students to cooperative learning groups (Johnson, Johnson & Smith, 1995) and help group members work together to develop multiple-intelligence learning activities (Gardner, 2000) that will lead to the accomplishment of goals or standards. Students, themselves, take major responsibility for establishing objectives, designing activities and evaluating their work and thus free the teacher to facilitate group and individual progress by "asking higher-order questions, extending the group's thinking on its activities, and taking care of status problems." (Cohen et al., p. 90) Teachers who are successful with complex instruction are able to help students use their multiple intelligences, personal interests and perspectives to work cooperatively on academic projects. They are also able to help students use the often unpredictable flow of group work to engage in higher order thinking. These teachers are likely to have developed the kinds of team building skills essential to successful service-learning.

An example shows how teachers can judge their abilities to use complex instruction as practice for service-learning team building. A math teacher wants students to understand the concept of average and its use as an interpretive tool. He assigns students to cooperative learning groups and asks for their help. Groups decide to use their textbooks and data ranging from sports scores to demographic information to review how to calculate an average and determine what an average can and cannot reveal about a particular set of scores or characteristics. They also decide to share their conclusions in an illustrated web page for other students. The teacher helps them parcel out tasks related to these two objectives in accord with the various abilities of group members. As they work in their groups, the teacher provides information as needed and at the same time, gauges his own abilities to 1) authenticate the differing contributions that students can make within their groups, 2) ask higher order questions that extend the groups' thinking and 3) guide the project to fruition without personally taking charge. By using an informal self-awareness scale of 1-4 for these three factors, the teacher can estimate his abilities to 1) bring diverse individuals together in a service-learning team, 2) help them work together on a project in the face of ambiguity and lack of structure and 3) guide team members toward accomplishing service-learning objectives while functioning as a team member himself.

Supportive Communication

Successful teachers recognize the centrality of supportive communication to their own and their students' success and consistently strive to employ and improve their communication skills. These teachers are well-equipped to communicate effectively within service-learning teams. As they do, four fundamental communication strategies will be important in their work: 1) active listening, 2) reinforcing self-esteem, 3) anchoring expectations in shared goals and 4) providing specific feedback and suggestions. Each of these basic strategies can be accomplished in a number of ways. Active listening, for example, can involve body language, paraphrasing, appropriate questioning and summarizing as well as other techniques. Reinforcing self-esteem can involve use of appropriate praise, empathy and humor, and requests for assistance. The use of questioning to develop group consensus is essential to anchoring a groups expectations, and specific feedback derives from careful analysis and observations of whatever is being critiqued.

The particular strategies a teacher employs to listen actively, reinforce self esteem, anchor expectations and provide feedback makes up his or her communication style. Essentially, though, service-learning teachers need to be confident that they can employ strategies in all four areas with their students and with administrators, parents and community partners. Opportunities to develop a sense of one's supportive communication skills abound—in the classroom, of course, but also in faculty and PTA meetings, in everyday encounters in the community and above all, in the multitude of family situations where communication is so central to the maintenance and enrichment of relationships. Teachers can do much to become aware of their own supportive communication styles by asking supervisors and peers to observe them at work. Instructional supervisors' classroom observations are a standard practice in K-12 education, and nearly every classroom observation instrument includes opportunities to observe for the four skills of active listening, reinforcing self-esteem, anchoring goals in shared expectations and providing specific feedback. It is easy and appropriate for teachers to identify communication as a professional development area of interest and ask supervisors to observe for these skills and collect relevant data. Teachers and supervisors can then analyze the data and set goals for improvement. Post-analysis conferences can also provide opportunities for teachers to observe and reflect on ways both they and their supervisors model the target communication skills during their interactions. With confidence in their communication skills, teachers can move effectively to using service-learning.

Analytical and Creative Problem Solving

Problems arise in any project, and service-learning projects with their involvement of many people and many experiences are no exception. When problems arise, it is likely that teachers will need to play a lead role in guiding project teams in analytical and creative problem-solving. Teachers lay the foundational skills for this type of problem-solving in service-learning by helping their own students solve problems that arise within complex instruction projects. They do this by attending regularly to the effectiveness with which students working on group projects use the five cooperative learning elements which are described in Chapters V and X and include positive interdependence, face-to-face-promotive interaction, individual accountability, social skills and group processing. (Johnson, Johnson & Smith, p. 42). This means that teachers help students determine if they are successfully depending upon one another to complete learning tasks, interacting to help one another, taking individual responsibility within their groups, using effective interpersonal skills and thoughtfully evaluating what they are doing in their groups. It also means they help students find ways to use these elements analytically to solve problems that arise.

Prospective service-learning teachers can gauge their own analytical and creative problem-solving skills by judging the degree to which they help students engaged in complex instruction projects analyze their use of cooperative-learning elements in aid of group problem-solving. To do this, teachers meet with groups that are having problems, review the five elements and ask student members to describe how they are using each of them. When it becomes evident that students are not using one or more elements, the teacher asks students to suggest how they could use the missing elements to solve the problem they have identified. When students come up with a solution and put it into effect, teachers ask them to rate their satisfaction with the problem-solving process they have used on a low (1), moderate (2), high (3) scale.

For example, students in the learning-about-averaging project described earlier complain to their teacher that their elected group leader is not laying out clear subtasks for them and nothing is getting done. The teacher helps students analyze their use of the five cooperative-learning elements, and it becomes evident that group members are not interacting to decide what has to be done, rather, they are all waiting for the leader to figure out who has to do what. The group reviews the meanings of positive interdependence and promotive interaction and discusses ways to use these elements to solve this problem. They decide that the group could brainstorm all subtasks necessary, then members could volunteer to take responsibility for particular ones. Members agree that as cooperative learners they are obligated to accept this solution. They decide that once they have laid out subtasks and assignments, the leader will record them, then the teacher will meet with the group to critique their plan, suggest subtasks that may be missing and help identify resources they can use to carry out subtasks. The teacher asks group members to rate their problem-solving process anonymously, and they rate their overall satisfaction level between moderate and high.

In the example, students and teacher use cooperative learning elements analytically and creatively to find a solution that democratically distributes group process as well as group effort and keeps all working together as a team. Teachers who can use these element to help student groups solve problems will be more able, as discussed in Chapter XII, to use these same elements to help project teams analytically and creatively solve problems that may arise as they work together.

Time-Management Skills

Successful teachers, like successful leaders, manage their time effectively. They know how much time they have in each day, what they expect themselves to accomplish, and how to allot the time they have to what they want to do. On the one hand, they recognize that time management applies not only to work but to their personal lives as well, and they do all that they can to organize professional work, personal tasks and recreation and renewal into a manageable whole. On the other hand, they recognize that there is probably never enough time to do all that they would like to do, and they have the wisdom to make adjustments in their lives accordingly. Teachers who intend to use service-learning can review and strengthen their time-management skills by looking at the ways they do four things: 1) plan time use, 2) prioritize tasks, 3) maintain an efficient workplace and 4) use unexpected free time.

Teachers depend on written plans whether in lists, plan books, personal or computerized calendars or hand-held electronic organizers. These planning records make it relatively easy to assign specific amounts of time to particular tasks and to use personal codes such as numbering, asterisks or underlines to prioritize then. Most teachers, too, quickly become skilled in using unexpected time. They invariably have clip boards, brief cases or tote bags handy so they can grade papers, outline lessons or design learning activities while waiting—for appointments, car repairs, or to pick up children, for example. What often seems less easy for even the best teachers is maintaining an efficient work space—probably because their desks are continually and legitimately besieged by students. But being able to find necessary materials promptly is so important in time management that many teachers find they can save time by having a work table separate from the "teaching desk" and keeping special projects in three-ring binders with related, labeled boxes for ancillary materials. For instance, a social studies teacher whose students are helping the local social services agency conduct a neighborhood needs assessment sets up a project notebook. Here she keeps each of her student's applications to take part in the project, a progress record for each student, a one-page directory of collaborating personnel that includes social-service liaison people, school administrators supporting the project and parents involved. The notebook also contains a running chart for recording dates of student visits to the social services agency, the purposes of the visits and their outcomes. In a large, labeled plastic box the teacher keeps related teaching materials, copies of the needs assessment itself and student and site-representative evaluation forms developed for the project. She keeps all of these materials on her teaching table.

Teachers can make sure their time-management skills will be adequate for service learning by visualizing, then describing in writing the strategies they intend to use to ensure their own planning, prioritizing, and efficient time and materials management. This may alert them to changes they need to make in their own behavior and work settings in order to meet the time demands of developing and implementing service-learning projects with a team comprised of students, one or more community partner representatives, parents and others.

In summary, by virtue of their education and experience, teachers are likely to possess the management skills they will need to use service-learning effectively. By identifying the kinds of motivation strategies they employ, assessing their abilities to build teams for complex instruction and determining their strengths as supportive communicators, problem solvers and time managers, teachers can prepare to work effectively with their students, parents, administrators, community partners and others in service-learning project teams. Teachers who wish to explore their own management skill profiles in greater depth can go to the Whetten and Cameron website at www.prenhall.com/whetten_dms/ where these authors provide self-assessment surveys related to all the management skills they identify. Table 3.1 below summarizes the five management skills for service-learning discussed here in Chapter III with teacher indicators of the skills, and strategies for reflecting analytically upon them.

Table 3.1 Instructional Management Skills for Service-Learning with Associated Indicators and Self-Profiling Strategies

Management Skills for Service-Learning	Skill Indicators	Self-Profiling Strategies
Motivating Others	• Knowledge of attraction, intrinsic and extrinsic motivation strategies • Emphasis on use of attraction and intrinsic strategies	Analyze lesson plans to 1. identify motivation strategies used 2. determine own pattern of emphasis in use of strategy types
Team Building	• Knowledge of Cooperative Learning • Knowledge of Multiple Intelligences Concepts • Use of Complex Instruction	Judge own abilities to 1. authenticate students' differing contributions, 2. use critical-thinking questions to extend groups' thinking 3. guide projects without taking charge
Supportive Communication	• Active Listening • Reinforcing Self-Esteem • Anchoring Expectation in Shared Goals • Providing Feedback and Suggestions	Ask supervisors and peers to rate communication skills using school-system evaluation instruments Observe own use of skills in post-observation conferences
Creative-Analytical Problem Solving	• Guiding Student Analysis of Use of Cooperative Learning Elements • Helping Students Use Elements to Solve Problems	Rate own abilities to locate problems and solutions in students' use of 1. positive interdependence 2. promotive interaction 3. individual accountability 4. social skills 5. group processing
Time Management	• Planning • Prioritizing • Workplace Efficiency • Unexpected Free Time Use	Determine own use of 1. planning devices 2. priority indicators within plans 3. project-dedicated workplace 4. unexpected-time materials

In concluding this discussion of instructional management skills for service-learning, it is important to state again, that the best way teachers can learn to use these skills and strengthen their development of them for use in service-learning is to utilize complex instruction that engages students in cooperative learning with multiple intelligences activities. This approach in the classroom provides teachers and students with a laboratory in which they can learn about and test the skills they will need to move into the larger arena of service-learning.

Students' Service-Learning Competencies

In addition to being in some measure messy, service-learning is also risky because it often takes students out of the classroom and involves them in experiences beyond the standard curriculum. Because service-learning entails some risk, teachers need to assemble information about students' capacities to move beyond the familiar to what may be new and even strange. Developing an understanding of students' capacities for undertaking any new learning approach—including service-learning—is a common sense activity in which teachers engage as a matter of course to determine if students have the maturity, skills and attitudes that will help them use the new approaches effectively. Typically, teachers use simple data collection and analysis combined with observations of behavior to determine if students have the requisite capacities for new learning approaches. With resultant information in hand, they then help students develop the strengths they need to go forward with the new methods and adjust the methods themselves in ways that are appropriate to students' present developmental situations. For example, if a teacher plans to ask students to use the Internet to carry out research on snakes, he will first make sure that students have access to personal computers, know how to use search engines and can to some reasonable degree discriminate relevant from irrelevant information on snakes. He will also set up and supervise practice sessions for students who do not have personal computers or are otherwise not fully ready for this activity.

With respect to preparing for service-learning, individual student profiles can be extremely helpful. Teachers can easily assemble data that will help them gauge students' service-learning competencies and can add brief summaries of observations of relevant student behavior. Initially this information suggests the type of project design students can benefit from, and eventually, these profiles as a group help service-learning project teams decide what kinds of activities to include in their service-learning projects. Further, as projects progress and culminate, the profiles can also provide base-line information against which to estimate personal growth of individual students and students as a group. The following discussion outlines six student competencies for service-learning that can be used to develop these profiles: conceptual readiness, self-management skills, cooperative learning skills, information gathering skills, ability to work with authority figures, and ability to work with people from diverse cultures.

Conceptual Readiness

In order to engage productively in service-learning, students need to have cognitive structures for service—mental organizations of ideas related to service—that they can use to construct understanding from their service experiences. Teachers need to make sure the rudiments of these structures are in place in students' minds before they engage in service-learning. Then as students have opportunities to learn through service, these cognitive structures will elaborate, become richer and more extensive. Teachers can ascertain that students have initial concepts of service by asking them to explain in writing what service means to them and to describe services they have rendered or would like to render. Teachers can ask students, too, to explain how members of their families provide service within the family and in other ways. Results can then be discussed as a group with teacher and students speculating together on the meanings of three core service elements: genuine need, mutuality and community building. Most important here are reflections on mutuality. Students need to deeply explore the idea that service is an activity in which those who give benefit as much as those who receive. They need to understand and explore the difference between charity and service. With sufficient, careful reflection on the nature of service, students will almost invariably reveal a genuine sense of altruism, the desire to help others and a sensitivity to ways in which they and those they may serve walk together on a shared journey. With these ideas activated, students take a critical step toward success in service learning.

Self-Management Skills

When it comes to students' self-management readiness, teachers begin early in any school year to judge their students' capacities to 1) understand the goals they are working toward, 2) think through strategies for achieving those goals and 3) work persistently toward accomplishing their goals. Teachers can combine their perceptions of students' skills in these areas with students' own awareness of them by creating brief self-report profiles. These ask students to anonymously rate themselves on a four-point scale ranging from "not very often" to "most of the time" on such statements as, "I make sure I know what I am supposed to do for a learning activity," "I try to think through the steps I will use to complete a learning activity" and "I keep working on a learning activity until I finish what I am supposed to finish." Class plots of responses in each of these areas tell teachers the kinds of service-learning-related, independent-work skills they need to build across their classes, and individual responses help them create structures for the particular kinds of service-learning activities in which will students eventually engage.

Cooperative Learning Skills

Cooperative learning is fundamental to service-learning. Students collaborate with their teachers, community partners and other adults and work together in groups to commit to service, identify desired outcomes, provide service and reflect upon it and evaluate and share results. Students who have developed cooperative learning skills will be far more able to manage the collaboration fundamental to service-learning and to achieve outcome expectations than those who have not. Thus it is essential that teachers who intend to use service-learning prepare their students by teaching them how to be cooperative learners. This means teaching students to help each other successfully complete learning tasks. It means teaching them interaction skills that will promote their shared task accomplishment. And it means teaching students how to take individual responsibility for their work, use interpersonal and social skills and thoughtfully evaluate their cooperative learning processes.

Cooperative learning is a widely used teaching and learning method; nearly every teacher is familiar with its general thrust, and many teachers actively promote cooperative learning in their classrooms. Teachers who regularly engage their students in cooperative learning are already prepared to take the natural next step to service-learning in the ways described in Chapter X of this book. Teachers who are not as experienced with cooperative learning will need to learn how to use the method and teach it to their students. This will take time, perhaps a full school year, but there is a wealth of material that can enhance their understanding and use of the method. Three books that are particularly useful because of the ways in which they link use of cooperative learning to elements important in service-learning are Slavin's (1995) *Cooperative Learning: Theory, Research and Practice*, Putnam's (1998) *Cooperative Learning and Strategies for Inclusion* and the *Handbook of Cooperative Learning Methods* (1994) edited by Sharan.

Information-Gathering Skills

As students participate on service-learning project teams, and as they provide service, they frequently need to independently gather new information from many sources. Teachers can easily assess students' specific competence in this area by using an adaptation of Torrance's (1962) time-honored alternate-uses technique. To do this a teacher lists 3-5 topics or circumstances for which information is needed, then has students brainstorm specific sources for this information. The teacher lists responses on the board or overhead and encourages students to work together and springboard from each others' suggestions. Once a good number of responses have been generated and listed, the teacher asks students to justify each suggested source in terms of its perceived usefulness in providing information relevant to the original topic. The teacher then looks at all the resources students suggest to see what sources they may not be aware of.

A high-school business teacher, for instance, asks students to generate information resources they can turn to as they seek to help families they are working with find out about tax-deferred, college-tuition investment programs. As students offer possibilities and justify them, the teacher categorizes them as human resources, traditional media, electronic media and public agency resources. In this example, the teacher determines that students need to become more familiar with electronic media resources both in support of their particular service-learning project and to aid them in all their academic work.

Ability to Work With Authority Figures

Students who engage in service-learning will interact with authority figures other than their parents and teachers. They will need to be able to make clear to these adults what their responsibilities as service-learners are, solicit appropriate assistance from them and accept evaluative feedback these adults may give them. One of the best ways to determine how well students do this is by using role playing as described by Joyce, Weil with Calhoun (2000). Teachers use this technique by creating scenarios in which students try out—role play— different ways of interacting with adults who control the resources they need in order to meet service-learning expectations and who evaluate how well they meet the expectations. Teachers and other students observe how the role players manage, then all discuss observations and make suggestions for improvement which are then tried out in new role plays. The cycle of role play, discussion and suggestions for improvement is repeated as many times as necessary for students to feel confident in their abilities to work with authority figures who control resources and often evaluate aspects of their service.

For example, a ninth-grade science teacher is hoping to involve her students in a service-learning project in which they will respond to a request for assistance from the county's mosquito control unit. She envisions linking the project to her students' learning about animals and insects as vectors in the spread of infectious disease. Her project has yet to cooperatively evolve, but to gauge their readiness for such a project, she uses a role play in which students imagine they are attempting to identify area disease hosts by interviewing a county health-services research physician. The teacher's instructional supervisor, who is unknown to the students, agrees to play the physician's role. As part of his role, the supervisor will begin the role play by saying he doesn't know what students want, but will help them if he can. When students explain their tasks, he will list one or two disease hosts, then refer students to a highly technical report for more information. Finally, he will tell students that they ought to identify the two or three disease hosts that are most dangerous to the public and forget the rest. After three repetitions of the role play cycle, the teacher uses a four-point scale described in the earlier section on self-management skills to determine how effectively students are able to 1) make clear the information they are seeking and explain why, 2) relate the information they receive to their task and 3) accept and use evaluative feedback in ways that keep them on task.

Ability to Work With People From Diverse Cultures

Students involved in service-learning will need to interact and work with people whose cultures differ from their own in a variety of ways. These may be people of different national or ethnic origin, people of different ages and people whose lifestyles differ from theirs. Fortunately, schools everywhere emphasize the importance of diversity in some way—either generally through the interpersonal attitudes and behaviors expected in all school transactions, or through multicultural curriculums that teach students specific skills for relating to people of all types. Teachers can observe the degree to which students practice respectful multicultural interactions in the classroom, but also can observe students' interactions with people they encounter on field trips and with school visitors. Students who can consistently employ three behaviors in their interpersonal interactions are likely to be able to move with reasonable confidence into the multicultural arena in which service often takes place, and once engaged there, become increasingly comfortable with learning from diversity. These three behaviors include 1) polite, substantive requests for information and assistance, 2) good listening skills and 3) courteous acknowledgement of responses they receive. Teachers can help students strengthen these behaviors by using role playing with discussion and replay as described in the preceding discussion. Students who master this small triad of interaction behaviors through real practice with each other and adults in their school environment are likely to succeed in the kinds of multicultural engagements that service-learning so often entails.

Integrating Student Service-Learning Competency Profiles

Because service-learning extends teachers' responsibility for their students beyond the classroom, teachers who plan to implement the method often want to develop a sense of their students' competencies in a fairly formal way. They can do this by setting up a check sheet based on the summary of student readiness indicators and associated information gathering strategies in Table 3.2. They can use the check sheet to profile each student's service-learning competencies on a four-point (low-high) scale, then summarize these in a class plot which will help reveal the kinds of skills students as a group need to develop in order to undertake-service learning.

In concluding this section, it is important to reiterate that successful teachers already use many, if not all, of the techniques described here and summarized in Table 3.2 to determine if students have the competencies they need for the profitable use of new learning approaches. Teachers who use these techniques to profile the particular competencies students need for service-learning will be determining if they have the skills necessary for dealing with increased amounts of information, more people and more ideas in settings that are different from the classrooms to which they are accustomed. Happily, as teachers assess students' competence in these areas and work to increase that competence, they will be readying students not only for service-learning but for life.

Table 3.2 Student Service-Learning Competency Indicators with Associated Information Gathering Strategies

Student Readiness Indicators	Information Gathering Strategies
Concept of Service	Ask students to define service and give examples of service they, family members and friends have performed. Reflect with students on service as a mutual endeavor.
Self-Management Skills	Have students rate their abilities to 1. understand the goals they are working toward 2. think through strategies for achieving those goals 3. work persistently toward accomplishing the goals
Cooperative-Learning Skills	Use prior experience with cooperative learning to determine students' abilities to 1. complete learning tasks interdependently 2. use positive, face-to-face interaction in pairs and group work 3. be individually accountable for their share in group work 4. use social and interpersonal skills in group work 5. analyze and improve their own group processes
Information-Gathering Skills	Use alternate-uses technique to determine students abilities to 1. identify resources relevant to topics/issues 2. justify relationships between named resources and topics/issues
Ability to Work with Authority Figures	Use role playing to determine students' abilities to 1. communicate own goals and responsibilities 2. elicit relevant information from supervisors 3. accept and use evaluative feedback
Ability to Interact with People from Diverse Cultures	Use observation of students in daily interactions with adults and role-playing cycles to determine their abilities to: 1. politely and substantively request information and assistance 2. listen carefully 3. courteously acknowledge responses received

Service-Learning Support Networks

Implementation of service-learning depends on the network of support for the method within the school system, among parents and in the community where it will be used. In some settings there may be only rudimentary support while in others, service-learning may be a continuing school-community initiative that parents support, and is part of the life of the community. Teachers need to have a good sense of the kind of support network in their own situations in order to effectively design, implement and evaluate service-learning projects. Three concepts from Bringle and Hatcher's (1996) work on the institutionalization of service-learning in higher education can help them do this. These concepts are awareness, planning and resources (pp. 275-6), and they can be applied to service-learning in middle and high schools in the following way. Situations in which school system leadership, parents and the community know about and are interested in service-learning, but are not actively using the method can be thought of as having awareness support networks. Situations in which these constituents engage collaboratively in planning for the use of service-learning can be thought of as having planning support networks, and situations in which constituents consistently commit resources to service-learning can be thought of as having resource support networks. Table 3.3 describes behaviors in which school system personnel, parents and community agencies engage to create awareness, planning, and resource support networks for service-learning

Table 3.3 School, Parent and Community Partner Behaviors that Comprise Support Networks for Service-Learning (Adapted from Bringle & Hatcher, 1996)

Support Network	School-System Leadership	Parents	Potential Community Partners
Awareness	Express interest Attend service-learning conferences Hold awareness sessions Survey teacher, parent and community interest	Receive informative publications Raise questions Call for discussion	Receive informative publications Publicize service needs Attend service-learning conferences
Planning	Join national organizations Establish initiatives Develop policies Create planning groups Create advisory groups Provide planning time	Visit exemplary programs Participate in planning or advisory groups Help children identify community needs Provide service	Participate in inter-agency councils Participate in planning or advisory groups Provide education on service-learning to agency personnel
Resource	Provide support personnel Assign space Provide funding Provide ongoing professional development Apply for grants Encourage action research Include service-learning participation in reward structure Create coordinating body Institutionalize service-learning programs Evaluate and publicize outcomes	Assist in service-learning program design and implementation with own services and/or material and financial resources Publicize outcomes	Provide service sites Provide support personnel Assign space Provide funding Help create coordinating body Recognize personnel participation Collaborate on service-learning research Institutionalize service-learning programs Evaluate and publicize outcomes

Teachers can use Table 3.3 to estimate the extent and strength of their support networks by determining how many of the awareness, planning and resource-commitment behaviors the constituents in their situations exhibit. They can then use results with community partners to determine the nature and scope of their service-learning projects.

Table 3.3 shows that service-learning networks enrich and integrate as constituents move from awareness of the method through planning for its use to committing the kinds of resources that will make it possible to institutionalize service-learning. When constituents are primarily at the level of awareness, resulting support networks are simple and loosely connected. When constituents reach the planning stage, networks are characterized by greater integration, particularly through planning, advisory and inter-agency groups. When constituents attach specific resources to service-learning, they create integrating elements such as coordinating offices and action research cycles that make it possible to institutionalize service-learning within school systems and in communities. As shown in the examples of the five service-learning designs in Chapter II, the kind of design possible within a school system depends directly upon the service-learning support network in that system.

Putting It All Together

Teachers need to prepare to use service-learning by analytically reflecting on their own and students' relevant skills and abilities and the level of support for service-learning in their own school systems and communities. They can do this in a simple and straightforward way by thinking through the three areas and summarizing each in a brief paragraph. They can also do this in a more detailed way, using check sheets that they derive from the variables and indicators for each area shown in Tables 3.1, 3.2 and 3.3. Whichever way they choose to reflect, they need readiness information to go forward with the next step in a service-learning project, helping students commit with a community partner to a service-learning relationship. They can do this with a good measure of confidence by using the process shown graphically in Figure 3.1.

Figure 3.1 Process for Preparing to Commit to a Service-Learning Relationship With a Community Partner

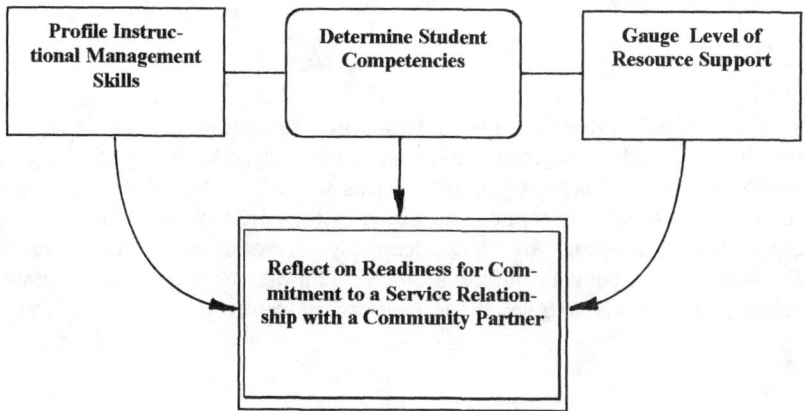

In thinking about the process that Figure 3.1 represents, teachers need to recognize that the three service-learning readiness factors are not simple yes-no switches. Rather they are multidimensional. Thus, while more experienced teachers are likely to have more and stronger instructional management skills, less experienced teachers and even teaching interns possess these skills in sufficient degree to transfer to service-learning. Similarly, students' self-management, cooperative learning and information gathering skills and their abilities to work with authority figures and people from diverse cultures are often a function of the instructional management skills of their teachers. Thus, students who are immature in some ways, but who are working with teachers who are good instructional managers may possess and be able to demonstrate these competencies to the degree necessary for success in service-learning. And in the same vein, the orientation toward service-learning that exists in the situation where the method will be used is likely to be multifaceted. Even though teachers may determine that service-learning infra-structure and material support are low in their situations, they may also find that the enthusiasm that surrounds developing awareness of the method provides a wellspring of psychological support that makes up for lack of money, space or formal organization.

As the figure shows, analysis of these three elements helps teachers think through and reflect upon the factors essential to committing with a community partner to a service-learning relationship. When they have reflected in this way, teachers must then use their own judgment. They must decide if their unique profiles of readiness factors support their use of service-learning, and on the basis of those profiles, which service-learning designs are likely to work best for them and their students. In many cases this reflective and personal judgment process will convince teachers that with the help of an appropriate design they can move forward with others in service-learning projects relevant to their own management skills, their students' skills and abilities and the resources available. In some few cases, teachers may find that they and their students need to lay additional foundations for using service-learning. They will be able to lay these foundations quickly and effectively because their analytical reflection has revealed the service-learning readiness elements that need attention in their own situations. They can address these directly and soon be ready to embark on service-learning with students and community partners.

In Conclusion

Teachers can prepare to undertake service-learning by analyzing their own instructional management skills, their students' readiness to deal productively with the wider arena of people, places and information that service learning entails, and by determining the kinds of support their particular teaching context makes available for service-learning. By carrying out this reflective analysis, teachers generate information they can use to guide their students in committing to productive service-learning relationships. In some instances reflective analysis may reveal needs to strengthen skills and resources for service-learning.

Activities for Increasing Understanding

1. Explore your own understanding of the concept of service by creating a collage, poster or sculpture that expresses your ideas of the meaning and relationships of genuine need, mutuality and community building within service. Accompany your work with an explanation of no more than 50 words of how your work's elements and total effect relate to the meaning of service for you.
2. Use techniques described in this chapter or appropriate surveys from the Whetten and Cameron website to reflect on your instructional management skills. Summarize your findings and suggest three personal goals for strengthening these skills in a paper of no more than 200 words.
3. Profile a group of students—either your own or those of a teacher you know—to estimate their readiness to undertake service learning by using at least three of the strategies described in this chapter's section on student readiness. Summarize the group's overall readiness as low, moderate, strong or high.
4. Outline a complex instruction activity that incorporates multiple intelligences and cooperative learning (see Chapter X) that you could use to teach an academic objective in ways that would exercise your own instructional management skills and students' skills for engaging in service-learning. Label components in your outline to indicate where they involve multiple intelligences, cooperative learning, and teacher and student skills for service-learning.
5. Use a copy of Table 3.3 with rows and columns labeled and cells empty to develop an overview of the service-learning support network available in your teaching context. Gather information for your table by interviewing a middle- or high-school principal, a parent of students at the school, a central office supervisor and a community social services director. Summarize the general character of the network you discern as primarily awareness-, planning- or resource-oriented.
6. Use the information you have gathered in activities 1-4 and the process described in Figure 3.1 to reflect in a brief written statement on your own and your students' (either real or hypothetical) readiness to commit to a service-learning relationship with a community partner.

Chapter IV: Committing to a Service-Learning Project

"So. You're not supposed to pour used paint thinner on the ground—not even on a sandy spot away from the house. Most people where I live do it. Probably couldn't convince 'em not too either," tenth-grader Joe Holloway snorts.

"It's your ground water they're poisoning, Joe," replies Manny Garcia from the front of the classroom. Remember what that guy from the county Environmental Protection Agency said—how we can all do ourselves a favor by disposing of hazardous home chemicals in the right way. We just need to convince people of the harm they may be doing to themselves and all of us."

Chemistry teacher Lisa Moranowsky advances to the front of the room. "Good report Manny. If we all followed your guidelines, everyone would be a lot safer. And you're right. We want the same things the EPA wants—for everyone's health and safety. You know, your report makes me wonder if the EPA could use our help in some way." She turns to the class. "How about it? Could we use what we're learning about household chemicals to help our local environmental protection office reach the people in your neighborhoods? And how could we do it—find out if the agency really needs our help. And if they do, how could we team up with them in a project that connects to what we're studying and makes a difference in our own community?"

Chapter Focus

In this scenario the stage is set for a teacher, her students and a potential community partner to move into the first phase of the collaborative service-learning model, the phase in which they commit to a service-learning project that will connect what students are learning to real community needs. The teacher identifies the essential characteristic of such a project—that it will be "founded on a shared vision and clearly articulated values" (Campus Compact, 1998, Stage I, Designing Partnerships). She does this by making clear that the rationale for students' potential partnering with their local environmental protection agency is the conviction they share with the agency that when people in their neighborhoods safely dispose of hazardous household chemicals, their community will be a better place to live. Thus, the project will be far more than an exercise in using a new teaching-learning method. It will be an opportunity for students to develop skills for democracy, to learn to work with community partners to improve the place where they all live.

The teacher also asks students to think about how to gather information they will need to collaboratively develop a project with their potential community partner. How, she asks, can they find out what the agency really needs? How can they determine if they can help meet those needs in ways that relate to what they are learning? The purpose of this chapter is to respond to the teacher's questions. The chapter explains how students, their teachers and community partners arrive at a commitment to service-learning projects that are based on mutual goals, roles and responsibilities. The chapter does this by explaining how these constituents integrate information about 1) community needs and issues, 2) students' learning goals and 3) students' capacities and interests, to propose service-learning projects in which they collaboratively contribute to the growth and strengthening of their communities.

Community Needs and Issues

Teachers help their students gather community needs and issues information by first having them identify and analyze a community in which they are able to provide service, one that is relevant to their ages and abilities. For younger students a community can be the school they attend or schools like theirs, or the neighborhoods in which they live. Older students can identify these same communities for the purposes of service-learning projects, but can also extend their communities of interest to their town, city or state, and in some cases to the entire country. While these several communities differ in size and complexity, each has needs and confronts community-relevant issues. Each, too, is supported by groups that attempt to meet these communities' needs and address these issues. When students become aware of the service networks in their communities of interest, they can efficiently gather needs and issues information that will help them commit with appropriate community partners to meaningful service-learning projects.

Students who are looking forward to service-learning often have a strong sense of their community of interest. In the scenario, for example, the tenth-graders are concerned about the needs of their own neighbors to adopt safe chemical disposal practices. There is already dialogue among them about what the issue is and how to address it. In other cases, students who are younger or may not yet see themselves as members of communities in which they can give as well as receive, need to explore possibilities. They need to become aware of the concept of community itself in order to identify needs and issues in their own communities, and to recognize their own potential for helping to strengthen those communities. In either situation, teachers play a key role in guiding students to identify the particular communities in which they can effectively provide service and to understand ways service in general is vital to these communities. Three strategies detailed in Chapter VIII help them do this: mapping, fact sheets and exploring a community's service needs.

Once students have identified a community that is relevant to them, they are ready to ask and answer the two-part question "What are the needs in our community and what groups help meet those needs?" The way teachers and students answer this question depends upon their own service-learning support networks. As Chapter III points out, a school system and its community can be in a stage of awareness, planning or resource commitment with respect to its support for service-learning. These stages affect the nature and extent of service-learning needs information available to teachers and their students.

Where a school system and its community regularly commits resources to service-learning, structures for gathering and disseminating service-needs and community-issues information will be in place. Where a system is primarily engaged in planning for service-learning, preliminary service-learning connections may have been established with the community, but community needs and issues information is likely to be less formally available. Where a system is in the awareness stage, there may be a general sense that there are community service needs to be met and issues to be addressed, but little detail about them. Thus teachers and students gather needs and issues information differently depending on the resources available to them in their service-learning support networks. The following describes these differences. The discussion begins with situations in which support networks are at the resources stage and are well developed, moves to those at the planning stage that are moderately developed, and concludes with suggestions about how to collect information in situations at the awareness stage where there are few or no resources assigned to service-learning.

Gathering Needs and Issues Information in High Resource Situations

When a school system has established a resources-level support network for service-learning and institutionalized the method, there is likely to be a service-learning coordinating group—a council, committee, office or director. This coordinating group generally defines community in a broad sense that may reach from neighborhoods to the level of the state. The coordinating group includes representatives of community agencies that support service-learning as well as other interested community members. These agencies and members understand the nature and practice of service-learning—that students will work with them to serve and strengthen the community and to learn from service and from serving. Typically, the coordinating group does three things: 1) keeps an updated compendium of service needs in the community, 2) keeps abreast of major issues the community confronts and 3) involves agencies in committing to service-learning.

The coordinating group regularly profiles its member agencies' service needs in terms of agency mission and goals, the kinds of service agencies want help in providing and requirements that those who assist them in service must meet. The group then publishes this in a document such as a newsletter, report or directory or on a website. Teachers and students can use these service-needs publications to identify possible service-learning project partners. They can determine which agencies have service needs that best connect to academic goals they are working on, then invite these potential partners to commit to and develop service-learning projects. As they move through this process the coordinating group often provides technical and resource assistance.

Gathering Needs and Issues Information in Moderate Resource Situations

School systems that have planning-level support networks for service-learning and commit some resources to this planning usually have created advisory groups that include representatives of the schools and community agencies and often parents. While these advisory groups are often aware of their constituents' service needs and issues, they may not be formally documenting and disseminating this information. Teachers and students can meet with these advisory groups to determine what they know about service needs and community issues that service-learning might address. They then document this information by listing the names of agencies and organizations that the advisory group suggests together with particular needs and issues these entities address. As part of this, teachers and students may often need to do additional research— using community directories, phone calls and personal contacts—to annotate their lists with clear descriptions of the mission and goals of each agency, its specific service needs, requirements for those who help meet those needs and contact persons who will help ensure that learning is linked with service. They can then examine these lists, contact particular agencies who seem to be potential partners and work with them to commit to and develop specific service-learning projects. Because all are working within a planning-for-service-learning support network, they are often able to call upon lead school and community persons to help facilitate commitment and project development.

Gathering Needs and Issues Information in Low Resource Situations

Teachers and students in school systems that have awareness-level support networks for service-learning but assign few if any resources for its use must become their own service-needs-information coordinators. Several strategies detailed in Chapter VIII help them do this: finding success stories, community, gathering service-agency information and formal needs assessment. These strategies introduce students to many aspects of the communities in which they hope to serve and learn, and in this way, can motivate their community contributions both immediately and in the future.

In addition, gathering community needs and issues information involves students in educating potential community partners about service-learning and motivating them to commit to the method. In high and moderate resource situations, potential partners have already come forward to participate in service-learning councils and advisory groups and are likely to understand and support the philosophy and process of service-learning. They recognize that they will be working with students in ways that are mutually beneficial as they strengthen the community. In low resource situations, however, potential partners are often more familiar with service as it is provided by volunteers who usually do not have specific academic goals related to their service. In other words, potential partners may not have had opportunities to explore service-learning as a collaborative teaching-learning method and will need to be oriented to its educational character. Teachers and students in low resource situations who seek needs and issues information can help educate potential partners about service-learning by using the four steps described on pages 67-8 of this chapter in the section entitled "Putting It All Together in a Service-Learning Commitment."

Connecting Students' Academic Goals to Service

Students who gather needs and issues information, begin to identify potential community partners and speculate on possible service-learning projects need to understand how to operationally connect service with the academic goals and they are working on in the classroom. For example, the tenth-graders and teacher in the opening scenario generally agree that encouraging their neighbors to use safe disposal practices will help them learn about hazardous chemicals. This is only the beginning, however. These students and their teacher must go on to decide with their community partner—in this case, the state environmental protection agency—what specific activities students will use to develop necessary information about safe disposal of chemicals and how they will convince their neighbors to accept and use this information. In other words, to link real service to real learning, students need to learn how to develop their service-learning projects as service-learning curriculum. Teachers can help them do this by teaching them a basic curriculum-development process, then that process to think about ways to transform existing, classroom-only curriculum into service-learning curriculum.

Probably the most widely used curriculum development process today is based on the specification of goals for learners in terms of instructional objectives, learning activities and assessments. Teachers use the process by identifying the state, local and sometimes national standards that their students are expected to meet and setting these as academic goals. They then develop standard-based outcome objectives that partition the goals into learnable segments. Next, they design instructional activities (IA) that help students achieve the objectives and thereby meet the standards. They also design paper/pencil (P/P-A) and performance assessments (P-A) that measure the degree to which students accomplish objectives and meet standards. Figure 4.1 maps this basic process teachers use to develop curriculum that helps students achieve educational standards/goals.

Figure 4.1 A Map for Standards-Based Curriculum Development

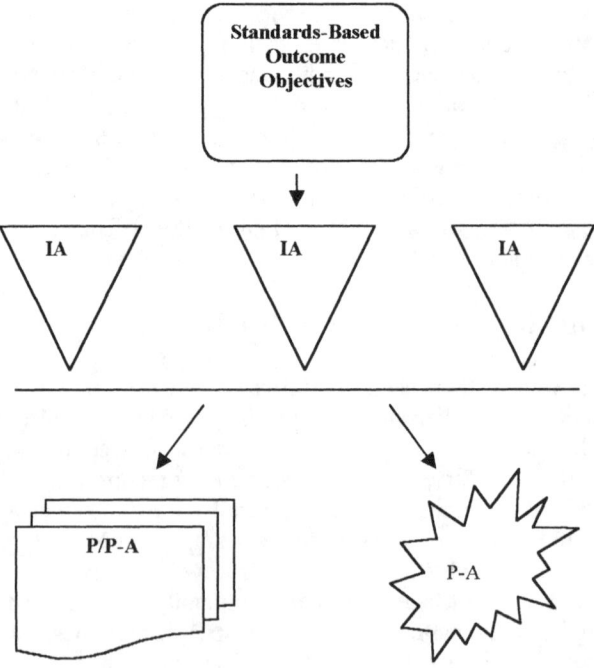

Most students are not fully aware of the process shown in Figure 4.1, and need to learn about it in order to collaborate in developing service-learning projects that tie service to expected academic outcomes. Teachers can help students do this by focusing them on an academic standard they have already studied, helping them recall and record the curriculum map for the standard, then challenging them to think of how they might adjust the map's learning activities to achieve its target outcomes through service. Once students have gathered information about service needs and issues in their community of interest, their teacher can use the following steps to teach them what they will need to know to collaboratively develop a service-learning curriculum.

The teacher begins by explaining that students can learn to develop a service-learning project by reviewing past units they have studied. The teacher reminds students that units are based on standards which are the goals for what students should learn, and writes on the board the standard for the unit which they are about to review. Students write the standard on worksheets. Next the teacher helps students recall the standard-related objectives they worked on within the unit and has them write these in an abbreviated form on their worksheets. Finally, teacher and students recall learning activities they used to achieve the objectives and tests they took to demonstrate achievement of objectives and note these briefly on their worksheets. The teacher now asks students to look over the service needs and issues information they have gathered for their community of interest and to imagine many service-based activities they might use to meet some of the community's needs. The teacher lists students' service activity suggestions on the board or overhead, then asks students to identify any of these activities that might have been used to accomplish the objectives of the unit they have just recalled and mapped. Students identify possible matches and list them on their worksheets. Examples of worksheets completed by younger, intermediate and older students show how teachers can use this process to teach students how to build service-learning projects by building from what they know to what is new.

Example One: Fifth-grade Study of Photosynthesis

Standard:	(Supplied by teacher) Understand plants as energy systems
Objectives:	(Recalled by students and teacher) Determine effects of light, water, air on plant growth
Activities:	(Recalled by students and teacher) Read about photosynthesis. Did experiments by growing plants with and without 1) light, 2) water, or 3) air
Assessments:	(Recalled by students) Reports on experiments, reports on own houseplants, multiple-choice test on how photosynthesis works
Service Links:	(Based on student identified community needs) City Park- Grow and donate flower packs. Arbor Day Observance- Develop citizen's guide to successful planting

Example Two: Ninth-grade Study of Novels

Standard:	(Supplied by teacher) Read literature to understand human experience
Objectives:	(Recalled by Students) Compare and critique central characters' problem in two novels
Activities:	(Recalled by students and teacher) Identified 1) goals 2) conflicts 3) problem-solving strategies of main characters in two personally selected novels.
Assessment:	(Recalled by students) Class analysis of types of goals, conflicts and strategies in all novels read, wrote essays on personal view of goals, conflict and solution in own novels.
Service Links:	(Based on student identified community needs) Nursing Home-Read to patients, talk about characters. Public Library-Create display of good summer books for teens.

Example Three: Eleventh-grade Study of American History

Standard:	(Supplied by teacher) Summarize issues of regional Native-American groups
Objectives:	(Recalled by students) Identify Native-American groups locally present during colonial period, identify issues raised by colonization
Activities:	(Recalled by students) Read text, talked with representative Native-American speakers, Used USA Index of Tribes website
Assessment:	Bulletin board on issues of each group, essay test on issues and similarities and differences across groups
Service Links	(Based on student identified community needs) Local historical society-Prepare albums, bibliographies about local Native-American groups. Prepare brochures about Native-American artifacts collection.

When teachers use this curriculum review process to help students understand how standards, goals and activities integrate in a unit they have already studied, they provide students with a model they can use to assist in coherently laying out new service-learning projects. With this in mind, teachers ask students to retain their worksheets for use with community partners.

Students' Capacities and Interests

When students first explore possible links between the service needs and issues they have identified and their academic studies, they may not always see direct connections between what is needed and what they, themselves, are able to do and are interested in doing. Teachers can help students become aware of and make connections by helping them understand and consider three kinds of service: direct service, indirect service and advocacy. By understanding and imagining activities in terms of each of these forms of service, teachers and students can envision and propose the kinds of service-learning commitments that will work best for them as unique learning groups.

Direct Service

Direct service means engaging face-to-face with individuals who are in need and assisting them to do something they might otherwise not be able to do. Examples include caring for children in a public agency waiting room, grocery shopping for shut-ins, teaching English to non-speakers of the language, helping people with tax forms, and providing computer tutoring to people of all ages. As these examples show, direct service often involves individual students in assisting individual recipients. In addition, direct service usually requires students to go to recipients' locations. If students are to provide direct service, they must be interested in one-on-one interactions, be able to move confidently through the community to get to the site where they will perform the service and be able to competently use skills they have learned or are learning as they deliver specific services. As a general rule, older students are usually more capable of developing and implementing direct, community-based service-learning projects. Younger students, however, can easily engage in direct service-learning projects if they serve within their own schools or in the general environs of those schools. They can also provide direct service in other schools within their school system if parents or the system itself can assist with transportation, and they can provide direct assistance in their own neighborhoods if their parents are willing to partner with them in service efforts that help neighbors in ways that incorporate school learning. Students who engage in direct service as part of service-learning need to recognize that as Sigmon (1996) asserts " the aim of a service activity is to engage with someone so that the service is one of mutuality, each serving the other, so that each can be more autonomous and more able to care for self and care for others" (p. 228).

Indirect Service

Indirect service provides the wide-ranging support that makes the delivery of direct service possible. Because there are so many ways to support service delivery, and because indirect service can be organized to minimize transportation needs, students of any age can provide this type of service. Whether students have their own transportation, depend upon parents, school busses or special field trips, they can use in-school, after-school and weekend time to provide indirect service. For example, they can work individually or in groups to raise funds for disaster relief, scholarships or medical equipment. They can clear land for neighborhood parks, or collect and test samples of soil, air and water for health agencies. They can write and mail newsletters, deliver flyers and take pictures in support of public service events and programs. In essence, indirect service provides students multiple opportunities to play meaningful parts within community partners' programs. Through indirect service, they can appropriately contribute to the kind of service-agency, cooperative community-building that as Morton (1995) explains, aims at identifying problems and developing and implementing solutions.

Advocacy

When students take a stand on an issue, work to promote a cause, a behavior, an attitude or idea, they are serving as advocates. Like indirect service, advocacy is flexible because students can advocate in ways that minimize demands for transportation. They can write letters to the editor, make persuasive video-tapes, perform plays and hold debates on relevant school and community issues. They can gather and transmit information to support their community partners' programs and events, and they can remind neighbors and friends of community responsibilities such as voting or attendance at important meetings. With its flexibility, advocacy also carries an imperative for informed decision-making. Students need to carefully explore the issues, needs and causes they join as part of service-learning so that the stands they take and the proposals they put forward are grounded in un-biased fact and reasoned judgment. For when students become advocates, they are often working for the kind of social change identified by Morton—more democratic distribution of resources and social capital and the transformation of the world as it is to the world as it might be.

In conclusion, teachers can help students find links between service needs and issues and their own capacities by helping them think in terms of direct service, indirect service and advocacy. They can do this by having students build on their curriculum model worksheets described earlier. Students set up a three-column chart on the back of their worksheets with cells labeled "direct service, " "indirect service," and "advocacy." Next, they place their imagined service-learning activities for their reviewed units in the appropriate cells and propose additional service-learning activities as necessary. Results for the three worksheets shown earlier on pages 63-64 might look like those in Table 4.1. Italicized activities are the additional activities students propose for types of service not already represented by activities on their worksheets.

Table 4.1 shows that students can use the concepts of direct and indirect service and advocacy to explore opportunities for linking service with their studies. By imagining direct service, indirect service and advocacy activities for units they have already completed they build their understanding of how to develop service-learning projects that link needed community service to their academic studies. As they do this, however, it is essential that teachers emphasize three things. First, the service-learning activities students suggest during curriculum modeling are tentative explorations of possibilities. Second, the actual service-learning activities students eventually use will be developed collaboratively with a community partner. Third, to go forward toward the development of these activities, they need to identify community partners and commit with them to a service-learning project.

Table 4.1 Examples of Direct, Indirect and Advocacy Service-Learning Activities

Example One: Fifth-grade Study of Photosynthesis		
Direct Service: Grow and donate flower packs for community park flower beds	Indirect Service: *Propose and develop plan for children's educational garden*	Advocacy: Design citizen's guide to successful planting
Example Two: Ninth-grade Study of Novels		
Direct Service: Read and discuss novels with nursing home residents	Indirect Service: Create public library, summer books for teens display	Advocacy: *Write book reviews for teen section of local paper*
Example Three: Eleventh-grade Study of American History		
Direct Service: *Contact Native-American group members about contributing materials to the society*	Indirect Service: Prepare Native-American albums, bibliographies for inclusion in local historical society collection	Advocacy: Prepare promotional brochures about society's Native-American artifacts

Putting It All Together in a Service-Learning Project Commitment

When a teacher and students have gathered community needs and issues information, have a general sense of how to incorporate service activities into standards-based curriculum, and understand the three ways to provide service, they are ready to commit with a community partner to the design and implementation of a service-learning project. In high and moderate resource situations, teachers and students can move fairly quickly into a service-learning relationship with potential community partners who understand the method. They invite one or more of these partners' representatives to attend an opening meeting to discuss service-learning possibilities and agree upon the general outlines for one or more service-learning projects. In low resource situations, however, potential community partners are likely to need orientation to service-learning. Teachers and students can accomplish this by cooperatively using the four following steps:

1. List the names of 1-3 groups and agencies students have identified as having service needs related to a standard they will be studying.
2. Confirm identified service needs with agencies, and arrange appointments with them to discuss service-learning as a way of meeting these needs.
3. Prepare and send to potential partners materials that confirm the appointments, share information about students, and provide examples of successful service-learning projects accomplished by other similar students.
4. Visit potential partners, explain service-learning as shared community development through service linked to study, and review pre-sent materials

as necessary. Invite agency representatives to come to a meeting to help students outline a possible service-learning project that responds to the agency's service needs and helps students learn.

While the four steps above are all essential to fully educating potential community partners about service-learning, the third may be the most critical because it helps motivate potential partners by providing them with in-hand, relevant material they can examine and re-examine. Chapter VIII details three strategies for developing these motivational materials which include class introductions, resource groups and class directories.

With steps in the list complete and the initial project-commitment meeting underway, teacher and students identify the academic standard and objectives they believe may link to participating agencies' identified needs. They describe the kinds of academic in-class activities they will use to accomplish these particular objectives and ask potential partners to suggest agency-needed, direct service, indirect service or advocacy activities that might also help them accomplish the objectives. As ideas emerge, the teacher guides students and potential partners in cooperatively completing commitment forms that outline possible service-learning projects. If several project outlines develop, the group discusses them and either selects the one that seems most appropriate in terms of students' and community partners' needs and resources, or if resources are available, the group agrees to go forward with all of the projects. The following example describes how an eighth-grade mathematics teacher and her students uses this service-learning commitment process to join with their community police department in outlining a collaborative service-learning project.

An Example of Collaborative Commitment to a Service-Learning Project

In September, the teacher who has decided to use service-learning has students design, administer and analyze a questionnaire about the service needs of the five community agencies in their small town. As they identify needs, she sees possible connections with the class's upcoming study of measures of central tendency. Students will be learning about use of the mean, mode and median as part of a state mathematics standard calling for competence in the use of data analysis tools. In October, the teacher provides students with a copy of the standard and proposes that they use service-learning to achieve it. The class agrees that to meet the standard, they will need to be able to show use of measures of central tendency in charts, graphs and tables that display data drawn from real life. The teacher now calls attention to the service needs list that resulted from their questionnaire. Discussion reveals possible links between the standard and three needs in their community: the board of education's need to reduce school vandalism, the police department's concern for teen driver safety and the county health department's campaign to improve children's eating habits. Students are most interested in the teen driver safety issue since it is something they will soon have to know about in order to get driving licenses. They decide to explore a service-learning relationship with the police department. Representative students visit the police chief and explain service-learning with examples of two successful middle-school projects found through the National Service-Learning Clearinghouse website. The chief agrees to send a representative to a project planning meeting.

At the meeting, teacher, students and the sergeant representative from the police department discuss the data analysis standard and its objectives. The teacher explains that in class, students will learn how to use means, modes and medians. The sergeant suggests that students could advocate for area teens' safe driving by creating displays of central tendencies in local statistics related to teen driving accidents and causes. Students agree to do this, and the teacher provides the following graphic organizer which contains the titles 'Standard," "Service Need/ Issue," "Objectives," "Type of Service" and "Service-Learning Commitment" in its five sectors as well as statements of the standard students are working on and the service need they have agreed to address (all shown in bold type). Students and the sergeant complete the organizer (shown in italics) to record their shared commitment to a service-learning project. As these constituents complete this form, they become a service-learning project team.

**Figure 4.2 Graphic Organizer for
Making a Service Commitment**

Standard **Use Data Analysis Tools**		**Service Need/Issue** **Teen Safe Driving**
	Service-Learning Commitment *Use charts, graphs and tables that display central tendency statistics for local teen driving accidents to help convince area teens to drive safely*	
Objectives *Display central tendency measures for real-life data in charts, graphs and tables*		**Type of Service** *Advocacy*

The graphic organizer in Figure 4.2 summarizes and records a collaborative commitment made by eighth-grade math students and their police department partner using four essential elements: an academic standard, its related objectives, a service need and a form of service for meeting that need. By integrating these elements, the organizer generates in its central cell a proposal for a service-learning project. Depending upon the teacher's experience, students' service-learning competencies and the service-learning support network available, the project can eventually take the form of an in-class approach, a community-based event, a prototype, a component in a curriculum design or a project within a service-learning program.

When members of a budding service-learning team have committed together to a summary outline of their service-learning project such as the one in Figure 4.2, they are ready to move forward to actually plan their project. This will involve them in determining the specific outcomes they want students to achieve in the areas of academics, service and personal growth, and developing reflective learning activities that can promote these desired outcomes. It will also involve them in evaluating their work together and celebrating the growth they discern. Throughout, they will work as a collaborative team in which all members "have the same information and plan of action and know and respect each other's role in the project" (Irizarry, 1996, p. 25).

In Conclusion

Committing to service-learning enlists teachers, students and community partners in laying foundations for shared project development. Together, they focus on service needs and issues, students' academic goals and kinds of service that can integrate these elements. This leads them to a proposal for a collaborative service-learning project and the formation of a service-learning project team. Teachers guide this integrative approach with their students in ways consistent with their own teaching experience, students' needs, interests and abilities, and the level of available service-learning support. Teachers may engage students and community partners in the service-learning commitment process through brief discussions of standards, service opportunities and possible types of service, or may work systematically through the commitment steps using a graphic organizer such as the one in this chapter (p. 69).

Activities for Increasing Understanding

1. Write a paper of no more than 500 words discussing your positive reactions to and reservations about involving students in service-learning curriculum development. Justify your position in your own teaching situation and your professional understanding of the students you teach or plan to teach.
2. Review the characteristics of service-learning support networks in Table 3.3, then assume that you are working in a situation where the support network is at the awareness stage. Identify (and imagine where necessary) the following information and integrate it in a service-learning commitment plan using a graphic organizer like the one presented in Figure 4.2.
    a. a standard that your students or those you plan to teach must meet
    b. 2-3 specific student learning objectives related to the standard
    c. a possible service-partner with needs related to the standard and its objectives
    d. direct service, indirect service or advocacy that your students could provide to meet the possible partner's needs.

Chapter V: Setting Goals in a Student Outcomes Plan

"OK everybody, let's arrange the desks conference style. Mr. Kincaid from the Neighborhood Watch Council, our parent volunteer, and the vice principal should be here in ten minutes to help us plan our project. Jeryl, you and your group need to set up the refreshments table." Ninth-grade civics teacher Darren Jackson, wipes his brow furtively and glances out the door.

"Don't be nervous, Mr. Jackson. We're with ya' on this. Student Augustine Arroyo gives his teacher a companionable wink as he pushes a desk into place. *"It'll be different—maybe even interesting. And no homework, no tests. Right Mr. J?"*

"Now, Auggie. We talked about this meeting in detail—you know we're going to work with Mr. Kincaid, our parent volunteer, and the veep to develop tests to determine what you learn from the project—different, yes, but we'll still be accountable for our learning and for our service."

"I know, I know, Mr. J. Just tryin' to loosen ya' up. Like I said, we're with ya'."

"Thanks, Auggie. I am a little nervous. This is my first try with service-learning."

Chapter Focus

Effective service-learning projects depend upon reciprocity, "the act of giving and receiving at the same time such that both parties in the service relationship teach each other and learn from each other." (Cumbo & Vadeboncoeur, 1999, p. 85) Reciprocity begins in the commitment phase of service-learning when a teacher, students and a community partner learn about each others' goals, capacities and interests and form a team to collaboratively develop an outline for a service-learning project. It continues as the team learns how to integrate the various goals they have for students in a plan that specifies what students should be able to do as a result of the project and describes how students' achievement of these outcomes will be measured. This chapter explains how a service-learning project team carries out this reciprocal outcomes planning process. The discussion is framed in terms of a team that is developing its first service-learning project within a school system that has a service-learning support network at the awareness level. It lays out steps the team takes to add key players, mutually agree upon academic, service and personal growth goals for students, and decide how to determine the degree to which students meet these goals. These steps, however, are not limited to use in limited support network situations. They are applicable across situations and can be used by teachers, students and community partners who have access to support networks that are at the planning level or at the full resources level. Examples that conclude the chapter demonstrate this generalizability.

Assembling Key Players

Service-learning involves key players in addition to teachers, students and community partners. These people include clients to be served, parents, school administrators and supportive community members. They have differing reasons for becoming involved and view service-learning projects and activities from different perspectives, and they will need to take on new roles and responsibilities within service-learning. Project teams can do much to assist these key players in moving into their new roles by assembling them from the outset in ways that help them define these new roles and function in them.

Clients to Be Served

Service-learning projects grow stronger when those whom students will serve can send a representative to planning meetings, or when the community partner can bring client needs and interests information to these meetings. An example of a small, but important point related to working with older people explains this. Many older people are hard of hearing and those who help them must raise their voices. Some, however, are not hard of hearing and feel shouted at if voices are raised. Students who will be serving in a senior center need to know this, need to be prepared to ask clients if they can hear and adjust their voices accordingly. While senior center clients may not be able to attend planning meetings, the community partner who represents their center can and should take responsibility for sharing client's needs and interest information. Once a project team is formed, the teacher on the team facilitates client's input by asking the community partner to bring either client representatives themselves or client needs and interest information.

Parents

Parents are key members of service-learning project teams because they can encourage support by other parents and help them gain confidence in service-learning as an educational method. Some parents may feel that service-learning is dangerous; others may feel that it is a time-wasting way to learn, and others may have no idea of how it works. Much can be done to allay these concerns by making sure that a parent selected by the parent-teachers association of the school or by the school administration serves on the service-learning project team. The basic criteria for selecting this person are 1) commitment to representing all parents, 2) participation in school support activities, 3) interest in service-learning and 4) good communication skills. This parent should also be willing to prepare brief reports on the project's progress for distribution to other parents in a letters home or a school newsletter.

School Administrators

Administrative support is essential to the success of any school project and nowhere is this more important than in service-learning. Teachers and students will engage in a variety of new activities in class and possibly away from the school; new people will be involved and may be coming and going to the school and classroom in new ways. Things will be different, and the school administration needs to be informed of what will happen in each step of a service-learning project from its earliest conceptualization. Equally important, administrators represent and control resources. They are educators themselves, have experience with planning and evaluation, know who among parents and community members might be called upon for personal and material support, and may have discretionary funds which they can grant under appropriate circumstances to a project. They are vital members of any service-learning project team.

Community Members

Community members widen the network of support for service-learning that teams using the method work to build throughout the project. They often come from a private, non-profit support group—perhaps a foundation—established to facilitate the goals of its local school system. But they can just as often come from business and industry in the community. Here again, administrators can be very helpful in finding one or two community members who have genuine interest in school-community relations and who are willing to serve on a service-learning project team. Once involved they often work assiduously to add resources to the particular project and to create the circumstances and structures that will help institutionalize service-learning.

Teams need to formally invite the participation of other key players. They can do this by sending them a letter similar to the one in Figure 5.1 based on the example from Chapter IV in which students plan to use measures of central tendency to advocate teen driver safety.

Figure 5.1 Sample Letter of Invitation to Additional Service-Learning Project Team Members

Three Oaks Middle School
1413 Three Oaks School Road
Middletown Illinois 12345

(Address and title of invitee)
Dear _____

*Our eighth-grade mathematics class is planning a service-learning project with the Middletown Police Department Division of Traffic Safety. We will use what we are learning about in math class to help convince Middletown teens to drive safely. Our specific service-learning proposal is to **use graphs, charts and tables displaying central tendency statistics for area driving accidents to convince area teens of the importance of driving safely.***

Would you help work on this community issue by becoming a member of our service-learning project team? Members of the team include our teacher Ms. Cheng, our vice principal Mr. Hartman, Sergeant Mendoza of the police department, two teens from Middletown High School, a parent from our school and a representative of the Middletown Better Schools Council.

Ms. Cheng will call you next week to see if you are willing to come to a planning meeting here at the school which we are scheduling for Tuesday, November 12 at 2:00 P.M. We look forward to hearing from you.

Sincerely,

Members of Ms. Cheng's Eighth-Grade, Fifth-Period Math Class

A letter like the one in Figure 5.1 should be sent to each prospective project-team member including any new representatives that the community partner wants to include. The text can be adjusted depending on the addressee, but all invitees receive the same basic information. Once letters are sent and commitments to attend returned, teacher, students and their administration representative attend to logistics for the meeting. Students can create nametags for all including themselves, and help produce an agenda that includes time for introductions, review of the service-learning project's purposed thrust, and a work session. Typically this first meeting will take two hours and once the agenda is developed it can be sent in advance to all participants.

The Initial Meeting: Focusing on Outcomes

It might appear the project team's initial task is to design learning activities students can use to combine service with learning. Increasingly, however, lead service-learning researchers such as Eyler (2000) propose that before a team can think about instruction, it needs to set outcome expectations that will create "scaffolding that supports student and teacher learning." Then, "the next step will be to identify the specific organizational and instructional strategies that increase the power of service-learning to add to these outcomes" (p. 13). To create a scaffolding for a service-learning project, the project team uses a "backward mapping" process (Compact for Learning and Citizenship, 2001, p. 14) to focus first on student outcomes and their measurement, then create instructional activities to help students achieve these outcomes. The team works together to help answer two questions: "What do we want students to know and be able to do as a result of service learning?" and "How will students show that they can do these things?" As the team answers these questions, it lays out an outcomes measurement plan that will make the following possible:

1. Efficient development of service-learning activities that help students achieve desired outcomes
2. Evidence of students' accomplishment of academic, service and personal growth outcomes
3. Information about how students outcomes might be improved
4. Contribution to the increasing knowledge-base for service-learning

To actualize these possibilities, service-learning project teams can use a "multi-constituency approach" to create a student outcomes plan. The approach was developed by Gelmon, Holland, Driscoll, Spring and Kerrigan (2001) to specify and measure college students' service-learning outcomes. It is also appropriate for middle- and high-school teams for two reasons. First, the approach uses a basic accountability paradigm familiar in secondary education. Second, it helps constituencies who come to service-learning outcome planning with different needs, interests and perspectives to identify and agree to a common set of outcome expectations for students To use the multi-constituency approach a project team conceptualizes service-learning outcomes in three areas. Two of these areas—academics and service—unite through the service-learning process in a third area—student personal growth. Figure 5.2 graphically describes the intersection of the academic and service outcome areas to produce the personal growth area.

Figure 5.2 Three Service-Learning Outcome Areas

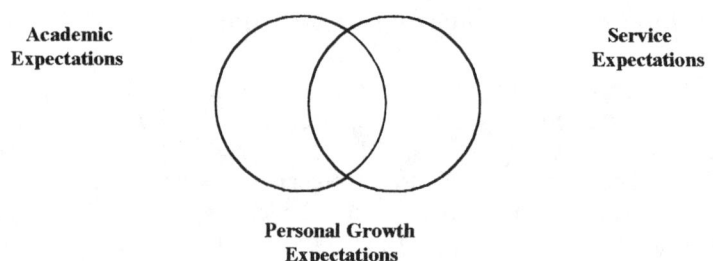

Project teams complete four tasks in order to decide upon the outcomes they want students to achieve in the three areas depicted by Figure 5.2 and incorporate these in a student outcomes plan. They 1) identify student outcome expectations in each area, 2) specify how students will indicate that they meet these expectations, 3) select strategies to measure students' meeting of expectations and 4) assign responsibilities for aspects of the measurement process. The following details these four tasks.

Task One: Identifying Student Outcome Expectations

In traditional, classroom-based instruction, expectations for students lie primarily in the academic area. In service-learning, expectations distribute across the three areas of academics, service and personal growth, and no one area generates all expectations. For example, sixth-grade students who study the universe in the classroom alone learn theories about and map the solar system, constellations and galaxies. Their teacher assesses their abilities to name and locate celestial bodies and find particular planets, stars and formations on a night star-gazing trip. Another group of sixth-graders learns through service as guides at a local planetarium. They learn theories in class and map the universe at the planetarium. They demonstrate recall of universe components on a classroom test, discuss theories of the universe in a joint school-planetarium symposium, and present information on astronomy careers during tours for elementary school children. Students in this second group are expected to accomplish somewhat more overall, but have more people helping them learn and more varied ways of showing what they've learned. Further, this second group is likely to learn in greater depth. It benefits from "a method that is ideally suited to help students develop a deeper understanding of subject matter, a practical knowledge of how community decision-making processes work and strategies for transferring knowledge and problem solving skills to new situations" (Eyler, 2000, p.12). This deeper learning results when a project team sets expectations in each of the three service-learning outcome areas.

Middle- and high-school service-learning project teams can select their outcome expectations for students from a basic set of widely accepted core expectations in the three areas. In the academic area, for instance, teachers, students, parents and the community agree that students need to acquire subject-area knowledge and skills and know how to use them. Academic tests measure students' abilities to 1) remember, 2) understand and 3) apply what they have been taught. Thus knowledge, comprehension and application first described for education by Bloom (1956) and updated by Anderson and Krathwohl (2001) are widely accepted core expectations for the academic area of service-learning. In the service area, service agencies expect students to help them accomplish their missions with clients by serving competently and in an appropriately caring manner. Ferrari and Worrall (2000) have worked with agencies that participate in service-learning to identify and describe behaviors these agencies see as indicators of competence, and Liddell, Halpin and Halpin (1992) build on Gilligan's (1982) work on the ethic of care to propose indicators of caring. In the personal growth area, reviews of service-learning research by Billig (2000a) and Eyler, Giles, Stenson and Gray (2001) together with the work of Gelmon et al. (2001) on service-learning assessment suggest many possible outcomes. Across these, four outcome concepts emerge as particularly appropriate expectations for middle- and high-school students engaged in service-learning. These can be labeled personal identity, problem-solving, career awareness and community commitment. Core expectations for the academic, service and personal growth service-learning outcome areas are shown in Figure 5.3.

**Figure 5.3 Student Outcome Expectations for
The Three Service-Learning Areas**

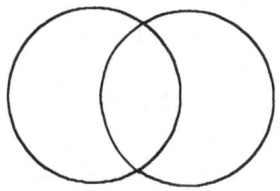

**Academic
Expectations**
Knowledge, Comprehension
and Application

**Service
Expectations**
Competence and Caring

**Personal Growth
Expectations**
Personal Identity, Problem-Solving
Career Awareness, Community Commitment

Service-learning project teams decide at their first meeting which expectations in each area they believe students should be able to demonstrate as a result of the envisioned service-learning project. They can do this by selecting among the nine expectations offered here, or they can identify other expectations they believe the students they are working with should meet. Whatever expectations teams elect to set for their students, they next make clear the behaviors through which students will indicate that they have reached these expectations.

Task Two: Specifying Indicators of Outcome Expectations

The nine proposed outcome expectations for service-learning students shown in Figure 5.3 are stated as names, labels or concepts and are not measurable in this form. To measure whether students understand something, can serve competently, or commit to their communities, project teams need to identify particular student behaviors generally accepted as indicative of student understanding, competence or commitment. Fortunately, the educational community in general and individual researchers offer many indicators of these expectations that project teams can use. Among them the following are especially useful in light of current trends in service-learning. Project teams may decide to use any or all of them and may also identify and use other indicators of the academic, service and personal growth outcomes they expect student to demonstrate.

Indicators of Academic Expectations

Showing academic competence through knowledge, comprehension and application is so basic in the field of education that the indicators for assessing these three outcome expectations have wide general acceptance. They can be stated as follows for use in service learning:

- knowledge – recalling information, ideas, principles and skills essentially in the way that they were originally presented
- comprehension – expressing learnings in one's own words and explaining the purposes of that information
- application – using previously and newly learned information in new situations to find best answers to posed problems

Indicators of Service Expectations for Competence and Caring

In the service outcomes area of service-learning, students can indicate their competence through behaviors Ferrari and Worrall find of particular interest to service agencies (p. 37). These include the following, and a service-learning project team can use any or all of them.

- attendance – adhering to schedules without unexcused absences
- punctuality – arriving on time for service without unexcused tardiness
- appearance – dressing appropriately for the agency and assigned work

- attitude – showing willingness to work and interest in what the agency does
- respect – acting with respect toward agency personnel and those it serves
- working relationships – being approachable and easy to work with on tasks
- dependability – accomplishing work in a dependable manner under appropriate supervision
- work quality – showing commitment to thorough and careful work
- work importance – showing understanding of the importance of the agency's work

Also in the service domain, project teams who wish to assess students' abilities to give caring service can use the following indicators of caring derived from the work of Liddell et al. (p. 326).

- responding to people in ways that cause the least pain or harm
- responding to people in ways that maintain relationships
- responding to people in terms of the shared situation.

Indicators of Personal Growth in Self Awareness

Mitchell (1992) offers four "key ingredients to a healthy adolescent identity" (p.136). Aspects of each of these ingredients suggest indicators that can be used by middle- and high- school project teams to measure students' growth in personal identity. Stated for the purposes of service-learning outcomes measurement, these indicators are:

- sense of self – recognizing own strengths and weaknesses
- sense of others – recognizing the need for social cooperation.
- values – holding beliefs with which to make important choices and decisions.
- self efficacy – having confidence in own ability to cope with life's adversity

Indicators of Personal Growth in Problem Solving

In service-learning, problem-solving includes but goes beyond the cognitive process of application. When students apply academic learning, they use previously and newly learned information in new situations to find problem answers that have in some measure been pre-identified as the "best" answers. Steinke and Buresh (2002) add a further dimension to problem-solving within service-learning. For them problem-solving means students' abilities to transfer and apply appropriate aspects of prior knowledge to new situations where no one has established a best answer. Whitfield's (1999) work on connecting service and classroom learning through problem-based learning specifies a set of behaviors that students can use in a systematic way to engage in effective service-learning problem solving (p. 106). These behaviors can be re-stated in the following way as measurable problem-solving indicators for use by middle- and high-school teams:

- identifying problems that are not easily defined or solved
- determining what more needs to be learned
- determining how to find appropriate resources
- exploring problem solutions
- evaluating use of information and resources at conclusion

Indicators of Personal Growth in Career Awareness

Billig's review of the K-12 service-learning literature finds that "Service-learning helps students to become more knowledgeable and realistic about careers." (2000a, p. 661) There are many indicators of this realistic knowledge but one that is fundamental and cuts across grade levels is the National Career Development Guidelines (1986) indicator "understanding how societal needs and functions influence the nature and structure of work." Project teams can look to students' increasing abilities to connect the work that they and others do in the agencies in which they serve to the needs and activities of their local, state and national communities as a primary indicator of their career awareness. A useful career expectation and indicator can be stated as follows:

- career awareness – understanding how the work people do and the way they do it relates to the needs and functions of their society

Indicators of Personal Growth in Community Commitment

Gelmon et al. suggest four indicators of service-learning students' community commitment (pp. 22-24). These can be appropriately adapted as indicators of middle- and high-school students' achievement of community-commitment outcome expectations in the following way:

- knowledge of community issues – recognizing community needs, strengths, problems and resources
- attitude toward service – personally expressing positive stances toward service and its component tasks

- sensitivity toward diversity – personally expressing positive attitudes about working with different people and confidence in and comfort with service
- commitment to service – planning for future service

Table 5.1 summarizes the student behaviors suggested here as measurable indicators of nine expectations that service-learning projects frequently seek to achieve. The table can help a project team decide at its initial meeting what to measure in order to determine if students meet or do not meet related outcome expectations.

Table 5.1 Measurable Indicators of Academic, Service and Personal Growth Expectations of Service-Learning

Outcome Area	Expectations	Measurable Indicators
Academic	Knowledge	Recalling facts, ideas, principles, skills
	Comprehension	Expressing and explaining learnings
	Application	Using learnings to propose best answers to concrete problems
Service	Competence	Adhering to schedules w/o unexcused absence Arriving on time w/o unexcused tardiness Dressing appropriately for agency and work Working willingly and with interest Respecting agency personnel and clients Being approachable and working cooperatively Working dependably under supervision Showing commitment to thorough, careful work Understanding importance of agency's work
	Caring	Responding to people in ways that cause the least pain or harm Responding to people in ways that maintain relationships Responding to people in terms of the shared situation
Personal Growth	Self-Awareness	Recognizing own strengths and weaknesses Recognizing need for social cooperation Holding beliefs to guide choices and decision making Having confidence in personal efficacy
	Problem-Solving	Identifying problems not easily defined or solved Determining additional learning needs Determining how to find appropriate resources Exploring problem solutions Evaluating own use of information and resources
	Career Awareness	Understanding relationships of work to society
	Community Commitment	Recognizing community needs, strengths, problems, resources Demonstrating positive attitude toward service Expressing sensitivity to diversity, comfort and confidence in service Planning for future service

Task Three: Selecting Strategies to Measure Indicators

Once project teams identify expectations they have for students in the three service-learning outcome areas and decide which indicators of those expectations they will measure, they are ready to select methods to measure them. The following discussion introduces eight strategies frequently used to measure service-learning outcome indicators, suggests which kinds of indicators they measure best and summarizes the logistics of their use. As project teams select particular measurement strategies, they can turn to Chapter IX which explains them in greater detail. In Chapter IX they will also find guidelines for creating their own instruments to operationalize the strategies. As teams become more experienced with service-learning they may wish to investigate and use other types of instruments beyond those described here and in Chapter IX.

Criterion-referenced Tests for Measuring Academic Growth and Problem-Solving Indicators

State Standards Tests - Nearly every state has developed paper-pencil and performance tests to measure students' progress at various grade levels on state academic standards. In many cases, these tests also assess students' personal growth in problem-solving. Service-learning teams that link their projects to state standards can often use post-project, state test information to get a sense of service-learning's impact on students' recall, comprehension and application of specific academic material and, in some cases, their abilities to frame and suggest solutions for open-ended, life-based problems.

Teacher-Developed Criterion Referenced Tests (CRTs) - Teachers create these paper-pencil and performance tests to measure the degree to which students demonstrate recall, understand and use particular information and processes in both convergent and divergent situations. In service-learning these teacher-made tests are particularly useful for measuring students' academic progress and their personal growth in problem-solving.

Observational Strategies for Measuring Provision-of-Service Indicators

Rating Scales - These instruments are designed to determine the degree to which students demonstrate delineated behaviors indicative of outcome expectations. Results of successive observations can be provided to students to help them shape their behavior toward target expectations and at a concluding point, to sum up their progress. In service-learning, rating scales are useful for gathering perceptions of students' abilities to provide competent and caring service.

Anecdotal Observations - These accounts record what students do and say in a specified period of time. Observer's records are analyzed to determine if what was said and done indicates situational dynamics that need attention or that students are not meeting outcome expectations. Within service-learning projects, records of anecdotal observations can provide indications of students' abilities to provide competent and caring service.

Self-Report Strategies for Measuring Personal Growth Indicators

Surveys - These instruments engage students in structured expressing their perceptions of the nature, quality and personal impact of their service-learning experiences. They encourage students to look back on service, inward on learning and personal growth, and forward to service-learning's implications for their lives by responding to prepared questions and/or stimulus items. Surveys can help reveal attitudes and values that indicate self-awareness, caring and community commitment across a student group.

Interviews - These one-on-one discussions also engage students in self-report of their perceptions of the nature, quality and impact of their service-learning experience. They may be structured as individual surveys that seek specific responses to questions, or they may be open-ended and exploratory of students' responses. Interviews help reveal students' attitudes and values about caring, self-awareness, career development and community commitment. Collective responses to interviews provide a sense of group orientation toward attitudinal outcome expectations.

Focus Groups - These group interviews engage students in guided, in-depth discussion of their service-learning experiences. Facilitator questions help students reflect with each other in ways that indicate cross-group attitudes and values about caring, self-awareness, career development and community commitment. Focus-group transcriptions are analyzed for patterns and relationships within revealed attitudes and values.

Experience Analysis - These essays ask students to recall notable or challenging service-learning experiences related to caring, self-awareness, career development or community commitment, then reflect on the experiences in ways that reveal their personal growth. Students' explorations of their own attitudes and values and their proposals for meeting the challenges they identify within remembered service-learning experiences provide indicators of their individual personal growth.

These eight measurement strategies require varying amounts of time to prepare, administer and analyze. As project teams select particular strategies for their student outcomes plans, they are aided by becoming aware of what Gelmon et al. call the "time and value considerations" related to them. These writers suggest that an array such as the one in Table 5.2 can serve as a decision-making tool for teams who are in the process of selecting particular strategies for use. Set-up and administration time estimates in Table 5.2 are based on the experience of the authors of this book. As explained in this chapter on page 88 and following, if the initial meeting of the team has been carefully set up, the team can make selections at that meeting.

Table 5.2 Time and Value Considerations for Service-Learning Outcomes Measurement Strategies

(Adapted from Gelmon, S. B. et al. *Assessing Service-Learning and Civic Engagement: Principles and Techniques*, Campus Compact, 2001, p. 18)

Measurement Strategy	Set-up Time	Administration Time	Analysis	Other Issues	Outputs
State Standards Tests	NA	2-4 days depending on state procedures	State performs, team culls out relevant results	Requires assistance of school or system assessment coordinator	Quantitative academic progress scores
Teacher's CRTs	1-8 hours	.5 -1 hour	With rubric, 5-10 minutes per response	Requires domain and item specification skills	Quantitative academic progress scores
Rating Scales	1-4 days	.5 -1 hour per observation	.5 to 1 hour per observation with conference	Provides formative, growth-over-time information when used several times.	Quantified description of performance based on qualitative judgment
Anecdotal Observations	.5 hours	.5 -1 hour per observation	.5 to 1 hour per observation with conference	Provides formative, growth-over-time information	Descriptive summary of performance and related dynamics
Experience Analysis	1 hour	.5 -1 hour	.5-1 hour	Requires holistic scoring skills	Descriptive summary of individuals' values internalization
Surveys	1-4 days	5 min to 1 hour per survey	Hand tally- 2-5 minutes per response	Benefits from statistical expertise	Quantitative summary of individuals' self-reported attitudes and values
Interviews	4 hours	.5 hours per interviewee	3 hours per interview plus synthesis	Requires basic content analysis skills	Quantitative summary of individuals' self-reported attitudes and values
Focus Groups	4 hours	1.5 hours per focus group	3 hours per focus group plus synthesis	Requires basic content analysis skills	Descriptive summary of group's self-reported attitudes and values

Task Four: Assigning Responsibilities

Outcomes Measurement Coordinator

Project teams share responsibilities for developing, administering and analyzing data from the instruments they use to measure outcomes. Sharing is greatly facilitated when a project team enlists the assistance of an outcomes measurement coordinator—an administrator, instructional supervisor or college/university consultant. The coordinator helps the team assemble and prepare the actual instruments they will use, helps supervise administration of the instruments and analysis of resulting data, and guides the team in interpreting results. Depending on instruments the team selects, and the depth of data analysis the team desires, the coordinator may need some statistical expertise or access to individuals who have it. Beginning teams, however, can derive a wealth of information about project outcomes by analyzing their outcomes data with totals, percents and basic central-tendency descriptors. Thus, at the beginning level, the coordinator serves most importantly as a facilitator and integrator of measurement strategies, rather than as an advanced-skills evaluator.

Test Administration Responsibilities

Once the team has identified its outcomes measurement coordinator, that individual can help the team decide who will take responsibilities for each measurement instrument the team plans to use. The simplest approach is to decide who will do what on the basis of outcome areas. Thus the classroom teacher in a team takes responsibility for obtaining relevant, standards-based, academic-outcomes information resulting from state-standards testing. The teacher also designs, administers, scores and summarizes classroom tests of students' recall, comprehension and application of academic material they learned in the project. Community partners take responsibility for determining students' on-site competence and caring. In the area of personal growth, responsibilities are typically shared. For example community partners may elect to measure students' increasing service commitment, an administrator on the team may be interested in assessing students' developing self-awareness and a parent may help measure their community awareness. In some cases, team members may share measurement responsibilities across areas with parents and administrators, for example, looking at diversity outcomes or teachers and community partners assessing problem-solving skills.

Once testing responsibilities have been assigned, the team goes on to document its outcomes measurement plan so that all can refer to it as project development and implementation go forward. Gelmon et al. provide a matrix approach for this documentation that is adaptable to middle- and high-school service-learning projects. Table 5.3 depicts such a matrix, one that comprehensively displays the nine service-learning outcome expectations for middle- and high-school students that have been identified in this chapter and the indicators associated with them. The table also displays the eight strategies useful for measuring these indicators and suggests who within a service-learning project can be expected to respond to the measurement strategies and thereby provide data about students' achievement of outcome expectations.

Table 5.3 Student Academic, Service and Personal Growth Outcomes Measurement Matrix
(Adapted from Gelmon, S. B. et al. *Assessing Service-Learning and Civic Engagement: Principles and Techniques*, Campus Compact, 2001, p. 28)

Student Outcome Expectations	Measurable Indicators	Measurement Strategies	Data Sources	Person Responsible
Academic Area				
Develop knowledge	Reproducing facts, ideas, principles, skills	State Standards Tests Teachers' CRTs	Students	Teachers
Comprehend information and ideas	Expressing and explaining learnings	State Standards Tests Teachers' CRTs	Students	Teachers
Apply knowledge, skills and understanding	Using learned information to propose best answers to concrete problems	State Standards Tests Teachers' CRTs	Students	Teachers
Service Area				
Provide competent service (direct, indirect, advocacy)	Adhering to schedules w/o unexcused absence; Arriving on time w/o unexcused tardiness; Dressing appropriately for agency and work; Working willingly and with interest; Respecting agency personnel and clients; Being approachable and working cooperatively; Working dependably under supervision; Showing commitment to thorough, careful work; Understanding importance of agency's work	Rating Scales Anecdotal Observation	Site Representatives Teachers Recipients of Service Other Team Members	Site Representatives
Interact with service clients in caring ways	Responding to people in ways that cause the least pain or harm; Responding to people in ways that maintain relationships; Responding to people in terms of the shared situation.	Surveys Anecdotal Observation Interviews Focus Groups Experience Analysis	Students Site Representatives Teachers Recipients of Service Other Team Members	Site Representatives

Table 5.3 continued

	Personal Growth Area		
Develop self-awareness	Recognizing own strengths and weaknesses Recognizing need for social cooperation of Holding beliefs to guide choices and decision making Having Confidence in personal efficacy	Observation Surveys Interviews Focus Groups Experience Analysis	Students Site Representatives Teachers Recipients of Service	Teachers Site Representatives Other Team Members
Use formal problem-solving strategies	Identifying problems not easily defined or solved Determining additional learning needs Determining how to find appropriate resources Exploring problem solutions Evaluating own use of information and resources	Criterion-referenced assessments	Students	Teachers Site Representatives Other Team Members
Increase career awareness	Understanding relationships of work to society	Experience Analysis	Students	Teachers Site Representatives Other Team Members
Strenghten community commitment	Recognizing community needs, strengths, problems, resources Demonstrating positive attitude toward service Expressing sensitivity to diversity; comfort and confidence in service Planning for future service	Surveys Interviews Focus Groups Experience Analysis	Students Site Representatives Teachers	Teachers Site Representatives Other Team Members

Real-life service-learning project teams, do not measure all possible outcome expectations shown in Table 5.3 Chapter-end examples of simpler plans for projects in awareness-, planning- and resource-level service-learning-support contexts show this. Broadly, Table 5.3 proposes a comprehensive model for service-learning student outcomes measurement. It also reflects the positive hypothesis emerging in the literature—that service-learning will affect students productively in their school work, as citizens and as growing persons.

Accomplishing Outcomes Planning at the Initial Meeting

Creating a student outcomes measurement plan for a service-learning project during a two-hour meeting is an ambitious goal for a newly formed project team. But it is not an impossible goal if team members themselves help all who will participate by carrying out the following facilitative steps:

1. Clarifying the project's goal, objectives and service focus in the initial commitment meeting (see examples in Chapter IV) and in letters of invitation to potential team members (see examples in this chapter).
2. Following up invitation letters with phone calls and e-mails that further explain project goals, objectives and service focus and confirm participation.
3. Preparing an agenda that lays out the four questions to be answered by the team at the first meeting:
   - What will we expect from students as a result of this project?
   - How will they indicate to us that they meet these expectations?
   - What strategies will we use to measure these indications?
   - Who will take responsibility for carrying out measurements?
4. Providing the team with information and support materials to answer the four questions as summarized in Table 5.4.

Table 5.4 Resources First Meeting Outcomes Planning

Question	Support Information	Support Material
Expectations?	Team can select among nine possible expectations in academic, service and personal growth areas.	Diagram of three domains with names of expectations shown
Indicators?	Team can select among indicators that describe demonstrable and measurable student behaviors	Table 5.1 Summary chart of areas, expectations and indicators
Measurement Strategies?	Team can select among measurement strategies different for each area: academic – CRTs service – observation & self-report personal growth – self report	List of strategies with definitions Table 5.2 – for time and value consideration of strategies
Assessment Responsibility?	Team shares measurement responsibilities in terms of individual strengths in the three areas.	Table 5.2 – for suggested distribution of responsibilities

5. Providing the team with a planning matrix based on Table 5.3 that includes the column headers "Expectations," "Measurable Indicators," "Measurement Strategies," "Data Sources," and "Person Responsible," as well as the "Academic," "Service" and Personal Growth" titles to divide the worksheet into three sections.
6. Working with the team to fill out the matrix to show which expectations will be set for the project, which indicators will be measured for each expectation with which strategy, as well as who will respond to each measurement strategy and who will be responsible for administering the strategy.
7. Reminding the team that as beginners they need to keep their outcomes plan simple by doing the following:

   a. Identifying only *two or three* outcome expectations for students
   b. Specifying *one or two* indicators of each expectation
   c. Selecting *one* strategy to measure each indicator

Student Outcomes Planning and Service-Learning Support Networks

A team's student outcomes measurement plan complements the type of service-learning project it designs, which, in turn, depends upon the team's service-learning support network. Where the network is in the awareness stage, teams develop simple outcomes measurement plans for in-class approaches or single events. Where the network is in the planning stage, a team may develop a prototype service-learning unit, and often needs help from an outcomes measurement coordinator for its more comprehensive outcomes plan. Where the network provides full resources for service-learning, a team may mount a continuing, annual project and will usually rely on an educational evaluator to lead development and implementation of its multi-featured student outcomes plan. The following examples sketch out how teams in these three situations might formulate student outcomes plans for service-learning projects.

Example One - Awareness Support Network: No Specific Resources for Service-Learning

Administrators, parents and neighbors of the Blue Mesa Middle School plan to testify at the county council hearing on traffic danger at the intersection of State Highway 41 and Blue Mesa Road, three blocks from the school. Last month, a twelve-year-old on his way to play after-school, pick-up baseball was hit by a truck and thrown from his bike as he crossed the intersection. He needs several operations to repair damage to his legs. The county budget can only afford stop signs at the intersection and parents have mounted volunteer patrols there from after school until six on weekdays. But people want a traffic light, and Mr. Vishinsky's seventh-grade math class wants to help persuade the county to install the light by testifying at the hearing. Mr. V. a second-year teacher, suggests a service-learning-event design for the project.

The class invites the Blue Mesa PTA president to a meeting and proposes to use learning related to their math standard "Using numbers in equivalent forms in problem-solving contexts" to help the PTA make a pro-traffic light presentation at the county council meeting. They offer to collect and present information about car, truck and pedestrian traffic through the intersection. The PTA president agrees, and Mr. Vishinsky and the class form a project team that includes a PTA parent, a traffic officer from the county sheriff's department, traffic division and the seventh-grade department chairperson. This team learns how to design an outcomes matrix and develops the plan shown in Table 5.5.

Table 5.5 Student Outcomes Plan for Seventh-Grade Math Class's Event Project Supported by an Awareness-Level Support Network

Expectation	Indicators	Measurement Strategies	Data Sources	Person Responsible
Academic Area				
Express numbers in equivalent forms (State Standard 2.3.7)	Convert real-life data into whole numbers, fractions and percents	State Standards Tests Classroom test: students set up given data in spreadsheets and show totals in percents	Students	Mr. Vishinsky
Service Area				
Demonstrate competent service	Dress appropriately during data collection and at council meeting	Observation	Ms. Selkirk (parent)	Ms. Selkirk
	Carry out thorough, accurate data collection	Observation	Sgt. Penders (traffic control)	Sgt. Penders
Care about varying points of view	Understand competing needs of those who want traffic light and the council	Focus Group	Students	Mr. Vishinsky, Sgt. Penders
Personal Growth Area				
Explore own integrity	Holds self to standards in completing group tasks	Experience Analysis	Students	Mr. Vishinsky, Sgt. Penders

The student outcomes plan in Table 5.5 is simple and manageable and distributes responsibilities across the team. At the same time, the plan makes sure students' academic, service and personal growth outcome indicators are all measured in ways that are appropriate to selected expectations and to a one-day event service-learning experience.

Example Two - Planning Support Network:
Moderate Resources for Service-Learning

Tenth-grade drama students at Peachtree High School respond to requests for "junior companions" from a local nursing home for the aged. With the nursing home staff director, their veteran teacher, their career education counselor, two parents and a member of the local commission on aging, they plan an eight-week, prototype service-learning project. The project will link students' service to their work on a state drama standard—conceptualizing and producing formal and informal performances. Students will read to and visit with patients, then use their experiences to develop and perform dramatic monologues about the meaning of old age in human life. Their school system will provide transportation and assigns the counselor to serve as outcomes measurement coordinator. The project team lays out the following student outcomes plan.

Table 5.6 Student Outcomes Plan for Tenth-Grade Drama Class Prototype Project Supported by a Planning-Level Support Network

Expectation	Indicators	Measurement Strategies	Data Sources	Person Responsible
Academic Area				
Apply knowledge of monologue elements and aging issues in own monologue performance (State Standard 1.6.2)	Identify characteristics at work in provided monologue	State Standards Tests	Students	Ms. Labelle (teacher)
	Create and perform monologue that identifies interests, concerns and views of aging people	Criterion-referenced Performance judged by panel	Students	Ms. Labelle Mr. Rachid and Ms. Holbrook, (parents) Ms. Barak (staff director)
Service Area				
Read competently to patients	Select appropriate reading materials for patients	Interviews	Patients	Ms. Barak
Respond in a caring manner to patients as persons	Interact with respect for and supportive communication with patients	Observation	Students	Ms. Labelle and Ms. Barak
Personal Growth Area				
Commit to community	Understand aging as a life stage of community concern	Focus Group	Students	Mr. Hildebrand (commission on Aging) and Mr. Jensen (career counselor)
Increase own career Awareness	Link health services careers to needs of the aging	Interviews	Students	

92 * CHAPTER V

The student outcomes plan for this prototype is more complex and involves more people in assuming assessment responsibility singly and together. Resources provided by the school system make this possible—especially time for the counselor to serve as the outcomes measurement coordinator—as does the experience of team members. The plan suggests that all team members are eager to assume responsibility as educational colleagues within the project.

Example Three - Resources Support Network:
Extensive Resources for Service Learning

Each year, seniors in the four Lincoln City high schools spend a semester working on their state's twelfth-grade civics standard—knowing ways citizens can influence public policy. This system-wide program was originally initiated by the city's media board as a way to build citizen confidence in media ethics. Currently, it is coordinated by the Lincoln Service-Learning Council, a school-community representative body. Four area-college faculty members serve on the council as program evaluators and assist participating schools in developing outcomes measurement plans. Within the program, each school's advisory board develops an interdisciplinary service-learning project with council-identified community partners listed under headings such as "Print and Broadcast Media Groups," "Governmental Service Groups," "Community Agencies," and "Citizen Action Groups." In each school, subject-area teachers and students identify key learnings they expect students to develop as they investigate how citizens use the media to influence public policy and explore related ethics. For example, at Greenmount High, science teachers expect students to use research methods, mathematics teacher expect them to use computer science learnings and English teachers expect them to use understandings about oral and written communication.

This year, the Greenmount High School Advisory Board teams with the Lincoln City Times, radio station KLCR and local TV network affiliate KVBC. They plan to have students rotate through three-week shifts in which they assist teams at these media outlets who are responsible for news and public affairs programming and broadcasting. Greenmount's advisory board which includes school personnel, students, representatives from the cooperating media, parents and other community members develops the plan shown in Table 5.7.

The student outcomes plan shown in Table 5.7 prefigures a massive project, yet outcomes measurement in the project is manageable. Classroom teachers carry out academic testing. Community partners use a uniform check sheet for students' general service competence together with classroom written experience analyses to determine students' understanding of media ethics; and evaluators from the Service-Learning Council assist with personal growth measurement through interviews, focus groups and problem-solving tests students can complete in the classroom. The outcomes plan also shows thorough-going cooperation between schools and collaborating agencies in the design of measurement strategies.

Table 5.7 Student Outcomes Plan for Cross-Disciplinary Senior-Year Civics Program Supported by Resources-Level Support Network

Expectation	Indicators	Measurement Strategies	Data Sources	Person Responsible
Academic Area				
Science - Use research strategies to gain information about TV influence techniques	Explain elements of a research plan for a media presentation that seeks to influence public policy	Criterion-referenced test Fill in missing research plan elements, justify all elements	Students	Subject Area Teachers and partnering research staff representatives
Mathematics - Use computer science understandings to learn about electronic influence techniques	Describe electronic techniques used to gather and distribute information	Criterion-referenced posters, pamphlets, fliers, fact sheets, computer presentations, videos	Students	Subject Area Teachers and partnering electronic staff representatives
English - Explain use of oral and written strategies in media to influence public policy	Explain use of psychological, sociological and economic elements to influence public policy	Criterion-referenced essays, speeches, dramatic presentations, symposia	Students	Subject Area Teachers and partnering writing and broadcast staff
Service Area				
Work competently with respect to media ethics.	Respect agency personnel and clients Work dependably under supervision Show thorough, careful work Understand agency's work	Cross-project observation check-sheet developed by advisory group subcommittee consisting of student, school and partnering agency representatives Experience Analysis	Partnering Agency staff	Partnering Agency Internship Coordinators
Personal Growth Area				
Commit to community involvement	Express community commitment through recognition of and orientation to community needs	Interviews and Focus Groups	Students	Evaluators from Service-Learning Council
Demonstrate problem solving skills	Identify civic awareness problems Determine problem-related information needs Determine how to find problem-relevant resources Explore ways to use media to address problems Evaluate own use of resources	Criterion-referenced team problem-solving based on the task of designing a persuasive media presentation about a complex problem	Students	Teachers-Partnering Agency Teams

94 * CHAPTER V

Looking Forward to Measurement Strategy Selection and Design

When a project team has developed its basic student outcomes plan, it can set up another meeting to select actual instruments for measuring these outcomes or learn how to design its own instruments using guidelines in Chapter IX. At that second meeting, team members can take varying responsibilities—some to look for instruments suitable for project use and some to design first drafts of instruments for review by the team at a final, assessment-instruments decision-making meeting. Again, all of this will be manageable if the team starts simply, assessing only one or two expectations, using existing instruments and regular classroom tests where possible and limiting new instrument design.

Measuring Indicators of Other Constituents' Outcomes

Consistent with this book's focus on using service-learning to enhance student outcomes, this chapter focuses on student outcomes planning. Project teams may also want to identify outcomes for other project constituents—community partners and their clients, parents, teachers and schools—and measure indicators of the outcomes. Teams know that together with student outcomes information this additional information will eventually help them evaluate their overall service-learning projects, strengthen future projects and gain support for continued use of service-learning activities, projects and programs. While comprehensive measurement of other-constituent outcome indicators is beyond the scope of this book, project teams can use surveys, interviews and focus groups described here and in Chapter IX to gather basic outcomes information from service-learning project constituents other than students. They can do this in a systematic way by developing outcomes measurement plans for the constituencies of interest then using surveys, interviews or focus-groups to measure indicators of targeted outcomes. Student involvement in developing these plans is essential and vital. Students strengthen their critical-thinking skills and deepen their community commitment as they think through ways to determine the wider impact of their service-learning activities. Several examples drawn from projects described in Chapter II summarize this process.

Example One: Anti-smoking One-Day-Event Plan for Measuring Booth-Visiting Client Outcomes

The project team for the one-day event in which students make anti-smoking presentations at their Community Wellness Day wants to assess outcomes for those who visited the booth. They prepare a five-question interview about the effectiveness of students' presentations in getting visitors' attention and about the presentations' anti-smoking persuasive power. Each team member, including student representative, agrees to interview three people who have visited the booth. Resulting information becomes part of the team's summative evaluation report. They develop the following client outcomes plan.

Client Outcome Expectations	Measurable Indicators	Measurement Strategies	Data Sources	Persons Responsible
Attend to presentations	Ratings of presentations viewed	Interview	People attending event and watching student presentations	Team Members
Strengthen anti-smoking attitudes	Self-ratings of change in attitudes			

Example Two: Illustrated Community History Prototype Plan for Measuring Community Interest Group Outcomes

The project team for the prototype project in which American History students work with community ethnic and interest groups wants to know about those groups' perceptions of the value of their participation in the project. The team develops a survey and arranges for students to administer it to members of the various groups at the conclusion of the project. With permission from each group, results will become part of an article about the project in the local paper. Their community group outcomes plan is as follows.

Community Group Outcome Expectations	Measurable Indicators	Measurement Strategies	Data Sources	Persons Responsible
Perceive group empowerment as a result of service-learning participation	Ratings of connections between service-learning participation, sense of inclusion and presence of group's contributions in final product	Survey	Community ethnic and interest group members	Student liaisons to groups

Example Three: Wacahatchee River Cross-Disciplinary Project Plan for Participating Teacher Outcomes Assessment

The cooperative school-community group that implements the Wacahatchee River project wants to explore the impact of school-wide service-learning on participating teachers' perceptions of the value of service-learning to their discipline areas. The team plans to conduct a series of focus groups in which teachers in each discipline discuss the advantages and disadvantages of the project in terms of their student's needs and abilities and the standards that organize their curriculum. Resulting information will be used to develop procedures that will increase discipline-area input in future project planning. The Wacahatchee project team develops the following participating teachers outcomes plan.

Participating Teacher Outcome Expectations	Measurable Indicators	Assessment Strategies	Data Sources	Persons Responsible
Recognize value of service-learning to discipline	Number and types of advantages and disadvantages identified by discipline	Focus Groups	Teachers participants in discipline-specific focus groups	Team Members

In Conclusion

Reciprocity is central to successful service-learning projects. Project teams ensure reciprocity from the outset by adding key school and community players to their teams. Expanded teams cooperatively establish a limited number of outcome expectations for students in academic, service and personal-growth areas. Teams then develop a formal plan that shows how students will indicate outcome achievement, how student indicators will be measured and who will take responsibility for finding and administering measurement instruments and analyzing results. Teams can develop outcomes plans along these same lines to gather information about service-learning outcomes for other constituencies with whom they and students work.

A project team's student outcomes plan represents its commitment to collaboration and full engagement in the second phase of the collaborative service-learning model. Now the project team is ready to move forward to the third phase of the model in which they will design an instructional plan. This plan will consist of reflective learning experiences that integrate classroom study and service activities in ways that provide students opportunities to accomplish the expectations specified in the team's student outcomes plan.

Activities for Increasing Understanding

1. Assume that the agency you identified will join with you in the service-learning commitment plan you outlined in activity # 2 at the end of Chapter IV. List other key players you intend to assemble to fill out your project team and write a draft of the sample letter of invitation you, your students and community partner will send to each of these key players.
2. Imagine the first meeting of your team and determine what outcome expectations the team would have for your students in the academic, service and personal growth domains. Use ideas from this imaginary meeting and material from Chapter V on expectations, indicators and possible assessment strategies to lay out a first-draft student outcomes plan as a matrix in the form shown in Tables 5.5, 5.6 and 5.7.
3. Speculate on how your team might secure the assistance of an outcomes-measurement coordinator. List the steps the team would use to find this person and convince him or her to take responsibility for helping your team develop and use its student outcomes plan.

Chapter VI: Linking Service and Learning With Reflective Learning Experiences

"We know what we expect students to gain from the project. Now we can design learning activities that help them accomplish our objectives." Tenth-grade biology teacher Susan Rhys emphasizes the word "we" as she looks around at her project team.

"Most of the academic activities are already in place in your regular instruction, Susan," department chair Bill Carter points out. "You'll be teaching students to use the microscopes, and sketch waterborne organisms before they work with the Water Quality Commission."

Greg Kostopolis from the commission chimes in. "And, as part of their service, we'll show students safe specimen collection, how to make wet mounts and log findings for analysis reports. We'll talk to them, too, about the new 2+2+2 biology careers program we have with the community college and the university."

"So what else do we need, Ms. Rhys?" Student representative Yvonne Belsky asks.

"Two more pieces, Yvonne," Susan replies. "Reflection and conceptualization. We need reflection activities that help students connect classroom learning and service experiences and conceptualizing activities that help them transform their reflections into personal growth."

"Just what do you mean by 'we,' Susan?" Parent Carline Brooks angles a glance across the table. "Are we all going to be involved in this reflection and conceptualization?"

Chapter Focus

As the scenario points out, establishing student outcome expectations—the second phase in the Collaborative Service-Learning Model—lays the foundations for its third phase—planning instruction that will link academic study to service experience and encourage students' personal growth. The scenario also points to the defining characteristic of this instructional planning, that it is a collaborative process in which all team members take part. The teacher on a project team takes a leadership role because of professional experience in instructional planning, but all team members have much to contribute to the design of learning activities and can enrich their own and students' service-learning by doing so. This chapter explains how teams can collaboratively and efficiently develop and implement instructional plans for their service-learning projects by doing the following: 1) using their student outcomes plans to state learning goals and objectives 2) designing reflective learning experiences that focus, connect and transform student classroom and service activity 3) sharing instructional responsibilities.

Using Student Outcomes Plans to State Goals and Objectives

Student outcomes plans set outcome expectations for students and specify the student behaviors that will indicate accomplishment of these expectations. As teams move to instructional development, their outcome expectations serve as the basis for students' learning goals, and indicators of the expectations serve as the basis for learning objectives. This mirroring of expectations and indicators in goals and objectives helps ensure that teams design learning experiences that help students achieve outcome expectations. For example, if the team in the opening scenario expects that as an outcome of service-learning students will be able to judge water quality, this expectation also serves as their instructional goal. When the team determines that indicators of judging water quality will include students' abilities to collect water samples, microscopically study wet mounts they make, find, sketch and identify organisms, and discuss organisms' effects on water, these indicators also serve as instructional objectives that help the team design appropriate learning experiences for students. Thus, by translating student outcome expectations and indicators into instructional goals and objectives a service-learning team takes the first step in instructional planning for its project.

A look at the "Blue Mesa" example from Chapter V shows how a project team uses expectations and indicators to state goals and objectives. In the project, seventh-grade students working on a mathematics standard join with community members to gather traffic data and make a pro-traffic light presentation to their county council. Table 6.1 displays the team's first step in its instructional planning work.

Table 6.1 Seventh-Grade Service-Learning Expectations and Indicators Stated as Instructional Goals and Objectives

Expectations as Goals	Indicators as Objectives
Express numbers in equivalent forms (State standard 2.3.7)	Convert real-life data into whole numbers, fractions and percents
Demonstrate competent service	Dress appropriately during data collection and at council meeting. Carry out thorough and accurate data collection
Care about varying points of view	Understand competing needs of the Council and those who want the traffic light
Become aware of own integrity	Hold self to standards in completing group tasks

Table 6.1 shows the Blue Mesa team's four outcome expectations—one for the academic area, two for the service area and one for the personal growth area—restated as four instructional goals. It also shows the five indicators of those outcomes restated as instructional objectives. These restatements make it possible for the team to move to the next step in service-learning instructional planning, the design of learning experiences that will help students achieve a mathematics standard, persuasively address their county council and move forward in their own growth toward self-awareness.

The design of learning experiences that will, in fact, give students opportunities to achieve goals and objectives and thereby meet outcome expectations can be a special challenge for two reasons. First, service experience is messy. As students engage in service, whether in controlled settings close to their school, or in the wider arena of the community, varying personality styles, unexpected events, new and strange environments whirl in a mix that may at times prevent students from seeing how their service and their classroom studies relate to each other and to instructional objectives. Second, particularly when students are in a larger service arena, they may find themselves drawn by the gravity of immediate need in a service situation to perform duties that have little or nothing to do with pre-established goals and objectives. Teams can do much to help students use their service—even its messy and seductive aspects—toward accomplishing goals and objectives and thereby achieving outcome expectations by designing integrated sequences of reflective learning experiences.

Reflective Learning Experiences

A project team's instructional plan consists of a sequence of reflective learning experiences that engage students in attending to their classroom and service experiences—those that they expect and those that are unexpected and may not seem make sense—thinking about those experiences, and deriving insights from their thinking. When students go through these three steps they integrate ideas, emotions, interactions and behaviors into new understandings and concepts, and this increases the likelihood that they will learn from service and that the perspectives they bring to bear on the world will be transformed. Three kinds of learning activities help students engage in reflective learning: focusing activities, reflection activities and conceptualizing activities. As teams plan and implement reflective learning experiences they help students progress toward accomplishment of instructional goals and objectives through an integrated process represented by the inverted triangle in Figure 6.1.

Figure 6.1 Reflective Learning Experiences as Service-Learning Instructional Plan Components

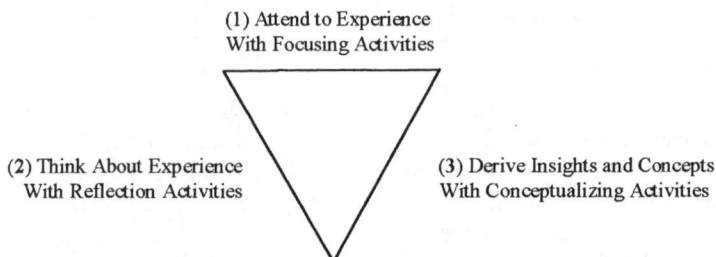

As Figure 6.1 shows, focusing, reflection and conceptualizing activities flow together in practice in unified reflective learning experiences. Individual discussions characterize each type of activity and show how project teams can integrate them within instructional plans to help students address academic and service experiences from which they can learn, guide them in interpreting that experience through reflection, and stimulate their capacities to derive new concepts from their reflections. Chapter X provides additional detail about these three types of activities.

Learning Activities That Focus Students on Relevant Experience

To develop learning activities that help students address academic and service experience from which they can learn, a project team asks a core question for each objective they state: "What activities will focus students on the information, ideas and skills they need to accomplish this objective? The Blue Mesa team, for example asks five such questions:

- What activities will focus students on the information, ideas and skills they need to convert real life data into whole numbers, fractions and percents?
- What activities will focus students on the information, ideas and skills they need to dress appropriately during service and at the council meeting?
- What activities will focus students on the information, ideas and skills they need to carry out thorough and accurate data collection?

- What activities will focus students on the information, ideas and skills they need to understand the competing interests of those who want the traffic light and the Council members?
- What activities will focus students on the information, ideas and skills they need to hold themselves to standards in completing their group work?

Restating this focusing-activity design question for each objective may appear to involve needless repetition, but it helps distribute responsibility for activity development across a project team. As each question is stated, team members can see which ones they can best answer, and they can thus collaborate in developing instruction for the project. In the Blue Mesa project, for example it is likely that once the five activity-design questions are stated along the lines shown above, Mr. Vishinsky as teacher will lead in answering the question for the academic, mathematics objective. He will propose learning activities he normally uses to teach to the mathematics standard upon which the academic objective is based. Sgt. Penders and Ms. Selkirk as team members associated with students' service in the project will probably lead in answering the activity-design question for the competence and caring service objectives. And in the same vein, all three team members are likely to answer the activity-design question for the personal growth objective.

Collaborative Design of Focusing Activities

No matter which team member leads in answering an activity-design question, the best activities result from collegial discussion that works to ensure that 1) each team member understands how each activity relates to its objective and can then knowledgably support student use of the activity, and that 2) the activities for each objective are necessary and sufficient in number but not excessive or unnecessary. With respect to knowledgeable support, for example, the Blue Mesa team is likely to require that students keep journals they can use to evaluate how well they contributed to group work. If all team members understand how, when and why students are to keep journals, they can all appropriately remind students to do this and thus increase the likelihood that when the time comes to reflect on journal entries, students will have material available. With respect to necessary and sufficient activities, Mr. Vishinsky may suggest using the discussion and practice of equivalent numbers that appears in his math textbook. But he may also suggest reducing the number of exercises students complete in class when Sgt. Penders proposes that students restate the traffic data they collect at the intersection as whole numbers, fractions and percents. Or, Ms. Selkirk may suggest that her understanding of parents' needs for the traffic light is only half the story and that students need additional opportunities to hear the council's budget-constraint position before they make their presentation.

Team members are able to see connections between the focusing activities they develop for their several objectives when they use a flexible, simultaneous approach. To do this, they write each activity-design question on an individual sheet of newsprint or section of a chalk board. The team then moves from one sheet to another, discussing ideas and possibilities and proposing learning activities without requiring themselves to develop all the activities for any one objective at once. Using this approach, teams often find situations in which activities central to one objective link to or blend with activities related to another objective—as in the case of students learning to express numbers in equivalent forms in both the classroom and as part of traffic data collection. They also find themselves less frequently blocked when they know they can leave an objective for which activities are slow in evolving and go on to work with another objective.

Using Multiple Intelligences and Cooperative Learning Principles to Increase the Power of Focusing Activities

Service-learning project teams increase the power of their focusing activities by designing them in terms of multiple-intelligences principles and sequencing them in terms of cooperative-learning principles. This means teams design activities that engage students in using the full range of their intellectual, social and psychological capacities and that they sequence these activities in ways that help students relate actively and interdependently with teachers, other team members and each other as partners in learning The following briefly summarizes multiple intelligences and cooperative learning principles and suggests how teams use them in focus-activity design. Further explorations of these approaches and guidelines for their use can be found in Chapter X as well as in materials cited in the references section.

Multiple-Intelligences Principles for Activity Design – Howard Gardner (1983, 2000) theorizes that all human beings possess eight distinct intelligences which have come to be labeled verbal-linguistic, musical-rhythmic, logical-mathematical, visual-spatial, bodily-kinesthetic, interpersonal, intrapersonal and naturalist. Gardner offers two intimately entwined, multiple-intelligences (MI) principles that are particularly relevant to the design of service-learning activities. The first is that "human beings have particular intelligences because of informational contents that exist in the world" (1983, p. xxi). The second is that intelligences manifest and strengthen themselves as human beings solve problems and create products that are valued within one or more cultural settings, or as lead developer of MI classroom applications Armstrong (1994) states, "in context-rich and naturalistic settings" (p. 2).

The statement that human beings have particular intelligences because of informational contents that exist in the world needs some clarification. The key words here are "particular intelligences." Gardner draws on research in biology and neurobiology to propose that from birth onward, the human brain differentiates into specific regions that take in and use the varying kinds of information the world generates. Thus, for instance, there is a language region in the brain that increases in complexity and organization as it takes in and uses language, a spatial region in the brain that increasingly maps the physical world, and so forth. This, then, relates to the second and remarkable principle in Gardner's theory, one that current, rapidly advancing brain research endorses. That is that the brain regions are, in effect, intelligences, and as human beings have experiences related to the regions, the regions become larger and more differentiated and the intelligences they control concomitantly strengthen.[1]

Project teams take advantage of these principles in several ways. By designing MI focusing activities for service-learning, they increase the likelihood of wider and deeper student involvement in their projects—motivate more students through activities that address and engage their particular strengths and interests. Use of MI focusing activities also helps teams take fuller advantage of the range of experiences that community-related and community-based learning makes possible. Above all, as students engage in a full range of MI focusing activities, all of their intelligences can be nurtured—those in which they are already strong as well as those which they have not yet so fully developed.

The ways a team uses MI principles in the design of focusing activities can be seen as the Blue Mesa team continues its work. As explained earlier, the team states each of its focus-activity design questions on a separate sheet of newsprint and works back and forth across sheets to propose activities that will answer the questions. The results of half-day session appear as follows:

- **What activities will focus students on the information, ideas and skills they need to convert real-life data into whole numbers, fractions and percents?**

    1. Attention-getter "commercial" for applying math to life (Musical-Rhythmic Intelligence)
    2. Reading text and working examples on equivalent forms, pp 79-81 in text book (Verbal-Linguistic, Logical-Mathematical Intelligences)

- **What activities will focus students on the information, ideas and skills they need to dress appropriately during service and at the council meeting?**

    1. Drawing posters of "dress for important occasions," and developing general guidelines from commonalities. (Visual-Spatial, Logical-Mathematical and Interpersonal Intelligences)

---

[1] The following researchers are leaders among the many who have conducted and continued to conduct major studies of brain regions and the influence of experience on their growth and development. Their extensive writings offer a comprehensive view of major advances in neuroscience and reveal the extraordinary potential of the work in this field for educators: Jonathan Cohen, Director, Center for Study of the Brain, Mind and Behavior, Princeton University; Adele Diamond, Director, Center for Development of Cognitive Neuroscience, University of Massachusetts Medical School; Gerald Edelman, Chairman of the Department of Neurobiology, The Scripps Research Institute, La Jolla, California; Jordan Grafman, Chief of the Neuroscience Section, National Institutes of Health.; Alvaro Pascual-Leone, Clinical Research Center of Beth Israel Deaconess Medical Center, Boston, Massachusetts, and National Institutes of Health.

- **What activities will focus students on the information, ideas and skills they need to carry out thorough and accurate data collection?**

    1. Using spreadsheets to collect and record data as whole numbers, fractions, percents and exchanging sheets to check for accuracy. (Logical-Mathematical and Interpersonal Intelligences)
    2. Preparing an illustrated class presentation for the council justified in percents of car, truck and pedestrian traffic through intersection from 4-6 pm during a one-week period. (Verbal-Linguistic, Logical-Mathematical, Visual-Spatial, Interpersonal Intelligences)

- **What activities will focus students on the information, ideas and skills they need to understand the competing needs of those who want the traffic light and Council members?**

    1. Interviewing parents and Council members via e-mail and role playing the discussion of the proposed traffic light. (Verbal-Linguistic, Interpersonal, and Bodily-Kinesthetic Intelligences)
    2. Presenting proposal to Council. (Verbal-Linguistic, Logical-Mathematical, Interpersonal, and Bodily-Kinesthetic Intelligences)

- **What activities will focus students on the information, ideas and skills they need to hold themselves to standards in completing group work?**

    1. Keeping daily personal journals that list own contributions to efforts for each day. (Verbal-Linguistic and Intrapersonal Intelligences)

It would be misleading to suggest that project teams effortlessly come up with activities such as these. Activity creation invariably involves give and take, advance and retreat. But good activities do emerge as teams speculate on ways to focus students on the information, skills and ideas they need to achieve objectives and then speculate on how proposed activities can individually and as a group be shaped to appeal to the range of students' intelligences. What is often very useful here is for teams to use a two-step brainstorming approach. In the first step, every team member tries to offer a possible focusing activity for each objective, then the one for which most resources are available is selected. In the second step, the team identifies the basic intelligence associated with the activity, then tries to associate at least one other intelligence with the activity.

For example, the Blue Mesa team wants its first focusing activity to create the context for teaching a math standard through service-learning. The team's parent representative suggests that the teacher should do this by reminding students they have a state standards test coming up and will have to solve problems based on life data. The sergeant suggests that just telling students "that's what math is all about" will do. The teacher suggests opening with a short class discussion, asking students what they think the ultimate purpose of mathematics is. The team's two student representatives suggest that since the team is trying to sell math for life, an attention-getting commercial might work. The team decides this suggestion is best and discusses whether the commercial should be presented as a poster or flyer, a video clip or a jingle. The group opts for a jingle as most quick and efficient when the students say they want to be responsible for the activity and will develop it in their free time using a familiar tune.

Cooperative Learning and Focusing Activities - Johnson, Johnson and Smith conclude from research on cooperative learning over three-quarters of a century that "cooperative efforts result in more frequent use of higher-level reasoning strategies, more frequent process gain, and higher performance on subsequent tests taken individually (group–to–individual transfer) than do competitive or individualistic methods" (1995, p. 30). They assert that these benefits result when teachers set up and use productive student groups and work with those groups in facilitative and consultative ways. Essentially, productive students groups require that students work together on tasks using positive interdependence, face-to-face promotive interaction, individual accountability, interpersonal and small group skills, and regular reflection on their own processes. Teachers—individually and in cooperative faculty teams—set up cooperative learning groups, explain group tasks and their relationships to objectives and provide the information groups need to work. Then they move to the facilitative and consultant role in which they "monitor students' learning and intervene within the groups to provide task assistance or to increase students' interpersonal and group skills" (p. 41).

The continuing Blue Mesa example shows how a team incorporates cooperative learning principles into focusing activities. As the team—including its student representative—develops focusing activities, they want the activities to work in a natural flow that moves students from orientation to the teacher, through cooperative work with team members and each other, to responsible individual learning. To make the activities function together in this way, the team decides to order the activities they have created thus far with academic activities first, service activities next, and personal growth activities last. They then decide how to engage students in each activity so that they move from depending on the teacher for control of learning, to learning with the team and from each other, and ultimately, to taking responsibility for their own learning. This again takes a half-day session and produces the results shown in Table 6.2.

As Table 6.2 shows, the Blue Mesa team has added cooperative-learning dimensions to each activity in an overall sequence that leads students toward independence. Its first activity, presented by students on the team, sets the math-for-life tone of the project. In the core activities that help students apply math to life (CL-3, 4, 5, and 7), the team facilitates cooperative learning by dividing the 30 students in the class into five groups of six students each that will work throughout the project with various team members. The teacher uses a traditional knowledge-giving role to provide students with the information they will need to carry out the project (CL-2). Near the end of the project students come together as a class in an independent, self-monitored group to gather information about and role play the positions they are likely to encounter at the council meeting (CL-6). They present their proposal in interdependent, self-monitored small groups (C-7). Throughout their project, they individually record their own contributions as cooperative learners in their journals (CL-8).

Table 6.2 Multiple Intelligences, Cooperative Focusing Activities for Instructional Objectives of Seventh-Grade Service-Learning Project

Expectations as Goals	Indicators as Objectives	Focusing Activities
Academic Area		
Express numbers in equivalent forms (State standard 2.3.7)	Convert real-life data into whole numbers, fractions and percents	CL-1 (MR, VL) Compose and sing "commercial jingle" for applying math to life (student project team reps)
		CL-2 (VL, LM) Read, discuss and work examples for Topic 9 in Today's Mathematics, pp 79-81 (pairs and individuals)
Service Area		
Competence	Carry out thorough and accurate data collection	CL-3 (LM, IP-1) Use spreadsheets to collect data and record as whole numbers, fractions and percents. (continuing 6-member groups set up in class, one assigned to each data collection day) Exchange to check accuracy (pairs within 6-member groups)
		CL-4 (VL, LM, VS, IP-1) Prepare illustrated class presentation for council justified in percents of car, truck and pedestrian traffic through intersection from 4-6 pm during a one-week period. (whole group outline, 6-member groups for components)
	Dress appropriately during data collection and at council meeting.	CL-5 (VS, LM, IP-1) Draw posters of "dress for important occasions," develop general guidelines from commonalities (individuals then 6-member groups)
Caring	Understand competing concerns of those who want traffic light and council	CL-6 (IP-1, VL, BK) Interview parents and council members via e-mail, then role play council discussion of proposal. (whole group with five student observer reps—one from each 6-member group)
		CL-7 (VL, LM, BK, IP-1) Present proposal to council (a component by each group)
Personal Growth Area		
Self-Awareness	Hold self to standards in completing group tasks	CL-8 (IP-2, VL) Keep daily personal journal listing own contributions to efforts for the day

Key: VL=Verbal-Linguistic, LM =Logical-Mathematical, VS – Visual-Spatial, BK=Bodily-Kinesthetic, M= Musical-Rhythmic, IP-1=Interpersonal, IP-2=Intrapersonal, CL=Cooperative Learning

The evolving plan shown in Table 6.2 is not intended to reflect a hard and fast approach to incorporating cooperative learning into service-learning. Project teams need to experiment with their own types of cooperative learning and the way they order activities. Table 6.2 does suggest, however, that once teams decide upon multiple-intelligences focusing activities, they can infuse those activities with cooperative learning opportunities and arrange them in flow that help students strengthen skills and abilities, increase understanding, and gain insight as they become independent learners.

Learning Activities That Engage Students in Reflection

Reflection activities provide "the transformative link between the actions of service and the ideas and understandings of learning" (Eyler, Giles & Schmiede, 1996, p. 14). They reside "at the core of service-learning, creating meaning out of associational experience" (Saltmarsh, 1999, p. 18). In a very real sense, there is no genuine service-learning without reflection, thus it is critical that each member of a service-learning project team understand reflection and contribute to its use by students and the team itself within the overall process of reflective learning. Team members can accomplish these ends by learning about the nature and characteristics of reflection activities in this chapter, by becoming familiar with particular reflection activities described in Chapter X and by using these reflection activities in ways also described in Chapter X.

Characteristics of Reflection Activities

Reflection activities that help students link the actions of service with academic ideas and understandings are purposeful, organized and disciplined. They consist of specific thinking steps that students know and use with increasing independence. Eyler, Giles and Schmeide point out that in their deliberate and analytical nature, these activities center on critical reflection and differ from the more casual and unstructured yet equally important reflection in which all human beings engage as they go about their lives. On the basis of college-student interview data, these authors identify four characteristics of effective service-learning reflection activities. These activities are continuous, connected, challenging and contextualized. The discussion in this section integrates the Eyler, Giles and Schmeide's foundational work on these "Four C's" (pp. 15-20) with additional ideas about reflection activities that help increase their efficacy in middle and high schools.

Continuous Reflection - Service-learning reflection activities are continuous in two ways: first, they take place before, during and after service experience, and second, by virtue of their regular and productive use, they increase students' propensity to use reflection throughout formal education and in their lives beyond schooling. Guiding student reflection before service helps orient them to service-learning itself. It also familiarizes them with the new environment in which they will be learning and maps out the particular aspects of the environment that will provide content for their learning. It elicits curiosity—about what will happen at the service site, what will happen to students themselves, what new skills and information they may need. Perhaps most important, it helps students begin to call up personal cognitive structures that have potential connections to the service experience. Students' reflection during service helps them directly address the experience as it takes place, increases their capacities to recognize and solve problems that may arise and take actions that will increase the capacity of their service to function as a source of learning. Students' reflection after service helps them understand specific ways service action integrates with classroom learning and with other experiences. It also helps them think about the implications that their service-learning experiences have for what they do and how they interact in the present and the future. As they conclude by reflecting on their own past, present and future use of reflection, students lay the ground work for making reflection a continuous part of their lives.

Connected Reflection - Effective reflection activities also work for connectedness in two ways. First, they help students establish links between service actions and information, skills and ideas within the academic area of study in which they are engaged. Thus students may come to recognize how geometry aids urban planning, how expository writing aids public awareness, how knowledge of bacteria protects water supply, or how education tracks economic advantage. Second, these activities help students gain expanding perspectives on their world and awareness of the broader and deeper connections within that world. For example, Blue Mesa students who reflect on the competing views of pro-traffic-light parents and a fiscally responsible county council may gain insight on the nature, value and complexity of participation in representative government for citizens as well as for those who govern.

Challenging Reflection - Service-learning reflection activities challenge students to think beyond their familiar comfort zones, when teachers, parents, agency representatives and others use them to "pose questions and propose unfamiliar or even uncomfortable ideas for consideration." (Eyler, et al., 1996, p. 19) This does not mean frightening or humiliating students. On the contrary, challenging reflection activities can only function effectively when students are confident that they are respected as individuals, that their contributions are sought and valued and will be treated with appropriate confidentiality. For example, tenth-grade drama students working with patients in a nursing home might need to recognize and reflect on patient anger, their own irritation with patients, or uncaring behavior of patients' families. Through reflection they can come to grips with the need to develop tolerance for themselves and others as complex personalities. The reflective discussion that helps students do this must be carefully framed and sensitively conducted so that students understand that neither they nor guiding team members are accusing or judging, rather, that all are seeking to understand. Essentially, the reflection facilitator calls attention to ideas, feelings and actions that may be disturbing, troubling or shocking, but does so in a way that supports and nurtures each student's exploration and analysis.

Contexualized Reflection – Contexualized reflection activities are appropriate for the content they address and the settings in which they take place. Thus as an eleventh-grade American History class develops a town history, they may reflect differently on academic material in the classroom than they do when summing up with local ethnic and interest groups that participate in the project. In both situations reflection is deliberate and purposeful, but in the classroom it is likely to be more formal and systematic with one question following upon another, while in the community group it may begin with a single direct question, then move in a spontaneous and less formal way, building from idea to idea toward insight and understanding. Additionally, it is not likely that students in such a project will reflect on academic content while they are summarizing with a community group setting. On the other hand if they need to reflect on and understand tensions within community groups, it is likely that they will reflect most fruitfully back in the classroom or in a setting away from the group.

Types of Reflection Activities

There are many types of reflection activities: some that can be used in nearly any subject area or setting and others which serve best in particular subject areas or settings. Essentially these activities use questions that help students reconstruct, reorganize and think about their academic and service experiences and link them together in meaningful ways. Reflection activities useful in middle- and high-school service-learning projects can be labeled as interrogative, emotion-based, critical-thinking, metaphoric, and symbolic activities. The following briefly describes these types of activities and Chapter X provides specific examples of each with guidelines for their use.

Interrogative Reflection Activities ask questions using single words or very brief phrases to help students mentally encompass an experience, then address components within it that are meaningful in terms of their targeted service-learning outcomes. The most familiar example of this type of reflection activity is the "What?" "So What?" "Now What" design developed by the Campus Outreach Opportunity League (COOL). Any member of a project team can facilitate use of these three questions with almost any academic or service experience.

Emotion-based Reflection Activities build upon students' affective responses to their academic and service experiences. Human beings derive much of their advantage as creatures from the existence of their forebrains—their powers to reason and consider before acting—but people tend to respond to experience first in terms of the animal brain, the amygdala or seat of emotions. Reflecting on personal emotive responses to experience helps students understand how their own feelings color their perceptions and shape the limits of their understandings. They can then often go on to rational types of reflection. While it might appear that emotion-based reflection activities are most suited to use with service experience, thoughtful consideration suggests that they may be equally fruitful when students use them to reflect on academic experience.

Critical-thinking Reflection Activities draw upon specific critical-thinking heuristics to help students use deductive and inductive thinking with academic or service content. An example of this type of activity is questioning that helps older students recall and categorize key items of information from their experiences, use categories to develop concepts, then relate concepts in propositions. Because these kinds of activities help bring order to complex situations that often appear to be disorganized they are especially useful when students seek to derive meaning from naturalistic service settings.

Metaphoric Reflection Activities help students objectify experience by comparing it to something else. The element to which experience is to be compared may be suggested by the reflection facilitator or by students themselves. As students make comparisons, a kind of displacement results, and this often helps create a safe distance for challenging reflection. Thus these kinds of reflection activities are especially useful when students need to think about sensitive matters or issues that are disturbing to their own sensibilities.

Symbolic Reflection Activities are similar to metaphoric activities in that they help create displacement and a sense of safety and thus increase students' capacities to objectively consider situations and events that are emotionally loaded for them. Because symbols are innately powerful, they can also be used to help students reflect productively on academic material that may be necessary to their service-learning success, but may seem dry and boring. Symbolic reflection activities differ from metaphoric activities in their reliance on the use of unique real-world or abstract items that can be named and represented as objects. Symbols may be suggested by reflection facilitators or by students themselves.

In concluding this section it is important to explain that reflection activities are frequently used as a distinct second phase in an overall reflective learning experience. Students begin with focusing activities in which they read, see, hear or research academic material and witness or participate in service events and interactions. Then they apply reflection activities to these various contents. In some instances however, focusing and reflection activities may be more tightly integrated. For example when project teams help students focus on academics and service using panel discussions or symposiums, or involve them in discussion experiences with community groups, they may intersperse discussion with reflection. In these situations students work with particular content and reflect as they work with it, altering and adjusting their course toward insight and understanding as they move forward along this duel track. Project teams can use the reflection questions detailed in Chapter X in both ways, as the second step in a three-part reflective learning experience, or interwoven with a focusing event.

Learning Activities That Help Students Construct New Concepts

Conceptualizing activities bring reflective learning experiences to fruition by helping students stabilize understandings gained from focusing on and thinking about their academic study and service experience. These activities involve students in expressing their new understandings so that they internalize them, and in sharing the understandings with others so that they publicly commit to them. Conceptualizing activities thus simultaneously engage students in personal and social constructivist learning. As they internalize understandings gained from service-learning, students construct their own intellects in ways theorized by Piaget, Bruner and Vygotsky (see Chapter I). As they share "exhibits" of what they have come to know (Gagnon & Collay, 2000), they strengthen their knowledge by communicating it to others.

The Nature of Conceptualizing Activities

Conceptualizing activities help students transform internal understandings they have gained from reflecting on their service-learning experiences into visible products that express these understandings for themselves and for others. Products that represent conceptualizations can be oral, written, constructed or performed or can combine these features, and students are encouraged to fashion them within a brief time limit. Once created, conceptualizing activity products are shared with others and explained to them as necessary.

Types of Conceptualizing Activities

Conceptualizing activities can facilitate students' derivation of six types of concepts from their service-learning experiences: summaries, insights, propositions, problems, values and commitments. The following outlines these types of conceptualizing activities while Chapter X explores them in greater detail and provides guidelines for their use.

Graphic Summarizing Activities – These activities guide students through steps that can be mapped or visualized graphically. Within service-learning, probably the most familiar example of this type of activity is the Kolb wheel based on David Kolb's experiential learning theory (1984). The wheel shows the process of learning from experience as a continuous cycle of reflecting on concrete experience, conceptualizing from reflection and actively experimenting with resulting concepts. By converting the wheel into questions, reflection facilitators and students can engage in a systematic process that helps transform experience into learning. Graphic summary activities work to bring order to the complex and apparently disorganized situations that service experience often entails. When facilitators encourage students to include academic as well as service experience in their graphic summaries, significant insight and understanding can result.

Insight Identification and Sharing Activities – These activities help students identify understandings they have gained from organizing information, ideas and interpretations of experience in new ways. Students often recognize insights they have from their own sense of suddenly "seeing" meaning in a field of information that had no meaning for them before. Insights are also often accompanied by a sensation of mental light and physical excitement.

Proposition Identification and Sharing Activities – These activities help students express testable ideas that they have derived from their service-learning experiences. These ideas often begin as students' personal opinions and assumptions that are either strengthened or eroded by events and actions over the course of an experience. They can also arise from the suggestions of others with whom they interact during service-learning.

Problem Identification and Sharing Activities – These activities help students identify and state problems that their service-learning experiences have made them aware of and that may stimulate commitment to self-improvement or to improving the situations of others. Students often recognize problems by the fact that they arise from discrepant, disturbing or even shocking information, events or actions.

Values Identification and Sharing Activities – These activities help students express moral and ethical principles that their service-learning experiences have either supported within their existing value systems or newly contributed to those systems. Students often recognize values as principles they can use to guide their own behavior in a broad range of situations.

Commitment Identification and Sharing Activities – These activities help students identify particular personal or community projects to which they are realistically able to contribute. These projects may relate in a positive way to some aspect of their service-learning experience or may involve a negation of some aspect of that experience. Students recognize possible areas of commitment through a sense of intense concern about a particular project combined with the ability to identify specific ways they can contribute to the project.

Using Conceptualizing Activities Within Reflective Learning Experiences

Conceptualizing activities are most effective and help students enjoy thinking—which is their nurturant effect—when teams use them artistically and happily, not in a grimly mechanical fashion. This means using them only when they can genuinely contribute to students extended and deeper thinking. Often, reflection activities themselves will lead students to solid and useful concepts and additional conceptualization is forced and not genuinely productive. When used, reflection activities need to guide individuals to draw conclusions, then share these conclusions with others—all within a brief space of time. As students become increasingly skilled at working in cooperative-learning groups, they can use conceptualization activities within their groups and enhance the power of their groups to promote the positive educational outcomes recorded by Johnson, Johnson and Smith and summarized on page 105 in this chapter.

A return to the Blue Mesa example shows how a team might use reflection to help students link academic study to service experience, then use conceptualizing to construct knowledge from reflection. Table 6.3 represents the Blue Mesa's reflective-experience outline showing when the team plans to use reflection and conceptualizing activities with its multiple-intelligences, cooperative learning focusing activities.

CONCEPTUALIZING WITH REFLECTIVE LEARNING EXPERIENCES * 113

Table 6.3 Reflective Learning Experiences for Instructional Objectives of Seventh-Grade Service-Learning Project

Expectations as Goals	Indicators as Objectives	Focusing Activities	Reflection & Conceptualizing Activities
Academic Area			
Express numbers in equivalent forms (State standard 2.3.7)	Convert real-life data into whole numbers, fractions and percents	CL-1 (M, VL) Compose and sing applying math to life "commercial jingle" (student project team reps.) CL-2 (VL, LM) Read, discuss and work examples for Topic 9 in Today's Mathematics, pp. 79-81 (whole group)	Reflect in class to prepare for use of academic learnings in service project and conceptualize propositions about possible effects of SL on own learning
Service Area			
Competence	Carry out thorough and accurate data collection	CL-3 (LM, IP-1) Use spreadsheets to collect data and record as whole numbers, fractions and percents (continuing 6-member groups set up in class, one assigned to each data collection day) Exchange to check accuracy (pairs within 6-member groups)	Reflect on cooperative group processes on site
		CL-4 (VL, LM, VS, IP-1) Prepare illustrated class presentation for Council justified in percents of car, truck and pedestrian traffic through intersection from 4-6 pm during a one-week period. (whole group outline, 6-member groups for components)	Reflect in whole group in class on audience needs and conceptualize propositions re vehicle types
	Dress appropriately during data collection and at council meeting	CL-5 (VS, LM, IP) Draw posters of "dress for important occasions," develop general guidelines from commonalities (individuals then 6-member groups)	Reflect in task groups on personal feelings about dress
Caring	Understand competing needs of those who want traffic light and council	CL-6 (IP-1, VL, BK) Interview parents and council members via e-mail, then role play council discussion of proposal (whole group with five student observer reps—one from each 6-member group) CL-7 (VL, LM, BK, IP-1) Present proposal to council (a component by each group)	Reflect on emerging positions w/ council members and conceptualize insights
Personal Growth Area			
Self-Awareness	Hold self to standards in completing group tasks	CL-8 (IP-2, VL) Keep daily personal journal listing own contributions to efforts for the day	Reflect in CL groups on own values and conceptualize commitments

Key: VL=Verbal-Linguistic, LM=Logical-Mathematical, VS=Visual-Spatial, BK=Bodily-Kinesthetic, M= Musical-Rhythmic, IP-1=Interpersonal, IP-2=Intrapersonal, CL=Cooperative Learning

Table 6.3 shows continuous use of reflection that is connected to the content of focusing activities. Several reflection activities challenge students to understand their feelings and behavior as dynamics within their service-learning project, and each takes place in a context that should increase its efficacy. Conceptualization activities are used with each outcome area, but not with each focusing and reflection activity. This gives students opportunities to explore many ideas and feelings, then bring these together to form concepts that contribute to their intellectual growth through internalization and sharing. When teams build reflective-learning experiences like these, they help students progress toward accomplishment of goals and objectives using the integrated process depicted earlier in Figure 6.1.

The Blue Mesa team will transform the outline shown in Table 6.3 into a full instruction plan by doing two things. First, they will complete its reflective learning experiences by choosing specific reflection and conceptualizing activities such as those named in this chapter and detailed in Chapter X. Then they will decide which team members will be responsible for implementing each reflective learning experience.

Sharing Instructional Responsibilities

The discussion up to this point makes clear that as teams develop integrated reflective-learning experiences, they have many options. These options can be liberating rather than confusing when teams select among them in ways they believe will best guide students toward accomplishment of goals and objectives derived from outcome expectations. Figure 6.2 provides an overview of this way of thinking about service-learning instructional planning process.

Figure 6.2 Service-Learning Instructional Planning Process

Use Outcomes Plan to State Goals and Objectives

Design Reflective Learning Experiences

(1) Focus Students on Academic, Service and Personal Experience

Multiple Intelligence-Cooperative Learning Activities

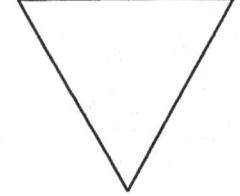

(2) Guide Students' 4 C's Reflection on Experience

Interrogative, Emotion-based, Critical-Thinking, Metaphoric, Symbolic, Activities

(3) Help Students Conceptualize from Reflected-Upon Experience

Activities That Elicit Summaries, Insights, Propositions, Problem Identification, Values, Commitments

Figure 6.2 summarizes the first two steps project teams use in the service-learning instructional planning process—stating goals and objectives, and designing reflective learning experiences. The process is not complete, however until team members take a third and critical step, sharing responsibility for engaging students in reflective-learning experiences. When team members cooperatively implement instruction, they bring the instructional planning process to fruition and concomitantly round out the third phase of the Collaborative Service-Learning Model. The following discussion explores ways team members can cooperate in the implementation of their team's instructional plan.

Two Ways to Share Instructional Responsibilities

Project teams that share instructional responsibilities increase opportunities for students to accomplish outcome expectations. They also increase their efficiency, strengthen collaboration skills and grow as service-learning educators. Team members share instructional responsibilities by taking both in-common and individual responsibility, and they bring closure to instructional planning by agreeing upon what all members will similarly do to help implement instruction and what each will do from his or her own unique perspective.

Common Responsibilities for All Team Members

The most important in-common responsibility that project team members take is keeping a record of their own work in the project and their reactions to it. Different team members may use different formats for keeping these records, but all members need to keep them regularly and consistently. This usually means that each time a team member works on the project—in planning meetings, preparation activities, sessions with students, co-workers, clients and so forth—he or she succinctly summarizes what happened and annotates this summary with related thoughts, ideas, perspectives. These in-common personal records serve three critical functions within a service-learning project. First they work as a management tool that keeps the team aware of the project's progress, its successes and its snags. If activities are unfolding smoothly and as planned and team members shares this information, they enhance the climate and process of the project. Or if a key learning activity is not implemented for some reason, the team can make adjustments that provide students the experiences they need. If new resources for the project appear—books, websites, experts, relevant extensions of service activity—the team can integrate them with appropriate aspects of the project. Or if logistics such as transportation or supervision go awry, the team can re-arrange plans as necessary.

Second, in-common personal records often provide content that team members can use to enrich already planned focusing, reflection and conceptualization activities and to help solve problems. Summaries of students' performance in some aspect of service may suggest where they need additional information through demonstrations and direct instruction. Records of unexpected, upsetting or negative events and behaviors may point to a need for additional student and team reflection. Records of the results of student reflection may imply nascent alternate concepts that students might usefully explore.

In-common personal records are critical in the fourth phase of the Collaborative Service-Learning model as they provide indications of the team's growth as a team. As discussed in Chapter XI, project teams review records team members keep over the course of the project in order to develop a picture of how the team functioned and of behaviors and attitudes that contributed to its progress. This information can be shared with others who are interested in using and supporting service-learning. Team members can also analyze their records with reflection strategies described in Chapter X and develop insights about themselves and new perspectives on their relationships with others.

Individual Team Member Responsibilities

Team members who take appropriate responsibility for focusing activities can contribute to students' deeper learning and to the team's success as a team. This usually evolves naturally with classroom teachers assuming responsibility for academic focusing activities and agency representatives assuming responsibility for service focusing activities. Administrators who serve on teams usually have teaching backgrounds and can serve in much the same way as teachers, and school counselors by virtue of their service orientation and training can often take responsibility for focusing activities related to service. Parents and community members whose background and training are not so clearly related to the elements of a service-learning project can assist as team teachers and in doing so gradually develop their own service-learning teaching skills. Sharing responsibilities for focusing activities in this way ensures collaboration and distributes the work load. But above all, it promotes an important global outcome of service-learning that Gelmon et al. identify as "valuing multiple teachers." (2001, pp. 23-24). As students learn from all project team members, they are more likely to recognize that many people in their lives can be their teachers.

Team members who also share teaching responsibility for reflection and conceptualizing activities can contribute to the depth of student learning and project team success. Again this sharing encourages students to learn from multiple teachers, ensures team collaboration and partitions the work load. In addition, it can bring the benefits of reflection and conceptualizing to team members themselves. Team members who help students think about particular experiences and gain insight and understanding may, themselves, develop new ideas and perspectives. They may become more aware of the work and mission of schools, the needs and strengths of their communities, and the power of human relationships to solve problems and productively shape society. As with focusing activities, team members can either lead or assist in teaching for reflection and conceptualization and by gaining expertise with these kinds of activities can develop competence in two skills they can use as they interact with others in their own lives.

In Conclusion

Service-learning project teams collaboratively develop instruction by restating student academic, service and personal-growth outcome expectations and indicators as instructional goals and objectives. Teams then design reflective learning experiences that help students achieve these goals and objectives. Reflective learning experiences consist of focusing activities, reflection activities and conceptualizing activities. Focusing activities use multiple-intelligences and cooperative learning techniques to help student acquire the knowledge, skills and understandings they need to accomplish academic and service objectives. Reflection activities use questioning to help students relate the knowledge, skills and understanding they are gaining from academic study and service to personal growth and their lives as community members, and conceptualization activities help students make manifest their new insights and perspectives through exhibits they share. Project teams complete the instructional development process by cooperating in the actual implementation of the reflective learning experiences they design.

Activities for Increasing Understanding

1. Begin developing instruction for your practice service-learning project by setting up a matrix using Table 6.3 as a model. In the first two columns write the instructional goals and objectives for your project using the students outcomes plan expectations and indicators you developed for Activity 2 in Chapter V.
2. Imagine using your goals and objectives matrix with your project team to develop focusing activities that will help students accomplish your goals and objectives. Use ideas from this imaginary meeting and information about focusing activities from this chapter to describe in the third column of your matrix one focusing activity for each objective in the second column.
3. Use information about reflection and conceptualizing activities from this chapter to describe in the fourth column of your matrix how you would use these two types of activities to help students think about and gain insight from their work with your focusing activities. Use entries in the fourth column of Table 6.3 as a guide to your descriptions of how you intend to use reflection and conceptualizing activities.

Chapter VII: Evaluating Projects and Celebrating Growth

"I suppose we could wait to develop our evaluation plan—till students are actually involved in the Seeds For Sustenance project." Social Studies teacher Pete Cohen leans back with crossed arms. *"It might give us time to catch our breath."*

"But Mr. Cohen. What more do we need? We have the tests we'll take to show what the class has learned. And we agreed who'll take responsibility for each one," says student representative Micah Arnot.

"There's a bit more to a project evaluation than student outcomes—although that is most important. Let me explain, Micah." guidance counselor Krista Reeves, says. *"We developed our students outcomes plan to find out about what students gain from the project. But we also want to find out how the project benefits the SFS people and how effective our project team is. If we gather this information, too, we can put it all together and decide what it tells us about the overall value of this project."*

"There's another piece, too," adds Gil Lehman, of the Seeds For Sustenance Coalition. *"It can wait till near the end, but we've got to start thinking about it now. Great things are going to happen in this project. We'll want to let people know about them."*

"Yes! We'll want to celebrate. All of us—the team, the kids, parents like me." Dot Mannix says.

Pete leans forward. *"So, we should do the evaluation plan now, then work on the celebration later. Makes sense to me. How about you, Micah?"*

Chapter Focus

In the fourth phase of the Collaborative Service Learning Model, project teams and their students evaluate their projects and celebrate new learnings and perspectives. To do this, they gather, interpret and share information from many sources including student outcomes assessment, client and partner feedback, and project team self- evaluation. Teams can assemble all of this information, construct meaning from it and celebrate that meaning with a wide variety of audiences by carrying out three steps: 1) developing and implementing an evaluation plan, 2) using inductive thinking to analyze and interpret the information the evaluation plan generates, and 3) integrating information from reflective learning experiences and evaluation in celebratory activities. The chapter describes basic procedures for carrying out these steps.

Developing Service-Learning Evaluation Plans

Popham (1993) explains that the purpose of educational evaluation is to make decisions about the worth of a particular program in order to improve it as it currently exists or as it might be implemented again in the future. This local, value-oriented emphasis discriminates educational evaluation from educational research, which emphasizes drawing conclusions that can be widely generalized to many programs in many settings. Educational evaluation and educational research use many of the same techniques to gather information, but they use the information they collect in different ways to support their different purposes. For example a service-learning team that is evaluating its project uses classroom test performance to decide if students in the project actually accomplished their instructional objectives. If they did, this helps build the case that the project was worthwhile for the students involved. A service-learning researcher, on the other hand, compares test performance of students taught traditionally and matched students taught via service-learning to determine which method resulted in the highest achievement of instructional objectives. If the service-learning group performs at higher levels, the researcher may be justified in concluding that service-learning is an effective teaching method for all students with the general characteristics of those in the research study.

In accord with these ideas, the fourth phase in the Collaborative Service-Learning Model focuses on educational evaluation, not on educational research. In this phase, project teams develop evaluation plans that identify the information they will need to judge the worth of their particular service-learning projects and establish the procedures they will use to collect this information. Once they implement their evaluation plans, teams use the information they gather in two ways: for accountability within their professional settings and—as is the focus of this chapter—for celebrating the accomplishments that they and their constituents have achieved through service-learning.

Positive outcomes for students lie at the heart of any service-learning project. Therefore, evaluation plans for service-learning projects consist in good part of procedures for implementing planned student outcomes measures. In addition, the success of any service-learning project depends upon the involvement of community partners and the leadership of a collaborative team. Thus, service-learning evaluation plans also detail procedures for collecting two other kinds of information. These are community–partner and service-client feedback about their involvement in service-learning, and project-team self-analysis information about the effectiveness of the processes and products the project team used to manage and implement the project. Service-learning evaluation plans, then, include a student outcomes assessment component, a project impact component and a project team self-evaluation component. The following describes how a project team can detail these three components in ways that support their implementation and concludes with an example of a service-learning evaluation plan that shows how these components can be organized and documented.

The Student Outcomes Component of an Evaluation Plan

The student outcomes component of a service-learning project's evaluation plan guides administration and analysis of the student outcomes measures that a project team identifies in its initial students outcomes plan. The creation of that outcomes plan as described in Chapter V is the first step in a "backward mapping" process a team uses to identify its academic, service and personal growth expectations for students. In a second step described in Chapter VI, the team uses its outcomes plan to generate an instructional plan, a framework of goals, objectives and reflective learning experiences that will help students achieve outcome expectations. In a third step described here in Chapter VII, the team uses its outcomes plan to specify the actual instruments that will measure agreed-upon student outcomes indicators, the procedures for using these instruments and the ways the information the instruments produce will be organized for interpretation. This specification becomes the student outcomes component of the teams' overall evaluation plan. To develop this component, teams identify each measurement instrument and decide which team member will administer the instrument. They then describe the logistics of administration, the materials needed, scoring or coding guidelines, and formats for summarizing data.

Instruments and Team Member Responsibilities

Student outcomes plans as described in Chapter V name each strategy a team will use to measure students gains from its project and identify a team member who will take responsibility for developing or assembling the instruments that will implement each strategy—a criterion referenced test, a survey form, an observation scale and so forth. Outcomes plans do not initially detail these instruments because they have yet to be found or developed. After a team's student outcomes plan has been laid out, assigned team members go on to find or create its instruments using guidelines such as those in Chapter V and IX, and share their work with the team as they go forward. By the time the team is ready to develop its evaluation plan, instruments to measure student outcomes have been located or developed and team members responsible for them can describe them in detail. Because these team members know their instruments well, they usually volunteer to administer them or make arrangements for someone else to administer them. Thus, a project team comes to evaluation plan development ready to write a brief description of each instrument that will be used to gather information about students' academic, service and personal growth outcomes and to identify who will administer each instrument. The team is also ready to include a copy of each instrument in an appendix to its evaluation plan.

Logistics

Careful specification of the procedures that will be used to administer instruments helps ensure that outcomes measurement goes smoothly. Smooth administration helps those who respond to instruments to do their best and this, in turn, produces meaningful outcomes information. To manage logistics in ways that produce good information, teams need to state when in the course of their projects each instrument will be administered, identify who will respond to each instrument and state the length of time needed to complete the instrument. Determining when each instrument will be administered helps ensure that there is, in fact, a time period in which it can be used. Describing who will respond makes clear if instruments must be given to and returned from an entire group or only to some members of the group—information that will be important when the team looks at results. Indicating the length of time needed—for distribution, giving directions, administration and collection of materials—helps ensure a match between measurement as planned and measurement as conducted, whether in the classroom or in the more complex world of the community.

Materials

Materials for measuring outcomes consist of the tests that students will complete, writing implements they will use and any special stimulus materials such as pictures, objects, quotations and so forth to which they will respond. The evaluation plan lists these materials and indicates that copies of instruments can be found in the appendix to the plan. Whether materials are to be used in the classroom or on site, a clearly marked box or receptacle for collecting each kind of material is essential.

Instruments, themselves, need to be formalized on paper. Students who are being tested or those who are gathering information about students' performance should be given a common, carefully prepared form to use. This is simple and straightforward in the case of academic tests, observation scales, surveys, interviews and focus groups where the test items that students are to address or the questions that team members will ask are printed directly on the forms they receive. For anecdotal observations and experience analysis papers, teachers and students also need forms that have clear, simple directions at the top followed by ample blank space in to record observations or write about experiences. Users of the forms should be able to refer easily to the directions.

Scoring or Coding Guidelines

Teams state scoring guidelines for instruments that produce numerically scored responses such as criterion-referenced tests, rating scales and surveys, in their evaluation plans by indicating the number of points each response or response element can earn. For example, if students are to learn the parts of a microscope in preparation for service with the water quality commission, and each part they correctly identify earns them one point, this should be noted in the evaluation plan. Or if library patrons are to be asked to report their perceptions of service-learning students' interpersonal skills on a survey that uses 4-item Likert-scale responses, the value of each response should be indicated in the evaluation plan. For instruments such as interviews and focus groups that produce information that will be coded for concepts and ideas, the plan should indicate by name and symbol the concepts that are to be coded if the team has identified these in advance.

Formats for Summarizing Data

Team members need to summarize scoring and coding results in ways that facilitate eventual analysis with inductive thinking. They do this by identifying the most salient positive and negative features of the results. Where instruments produce quantified data, they can do this using frequencies and measures of central tendency. Where data is in coded form, they can indicate the relative weight of a particular type of response. For example, teams usually summarize criterion-referenced test data in terms of respondent's average score on individual items and on the total test, and the number or percent of students who achieved whatever cut score was set. Survey responses can be summarized similarly but do not include information about non-applicable cut scores. Focus group and interview data can be summarized in terms of the ideas respondents express ordered from most to least frequently stated. Again, these summaries will be central to the inductive-thinking process teams eventually use to interpret and share evaluation information, so it is essential that teams agree to guidelines for summarizing data and that all team members understand and use them.

The Project Impact Component of an Evaluation Plan

Many project teams want to use the expectations-indicators-measurement approach described in Chapter V to measure project outcome indicators for recipients of services, community organizations, schools and teachers. Other teams that are just beginning to use service-learning may not have the time and resources to assess outcomes of constituents other than their students in detail. They can, however, gain a good sense of their projects' impact by requesting feedback from the clients their students served and community partners who provide service experiences for students. Ferrari (personal communication, July 24, 2003) suggests that this feedback can be obtained by asking constituents to answer questions such as the following.

- What services did students provide?
- How do you rate the overall service experience – excellent, good, fair or poor?
- Would you like to participate in a service learning project/receive student services again?

Teams can detail use of these questions within the project-impact component of their evaluation plans with the same descriptors they used to specify their plans for implementing student outcomes assessment. They identify who will ask the project-impact questions and when this will be done, and they indicate logistics, materials, scoring/coding guidelines, and data summary formats that will facilitate question use and results analysis. By including use of these project-impact questions in their evaluation plans, teams prepare to gather information that enhances their picture of the overall worth of their projects. Chapter XI explores ways teams can develop feedback instruments using the three questions.

The Project Team Self-Evaluation Component of an Evaluation Plan

Everything that happens in a service-learning project flows from the work of its collaborating project team. Therefore, a full picture of the value of a service-learning project includes information about the work of the team itself—the processes it used and the products it developed. Project teams can develop an understanding of how they functioned as a team by finding evidence in their journals of their own use of five group processes that facilitate team success. They can develop an understanding of the worth of their instructional products by judging them in terms of three basic efficacy criteria. They can then use these understandings in the inductive-thinking analysis phase of evaluation.

Criteria for Evaluating Project Team Processes

Project teams are cooperative-learning teams, and the criteria for assessing their interactive, working processes come directly from cooperative learning theory and practice described in Chapter VI. As that chapter explains, there are five essential elements in cooperative learning: positive interdependence, face-to-face promotive interaction, individual accountability, interpersonal and small group skills, and group process reflection. Teams can rate their own cooperative-learning process by using material from their journals to decide how effective they were with respect to each of these elements. This can be done productively and collaboratively using procedures described in Chapter XI.

Criteria for Evaluating Project Team Products

Project teams can judge the value of their instructional products in terms of three service-learning efficacy criteria. The first criterion centers on the collaborative product planning that is a defining feature of service-learning, and that research and best practice identify as essential to service-learning success. The second criterion centers on clarity and coherence of a team's products. Products that students, team members and constituents can understand and that relate meaningfully to one another facilitate viable connections between service and learning. The third criterion for judging the value of project-team products centers on their usefulness to the people for whom they were designed. Products that remain on the shelf or confuse those they were designed to help do little to further service-learning. Teams find evidence for their judgments of how well their products meet these three criteria in the nature of the products themselves, their journals and by recalling use of the products.

Project teams can describe the procedures they will use to gather information about their own process and products with the same descriptors they use in the student outcomes and project impact components of their evaluation plans. They describe who on the team will be responsible for examining processes and products and when these two examinations will be carried out. Again, teams detail logistics, materials, scoring/coding guidelines, and data summary formats those responsible will use. By making provisions for a close look at their own cooperative-learning behaviors and at quality of their service-learning products, project-teams gather critical information for use in inductive-thinking analysis of the overall value of their service-learning projects. Again, Chapter XI further details how teams can carry out this essential self-analysis.

An Example of an Evaluation Plan

A continuation of the Blue Mesa example shows how a project team lays out an evaluation plan that includes the three components discussed above. As explained earlier, the Blue Mesa project uses a one-day event design in which seventh-grade students learn how to collect data about traffic flow through a dangerous intersection, then array that data in ways that will support their school PTA's proposal to the county council for the installation of a traffic light at the intersection. The Blue Mesa project team consists of two student representatives, the class's math teacher, an officer from the county's traffic safety division and a parent. This team developed its student outcomes-, instruction-, and evaluation plans during the teacher's planning period over a two-week period prior to the project's four-week implementation period. From the perspective of students in the class, the project implementation sequence is as follows:

Week One: Students learn relevant mathematics and prepare for service.
Week Two: Students plan their council presentation in class and collect data at the intersection after school.
Week Three: Students present justifications for a traffic light to the council and complete outcome assessments.
Week Four: Students plan and implement a celebration symposium and disseminate project outcomes information.

The Blue Mesa team designs an evaluation plan that gathers the majority of student outcomes, project impact and team process/product information during the third week of the project so that results are available in week four for use in celebration. The plan is shown in Table 7.1.

A first look at Table 7.1 suggests that evaluating a service-learning project—even one organized around a one-day event—involves a project team in using many instruments and collecting a wealth of information. While this is true, a closer look at the example reveals that assessment and feedback collection in the plan can be distributed in ways that keep the actual amount of testing and information gathering at reasonable levels. Students in the Blue Mesa project spend about an hour completing a traditional in-class math test and an essay. They spend just under an hour completing other, learning-activity assessments—data sheet checking, analysis of dress-for-the-occasion, and focus group discussion. Partners and clients together spend less than two hours providing feedback about students' service, and project team members spend two hours evaluating their processes and products. Essentially, it is possible to comprehensively evaluate a project without testing participants excessively because all involved assist in implementing assessments and other evaluation strategies.

Table 7.1 also reveals that service-learning evaluation plans are very detailed, especially when copies of assessment instruments and feedback strategies to be used are appended to the plans. Experience suggests that the level of detail shown in the example is critical for successful evaluation. Thinking through and recording the operational details of each instrument helps project teams plan evaluation that is clearly related to what actually went on in their projects, helps them ensure what Freeman (1998) calls " the ecological validity" of the information they gather. In the table for instance, a seven-item, in-class math test, three feedback questions for the council, traffic data sheets checked immediately on site, and 30-minute, in-class focus groups all clearly relate to the real world of the Blue Mesa project and its purposes. Additionally, knowledge of the operational details of each instrument helps project teams confirm that they are collecting evaluation information that will help them answer their central evaluation question, "What is the worth of this project to those who have been involved?" Finally, when team members are all aware of the purpose and process of each test and feedback collection instrument, they are likely—because they have come to the point of evaluation as a team—to create a climate of support for conscientious use of planned instruments.

Table 7.1 Evaluation Plan for Seventh-Grade, Pro-Traffic Light Service-Learning Project

Instrument and Team Member Responsible	Logistics	Materials	Scoring and or Coding	Data Summary Format
Academic Area				
State Standards Test – Items 33, 34, 45 – expressing numbers in equivalent forms Mr. Vishinsky	School staff administers state test three months after project completion. Obtain results for use next year in seeking new SL project support	State test forms	Each SL student's total score on 3 relevant items using state test-item score values: Item 33 - Percents, value = 3 Item 34 – Fractions, value = 4 Item 45 – Decimals, value = 3	Array of item scores and total scores for SL students vs. item and total scores for all students tested on items 33, 34, and 45
Criterion Referenced Test of ability to express numbers in food drive example in equivalent forms Mr. Vishinsky	Administer in regular class period to all students Allow 30 min. after 10 min. for review and questions– Week 3, Day 3.	Seven-item printed CRT based on stimulus material describing food and money collected in a food drive	24 points total score based on 14 number-conversion related tasks that range from 1 to 3 points each in value	Summary showing students' scores by task with class average for each task; total on all tasks for each student with average score on all tasks for class
Service Area				
Anecdotal Observation of students' dress at council meeting re CL group dress guidelines Student CL group reps and Ms. Selkirk	Ms. Selkirk takes photographs as appropriate throughout 2 hour council meeting. Student reps evaluate – Week 3, Day 1	Camera and film or disk for at least 5 photographs of students arriving at and presenting to council meeting	5 photographs scored for evidence of 3 CL group dress criteria, each instance receives 1 point	Summary showing criteria score for each photo, summary of all points for each criteria and statement ranking criteria in photos from most to least evident
Rating of student use of data collection and checking process Sgt. Penders	Implement as each group completes data collection on site daily Week 2, Days 1-5	Printed traffic record sheet sectioned for cars, trucks, motorcycles with columns for whole number total of each and, fractions and percents of all vehicles	Student data sheets scored 1 point each for correct record of traffic, counts shown as whole numbers, fractions and percents; and partner's accuracy certification	Summary showing students' scores by task with class average for each task; total on all tasks for each student with average score on all tasks for class
Focus Group – Identification of competing parent/ Council needs Mr. Vishinsky, Sgt. Penders	Conduct 2, 30-min. sessions during regular class period, half of class in each session – Week 3, Day 2	Printed booklet w/ facilitator directions, discussion questions, space for facilitator notes on process. Laptop and backup disk	Identified needs of parents (np), identified needs of Council (nc), conflicts (x) coded. Appropriate codes assigned to other statements	Summary based on needs frequencies in each category and description of other ideas generated by focus group participants by frequency

Table 7.1 continued

		Personal Growth Area	
Experience Analysis of students' perceived best CL group contribution Mr. Vishinsky & Sgt. Penders	Administer in regular class period to all students. Allow 30 min. for writing after 10 min. for student review and questions – Week 3, Day 2	Printed writing prompt: Use your journal to review your CL group work. Identify your best CL contribution and explain why it was best. Suggest ways you can build on this kind of contribution in future group work.	Papers rated on identification of CL elements (3 points each), number of justifications (1 point each) and ways to build on contributions (1 point each)	Summary describing elements identified and their frequency, kinds of justifications and their frequency and kinds of contributions and their frequency

		Project Impact		
Client Feedback – Council's perceptions of students' contributions Students Council	Distribute to all council members at beginning of council meeting, collect at end - Week 3, Day 1	5"x 8" cards asking council members to list student contributions to meeting, rate overall service and willingness to invite future student input	Contributions categorized and coded excellent, good, fair, poor ratings tallied; yes/no for inviting future student input tallied	Summary of contributions most/least frequently identified, percent of total for each, percent yes/no for inviting future student input
Community Partner Feedback – Traffic Division's perceptions of students' potential as future project partners Sgt. Penders	Complete in own office during Week 3 by end of Day 2	Form asking Sgt. Penders to list student contributions, rate overall service and possibility of student partnering in appropriate future projects	Number and types of contributions, rating 4-1 excellent, good, fair, poor, yes/no for future work with students.	Summary listing student services, rating overall service and describing division's willingness to involve students in future appropriate projects

		Project-Team Self-Evaluation		
Process Evaluation – Team rankings of use of cooperative learning elements All team members	Complete in 1-hour, after-school meeting – Week 3, Day 2	Form for team collaborative ranking of own use of positive interdependence, face-to-face promotive interaction, accountability, group skills, group processing	Evidence of use of elements found in journals coded by element and tallied	Summary ranking of use of process with anonymous interpretive comment from team members
Product Evaluation – Team rating of selected plans and activities on three efficacy criteria All Team Members	Complete in 1-hour, after-school meeting – Week 3, Day 3	Form for team collaborative rating of instructional plan & materials re CL group guidelines of collaborative development, clarity and coherence, use	Ratings for each material tallied using 4-1 for excellent, good, fair, poor	Group rating of instructional plan and materials with anonymous interpretive comment from team members

To sum up, service-learning evaluation plans are comprehensive and detailed. These plan attributes help project teams collaboratively implement evaluation in ways that are reasonable, not excessive and that realistically collect meaningful evaluation information. These attributes also help team members support each other so that they implement their intended evaluation strategies with fidelity and gather the information they need to determine the worth of their projects for their students, the people that students served, their colleagues and constituents, and themselves as service-learning facilitators.

Implementing Service-Learning Evaluation Plans

Implementation of a clearly described evaluation plan is a relatively simple matter. Individual team members prepare the instruments and related materials for which they are responsible in sufficient number for those who respond to the instruments. They schedule the time necessary for instrument administration with all who will take part and make necessary physical arrangements for administration. Students respond to outcomes assessment instruments as scheduled in class or are observed as they provide service, again as scheduled. Partners and service clients respond quickly and succinctly to feedback instruments as close in time to student's provision of service as possible, and project teams meet in privacy to evaluate the quality of their work together and the products that their work produced. Team members then make sure they collect, label and organize all results information in terms of guidelines in the evaluation plan so that they can easily access it when they are ready to analyze and interpret it with inductive thinking.

Analyzing and Interpreting Evaluation Information With Inductive Thinking

With evaluation information in hand, teams are ready to use systematic inductive thinking about the outcomes of their projects and to judge the value of those outcomes in terms of those who were involved. Teams use inductive thinking as a critical-thinking reflection strategy in much the same way that students do. Like students, they reason from specific information through observed patterns and relationships to generalizations. The difference is that when students use inductive thinking as reflection, their experiences—in the classroom and in service—serve as the information they analyze for patterns and relationships and from which they derive generalizations. When project teams use inductive thinking for evaluation, they analyze the information they have obtained from implementing their evaluation plans by looking for patterns and relationships within it. They then integrate what they discern into generalizations about project worth.

Using Inductive Thinking With Partners

Project teams strengthen the validity of their generalizations when they use inductive thinking with partners. Partners are school and community agency affiliates interested in service-learning—other teachers, students, parents, administrators, guidance counselors, instructional supervisors, agency workers, staff developers, program developers. Team members select partners to assist them in using procedures detailed in Chapter XI in reflecting on the results of student outcomes measurement, and on information gathered about project impact and team processes and products. Pairs find patterns and relationships in this material and integrate these into generalized summary findings for each instrument. Table 7.2 shows how pairs might record results of inductive thinking about five different instruments used in the Seeds For Sustenance (SFS) project mentioned in this chapter's opening scenario. In that project a tenth-grade biology class of 30 students learns about subsistence agriculture as they help the SFS group with its work of testing seeds and distributing them to subsistence farmers worldwide.

Table 7.2 records the steps the SFS team and its partners used to make generalizations about the information produced by implementing their evaluation plan. The validity of these generalizations depends, of course, on participants' capacities to see meaningful patterns and relationships within results. Inclusion of non-team partners in the inductive thinking process should aid this validity because outsiders can help reduce bias that team members may understandably bring to analysis of results of instruments they have personally shepherded throughout a project. Partners also introduce fresh perspectives, suggest patterns and relationships that team members may not see.

Engaging in the kind of disciplined inductive thinking that leads to the type of record shown in Table 7.2 is likely to be challenging for teams and their partners at first, just as disciplined reflection is often at first challenging for students. Teams and their partners have to learn to draw back from the details of results, to see where certain results cluster and are related to each other, then to derive warranted generalizations from these patterns and relationships. But inductive thinking can be learned, and Chapter XI includes suggestions and guidelines that will help participants become skilled in its use.

Expressing Results of Inductive Thinking as Value Judgments

Once project teams use inductive thinking to summarize evaluation results in a set of generalizations, they express these as positive value judgments and/or needs-improvement value judgments about their projects. Teams can use sentence frames such as the following to express positive value judgments.

The _____ project was valuable for _____ because it showed that_____.

Table 7.2 Inductive Thinking About Tenth-Grade Biology Service-Learning Project Evaluation Results

Instrument	Results	Patterns	Relationships	Generalizations
Academic test: Students recall arid-region subsistence farming strategies taught in class and reinforced in service activities	Cut score = 3 strategies Class Av. = 5 strategies 93% of class at or above cut score	Highest reported: Resistant Seeds, Water Management, Mulching, Windbreaks Lowest reported: Interplanting, Shelter, Resistant Animals	Patterns cluster as: Plant Related Strategies Animal Related Strategies	Students recalled more of the strategies reinforced by service
Comparison of actual and expected growth rates of 6 types of oat seeds in students' test plots after 2-weeks of drip water, mulching, cultivating. Analysis of student logs.	27 of 30 of student test gardens showed expected growth rate, 3 did not. 27 of 30 student logs show complete, daily cultivation records, 3 did not.	Students with expected growth rates kept logs, used elevated drips and large mulch chunks. Others had gaps in log records, poor drip runs and used mixed mulch.	Patterns cluster as: Competent use of subsistence growth techniques Incomplete use of techniques	Most students understood and used competent practice and were successful in helping SFS with its seed testing work.
Feedback from SFS Mentors re types of student service, service quality, future service	By frequency, students helped with: Sorting seeds for mailing, testing seed type growth, visitor tours, newsletter articles. 7 students showed unusual skill in test work and publicity	Overall Service Rating – Good Future Return – Yes Give special invitations to highly skilled students	Patterns cluster as: Students as a group did what was needed. Some students showed particular skill/interest in test work and publicity	Students directly or indirectly helped SFS subsistence agriculture mission; some showed particular potential as future interns.
Team Evaluation of its Instructional Products Academic: Readings and video about subsistence agriculture Service: Orientation package	(1-4 = low-high) Collab. Dev – 1 Clarity & Coherence – 4 Usefulness to Students – 2 Collab. Dev – 3 Clarity & Coherence – 4 Usefulness to students – 4	Academic material: Little collaboration in producing, is clear and coherent but not usefully related to SFS thrust. Service Material: Good collaboration, material clear and coherent, reflects actual SFS practices.	Patterns cluster as: Collaboratively developed material rated useful Clear and coherent material may or may not be rated useful.	Instructional materials that were collaboratively developed were rated most useful to students.

*132 * CHAPTER VII*

Teams complete these positive value judgment frames by writing the name of their project in the first blank, the constituents who are indicated by the generalization as beneficiaries in the second blank and the summary finding that the generalization states in the third blank. Using the positive value judgment frame for the generalizations from the Table 7.2 Seeds For Sustenance project results in the following statements of worth about that project.

> **The Seeds For Sustenance project was valuable for students because it helped them remember classroom learnings about arid-region subsistence farming.**

> **The Seeds For Sustenance project was valuable for students because it helped them learn how to help the SFS group in their seed growth testing work.**

> **The Seeds For Sustenance project was valuable for SFS because it helped the group carry out services they provide such as tour guiding, sorting seeds for mailing and publishing their newsletter.**

> **The Seeds For Sustenance project was valuable for the school and the SFS group because it demonstrated that they can together create instructional activities that help students learn material related to a state biology standard as they provide needed services.**

Teams can also use a sentence frame to make needs-improvement statements about their projects in much the same way. The following provides a useful frame.

_____ outcomes could be improved by _____.

The SFS project can make needs-improvement value judgments about their project such as the following:

> **Student outcomes in future Seeds For Sustenance projects could be improved by engaging students in additional academic or service opportunities that increase their knowledge of animal-related, arid-region subsistence strategies.**

> **Usefulness of learning material to student future Seeds For Sustenance projects could be improved by ensuring school and SFS collaboration in the design of all instructional activities for the project.**

When teams use the generalizations they derived from inductive thinking about evaluation results to make positive and needs-improvement statements about their projects, they carry out what Popham (1993, p. 7) defines as educational evaluation: "a formal appraisal of the quality of an educational phenomenon." In this appraisal, they have not attempted to compare service-learning with other educational approaches. For that they would need to engage in action research. Nor have they attempted to establish cause and effect or correlational relationships between service-learning and other variables. For that they would need to engage in experimental research. Rather, they have described what happened in their own, unique service-learning projects, asserted which aspects of what happened were valuable, and identified aspects that if improved would be likely to add value to future implementations of the projects. For example the Seeds For Sustenance project might well become a continuing component in a biology curriculum on the basis of its value to students and to their service partners. As teams implement the project again, however, they will undoubtedly find ways to better reinforce classroom learnings about animal-related subsistence strategies and to increase collaborative development of learning activities. As they look at the original team's inductive thinking record and note the special interest of some students in the work of SFS, they may add a pre-internship feature to the project.

In concluding this section, it is important to review the steps service-learning-learning project teams carry out in order to evaluate their projects. First, they develop evaluation plans that guide collection of students-outcomes information, project-impact information and team-process and product information. Next they implement their evaluation plans and collect and organize results. Third, teams use inductive thinking to generalize from the patterns and relationships they observe in evaluation results, and fourth, they express their generalizations as positive and needs-improvement value judgments. When teams complete these steps they are ready to celebrate the many outcomes of their projects with a wide array of constituents.

Celebrating New Learnings and Perspectives

Celebrating learnings and perspectives gained through service-learning involves project teams, students and others related to them in culminating activities that are essentially internal in nature and in disseminating information about project outcomes to external audiences. Culminating activities usually take place in the classroom or the school and include many project participants who individually or in groups call attention to and celebrate what they learned and the new ideas they gained from service-learning. Culminating activities tend to be creatively shaped, and while calling upon students to use multiple intelligences often channel these through visual or performance modes. Dissemination strategies also enlist multiple intelligences but are more often shaped in terms of standard conventions, tend to be text-oriented even when they incorporate visual elements, and are integrated in ways that send particular messages to particular audience. They often consist of stand-alone products that can be sent or delivered to target audiences, and even when they involve performance, that performance is usually organized in terms of standard models. Examples based on projects described in Chapter II help discriminate culminating activities and dissemination strategies as internal and external forms of celebration. The first example extends the personal health standards project from Chapter II in which students work with the American Cancer Society to host an anti-smoking booth for their town's Community Wellness Day. The second extends the writing standards project from that same chapter in which students help equip a children's corner at the new branch of their public library.

Example One: Culminating Activity for Smoking and Health Project

Service-learning students plan a symposium for students in the two other, tenth-grade health classes in their school. The symposium involves service-learning students, the American Cancer Society representative on their project team, and two representatives from the county public health agency in discussing the role of wellness in community development, their perceptions of the major cause of and reasons for health problems in their community, and things citizens can do to reduce these problems. Service-learning students decorate the media room they will use with snapshots of their work at the Wellness Day booth, and displays of educational materials they created for the booth to illustrate the dangers of smoking and convince booth visitors to stop smoking. Within a mural illustrating a healthy community, they center a class non-smoking pledge signed by the majority of the service-learning students.

**Example Two: Dissemination Strategy for
Children's Corner Library Project**

An eighth-grade class in this curriculum component project created and implemented an oral reading and discussion program for primary-school children. Class cooperative learning groups prepare dissemination strategies to inform their community about their project. One group writes an article for release to local papers entitled "Students Make a Difference." The article describes how the class surveyed parents and children to learn of reading interests and needs, and includes pictures of middle-schoolers reading to second-graders in the library corner. The article explains how choosing stories and conducting discussions helped the eighth graders achieve state language-arts standards while they helped children. It also explains that the reading program is a continuing, weekly, after-school event that middle-schoolers sign up for throughout the year, and it includes comments from primary-schoolers and their parents about the value of the program to youngsters' thinking and reading-skills development.

As these two examples suggest, culminating activities and dissemination strategies are differently developed and implemented. The following briefly outlines how project teams and students create and use these two kinds of activities. More detailed examples of particular culminating activities and dissemination strategies appear in Chapter XI.

Developing and Implementing Culminating Activities

Project teams use culminating activities for several reasons. One is to inform their affiliates about service-learning as an educational method and encourage them to develop service-learning projects. But the most important reason for using these activities is to help students, themselves, integrate the new understandings they have gained from the reflective learning sequences within their service-learning projects. Teams accomplish this purpose using four steps. First, they ask each student cooperative-learning group to recall and share the results of their reflection and conceptualizing activities with the entire class. This sharing often consists of exhibits that cooperative-learning groups created to summarize their experiences and the other displays they used to express, insights, propositions, concerns, values and commitments. Second, the class as a whole considers all shared exhibits and selects 3-5 among them they believe best capture the class's new learnings and perspectives and are most important to share in a culminating activity. Third, the whole group decides on ways it might elaborate on its selections and/or add other features to its culminating activity. The group also decides how to organize these selections and features within a culminating activity. Finally, cooperative learning groups agree to take responsibility for the various logistical arrangements for the culminating activity.

These four steps make clear that students, themselves, through their cooperative learning groups and as a class, take responsibility for putting together service-learning culminating activities. They develop the substance of their culminating activities from their own thought products. They organize the activities by dividing responsibilities among their own cooperative-learning groups and by calling upon the expert assistance of their own project team members and others as necessary. As they take on these responsibilities, students have opportunities to deepen their learning. They revisit and review conceptualizations developed by their cooperative-learning groups. They expand upon their conceptualizations as they plan to share them with others.

Two brief examples suggest how students in two different classes share the new learnings and perspectives they have gained from service learning in culminating activities. The first example describes fifth-grade students who completed the shopping-bag conservation-messages project described in Chapter II. As the intern, cooperating teacher and the class review small group reflection and conceptualization, they decide that their culminating activity should share two new perspectives students have gained. The first is students' conviction that knowing that their shopping bags would go into the community improved their efforts at correct grammar and spelling. The second is their conviction that shoppers' rapid use of their bags showed that students can send conservation messages to their communities. The class decides to make a giant shopping bag display for the hall outside their classroom door. One group is to construct the bag, one will illustrate it, and one will make a framed statement about the project's effect on grammar and spelling and students' sense of empowerment as citizens. One group will post a collection of the conservation messages that appeared on students original bags, and a fifth will make a cafeteria announcement about the display and offer to send representatives to other classes to give five-minute presentations about possibilities for future service-learning projects.

In a second example, students in the Chapter V dramatic-monologue project integrate cooperative-learning group's ideas into three new understandings to share in their culminating activity. These are that nursing homes must rely heavily on volunteers for the extra interaction and recreation residents need; that team-facilitated reflection helped students confront their discomfort, even fear of the aged and helped them see aging as part of their own lives; and that interaction with older people made their monologues deeply real. The class decides to share these insights in three new monologues on aging that they will create and present to students taking tenth-grade English. Three of the class's five cooperative-learning groups will develop the monologues, one group will lead a discussion about the new monologues with students who attend, and one will make arrangements for the presentation, send invitations to parents and administrators, and a mount a display of service-learning banners.

In each of these examples students review, integrate and express as a class the results of cooperative-learning groups' thinking. They creatively share these new learnings and perspectives with others who are educationally affiliated with them. They learn as they prepare their culminating activities, and they reach out to interest others in using service-learning as they implement those activities.

Developing and Implementing Dissemination Strategies

When students and project teams disseminate information about their projects, they shape information in ways that persuade individuals and groups to look favorably on service-learning and to support its continued use. Ultimately, dissemination activities seek to move schools and their communities toward the institutionalization of service-learning. "Institutionalization" does not mean that students and teams are trying to convince everyone to carry out their particular service-learning projects. Rather, they are attempting to persuade their schools and communities that service-learning, itself, is a useful and worthwhile educational method. They are hoping that records of their own service-learning experiences will convince their school constituents, parents, school systems, communities and others to support service-learning verbally and through participation, and with material and financial contributions.

Because students and project teams seek to persuade particular audiences via dissemination, they benefit from using dissemination strategies designed to reach particular audiences. For instance, a video presentation might be an appropriate strategy for reaching parents and community groups, whereas a formal evaluation report might be more appropriate for reaching professional educators. Happily, shaping dissemination strategies in audience-driven ways is easier than it may at first appear. Students' and project teams' daily experiences abound with examples of dissemination strategies aimed at particular audiences. Students and teams have but to turn to the media—radio, television, newspapers, magazines, journals, films—to see dissemination strategies aimed at and reaching particular groups. They can select among these in terms of the audiences they wish to reach, use their formats to shape their own messages about service-learning, and send them forth to their chosen audiences to do their good work.

Dissemination strategies useful to students and project teams can be loosely categorized as either academic or popular in form and content. Academic-type strategies generally follow conventions used by descriptive scholars and researchers to enlist rational, cognitive attention to their message. They enlist this attention by using clear, objective writing to focus on a project, problem or issue, describe how it was addressed, discuss results of what was done, and speculate on further possible activity. These concluding speculations are dispassionately framed, yet thoughtfully pointed spurs to future work on the original problem or issue or ones closely related to it. Popular strategies, on the other hand, seek to enlist the attention of a wider audience and employ the conventions of advertising including psychological appeals to motivation and emotion. Both kinds of strategies rely on integrity of information and thoughtful and careful use of formatting. An evaluation report exemplifies academic-type dissemination strategies and a newsletter exemplifies popular-type strategies. Chapter XI describes a number of these types of strategies that students and project teams can use to demonstrate the value of service-learning and enlist a wide array of community constituents in supporting it as a powerful educational method.

Students and project teams effectively disseminate information about their projects using a four-step process in which they 1) identify groups and individuals who might support service-learning, 2) select those they wish to address, 3) devise a plan for reaching them, and 4) follow up on results of dissemination. The following outlines these steps and provides brief examples of their use.

Brainstorming to Identify Dissemination Audiences

Brainstorming for dissemination is most effective when many participants are involved. Thus project teams will want to include all of their own members and all project students in the brainstorming activity as well as others students, teachers and administrators in the school who may not have been directly involved in the service-learning project itself, but who have expressed interest in learning about it. As explained earlier, brainstorming produces many responses because it is open-ended and non-judgmental, and participants feel free to make suggestions. When using brainstorming for service-learning dissemination, for example, a facilitator—a member of a project team—simply asks the question, "Who do we want to persuade to join us and help us in future service-learning activities?" Student assistants write responses on the chalkboard or newsprint as participants contribute them. Typically, this type of open-ended question results in a flurry of responses at first, then a gradual decrease in responses until there is silence. At this point, the facilitator waits, perhaps suggesting that participants take a few more minutes to think, then contribute resulting ideas. Again typically, waiting results in additional suggestions, and often these later suggestions are even more useful than those offered in the first round. As the second round of contributions gradually cease, the facilitator seeks group consensus that the process is complete and asks assistants to array results for all to see.

Selecting Audiences

The next step is to select specific audiences for dissemination. Resources almost invariably limit the number of dissemination strategies that can be used, so it is important for the facilitator and the group to narrow the audience pool to those most likely to be persuaded and most reachable within students' and project teams' capacities. Use of coding can help here with the facilitator first asking participants to use the values 1, 2, and 3 (low to high) to code audiences for their potential as contributors of verbal support, participation, material contributions and/or financial support. When this first coding reduces the pool, the facilitator then asks participants to code again using 1-3 (low to high) to indicate for each audience that remains in the pool the time, expertise and resources that students and the team have for reaching the audience. This second coding will usually reduce the pool to a near manageable number, but often students' and teams' enthusiasm may lead them to think they can reach more audiences than they actually can, and the facilitator needs to ask participants to reduce the target audiences to no more than five.

Writing Dissemination Plans

When project teams have identified the audiences they wish to reach, they write dissemination plans that name their target audiences, identify the dissemination strategy that will address each audience, and assign responsibility for developing strategies, and carrying out dissemination and results integration. Table 7.3 shows a dissemination plan that students and the project team developed for the novel-reading project outlined in Chapter IV. In that project, students collaborated with their public library to learn about novels as arenas for reflection on living and to increase other teens' reading of novels. They read novels to conceptualize writers' exploration of human experience and created a monthly "Good Books for Teens" display for the public library. They and their cooperating librarian collected data that showed an increase in checkouts of the displayed books compared to the previous summer, and 22 teens showed up to participate in a discussion of the books in late August. After brainstorming and narrowing the resulting audience pool, students and the team decided that their school board, the local chapters of the National Reading Association, local bookstores and local parents would be most likely to support future, similar projects. They designed the plan in Table 7.3 to reach these audiences. The plan uses three dissemination strategies to reach the four target audiences and distributes responsibilities among project team members and students who carried out the project.

Table 7.3 Sample Novel-Reading Project Dissemination Plan

Audience	Strategy	Creators	Administrators/ Integrators
School Board	Executive Summary of Evaluation Report	CL Group (1)	Teacher
Nat'l Reading Assoc. Chapter	Executive Summary of Evaluation Report	CL Group (1)	Librarian
School Parents	Newsletter	CL Group (2)	Parent
Bookstores (4)	Web Page	CL Group (3)	CL Group (4)

This dissemination plan is efficient and manageable. As a matter of accountability, the project team prepares a report of its evaluation findings for the school principal and other school system administrators. It is a simple next step for one of the class's cooperative learning groups to prepare an executive summary of this report and use it with an appropriate cover letter as a dissemination strategy for the two different groups shown in Table 7.3. With respect to parents, the newsletter can provide an engaging summary of reflective learning activities with pictures and names of students who were involved. It can also include project evaluation data regarding increased use of the library by teens, and in this way, can interest its parent audience in supporting future service-learning projects. The web page can reshape information from the newsletter using existing web pages as models. This will challenge the students who prepare it to learn a great deal about the uses of Internet communication and provide a familiar, time-saving medium for book store personnel to learn about the project. These stores may well be convinced to provide support to future projects if their contributions are to be noted on the web page.

Dissemination Follow-up

Often, audiences who receive dissemination information are immediately interested in the projects they learn about or in service-learning in general and contact project teams to learn more and even offer assistance. Other audiences, however, may not respond. Whether audiences respond to dissemination strategies or not, project teams and students aid future service-learning efforts by following up on their dissemination strategies with letters, e-mails, phone calls or visits. They contact those to whom they have sent material, describe what was sent and ask those contacted to agree to be included in a list of future potential service-learning supporters. While not all who are contacted will agree to be included, many will, and the result is a resource base for future projects.

As this discussion suggests, dissemination is an essential feature of service-learning. When students and project teams use selected dissemination strategies to reach external individuals and groups who are likely to be interested in and support service-learning, they start to build a resource base which over time can become available to teachers, administrators, students and parents across a school's grade-level spectrum. Also, as students identify audiences and select and create dissemination strategies, they learn key communication skills that will help them as learners and community members.

In Conclusion

Service-learning project teams develop and implement evaluation plans to gather information about the value of their projects. They use this information for professional accountability and to celebrate their own and students' growth in new learnings and perspectives. Service-learning evaluation plans integrate results of student outcomes assessment, feedback from partnering community groups and their clients, and project-team self-evaluation in a design that when implemented will produce overall pictures of the worth of service-learning projects. Teams analyze evaluation results using an inductive-thinking process to state generalizations based on patterns and relationships they see in the results. Teams then express these generalizations as positive and needs-improvement value judgments about their projects. Service-learning students and project teams celebrate reflective-learning insights and results of evaluation in culminating activities with their school and service-related affiliates, and in dissemination strategies for external audiences who are interested in service-learning and might provide future support to service-learning programs and projects.

Activities for Increasing Understanding

1. Use Table 7.1 as a model to create a modified evaluation plan for the practice service-learning project you are developing. Include in your plan:
   a. an instrument from the student outcomes plan you outlined in the exercises at the end of Chapter V,
   b. a 3-item questionnaire to gather feedback from the agency or the clients that the students in your practice project will serve, and
   c. a self-evaluation instrument for your team to judge its use of any two of the five cooperative learning elements on a 4-point scale.

   In the appropriate cells of your plan describe the logistics, materials, scoring/coding and data summary format necessary for the administration of each of your three instruments.
2. Reflect on the inductive-thinking process. Then suggest three to five thinking skills that can help members of service-learning project teams recognize patterns and relationships and use these to derive generalizations about the results of evaluation information in the three areas.
3. Lay out the schedule in weeks for your practice project. Include the time that will be allotted to each of the following:
   a. planning for outcomes measurement, instruction, and evaluation,
   b. implementing academic study and service experience,
   c. conducting evaluation and interpreting results,
   d. celebrating through culminating and dissemination activities.

Chapter VIII: Strategies for Encouraging Commitment to Projects

"So the ninth-graders helped the parks and recreation department lay out and prepare the family campsite. They used service-learning to create a community resource while they learned geometry." Teacher Seth Tobias' glance sweeps over his own ninth-grade class. "What about it?" he asks "Could we do something like that? Could we find and work with a community partner on something our community needs that's related to earth science?"

"Nobody in Bryn Falls needs us!" Colin Hays asserts scornfully.

"And earth science is about rocks 'n stuff—not about parks," Veronica Cass adds.

Sula McRae turns on the two naysayers. "How do you know! Maybe there are things we could do—maybe something with wind power, solar power. I don't know but, we could find out."

"My grandfather was in some kind of conservation corps when he was a kid," says Tim Gomer. "Maybe there's something like that in Bryn Falls."

Seth nods encouragement. "Sula's right, and good thinking, Tim. We could find out what kinds of service our community needs, then think about how we might match needs with what we'll be studying in the next couple of months. Can we vote on at least investigating?"

Chapter Focus

This chapter provides a range of strategies that teachers can use to help students and potential community partners implement the Commitment phase of the collaborative service-learning model described in Chapter IV. The strategies help students 1) analyze their communities of interest, 2) determine their communities' service needs and 3) motivate potential community partners to join with them in mutually beneficial service-learning projects. The strategies can be used by students who intend to serve in small, medium-sized and large communities, and they can be used in basic and amplified versions. Basic versions help students who will use service-learning within a subject area such as English, mathematics, sciences, foreign language and the arts, and can typically be used within one to three class periods. Amplified versions of the strategies help students who will use service-learning as part of courses that focus on education for democracy, and these versions of the strategies may take a week or more to complete.

The strategies are designed to help teachers and students get started with service-learning projects when they are working in schools systems that are at the awareness level and not providing extensive resource support The strategies can also be useful to teachers and students who have some experience with service-learning and access to planning or fully resourced service-learning support networks. In these situations, the strategies can help teachers and students increase the focus and coherence of their service-learning projects and strengthen the team functioning essential to project success. As with all resources offered in this book, teachers select strategies for use with students and potential community partners that best suit these constituents' needs, goals, and capacities.

Analyzing a Community of Interest

Teachers and students gather the most useful service needs and issues information when they begin by analyzing the communities in which they intend to serve. This community may be their school or school cluster, their neighborhood, town or city, or their state. The community they actually select will depend upon students' age and abilities and the logistical considerations associated with their movement beyond their classroom. Teachers usually help younger and less socially and psychologically mature students identify communities that are smaller and easily accessible to them, while they help more mature students define communities that are larger and farther afield. Within this general guideline, however, teachers understand that as explained in Chapter IV, students who are younger and less mature can often collaborate with partners from distanced and larger communities by using indirect service and advocacy. They can use these kinds of service in their classrooms and still help agencies in these communities meet their needs and build support for their efforts. In any case, once a teacher has guided students to select a community appropriate for them, they can analyze that community as an arena for service-learning by using three strategies: 1) mapping, 2) working with fact sheets and 3) exploring rationales for community services.

Mapping

Community mapping is particularly useful to younger and less mature students—fifth-, sixth- and seventh-graders or students with special needs—who are looking forward to learning through service in their own schools, neighborhoods and small towns. Mapping can give them a comprehensive picture of the place where they live and interact with others, and help them become more aware of ways their lives interconnect and depend upon others in their communities. To use the strategy in its basic form, the teacher provides students with a map of their community of interest. The map contains only street names and a few reference points, perhaps the school itself, its government offices and its major shopping center. Students locate and add to the map their own homes and the main educational, recreational, transportation and emergency centers in their community such as libraries, museums, parks, bus stations, airports, police and fire stations and hospitals. They save their maps for future reference during needs and issues information gathering and other aspects of service-learning. In an amplified form, students can create large maps of their community—wall sized or even painted large in their school parking lot. They can invite representatives of educational, recreational, transportation and emergency service centers to come and locate their own agencies on the map and to talk about how their agencies help integrate and support the community. Use of this longer form of mapping can lead directly to dialogue with community service representatives about service needs and possible service-learning projects.

Working With Fact Sheets

Students in eighth, ninth and tenth grades are increasingly ready to strengthen and extend critical thinking skills. Teachers can encourage this by having them analyze their community of interest—often their town, city or county—with fact sheets. In a basic version of this strategy, teachers obtain community facts from local government or community development agencies and prepare single-sheet summaries that include information about the community's location and layout, its population size, characteristics and distribution, its governance structure and any unique features it has. Students receive copies of the fact sheet, and in pairs, small groups or as a class, use the facts to speculate on the kinds of services the community is likely to provide. They then give examples of specific services and service agencies they and their neighbors use. In an amplified version of fact sheet use, students, themselves, create the fact sheet for their community using school and public libraries and area college and university libraries, as well as by directly contacting local government and community development agencies. With facts assembled, they design a website for their community of interest. As with mapping, students retain their work for use in gathering needs and issues information and for later activities within their service-learning projects.

The fact sheet strategy helps students explore and understand the existence and importance of diversity in their communities. As they work with information about their community's population distribution and characteristics, teachers can help students consider ways particular groups make contributions. They can become aware, for example, of senior citizens contributions—often supplying part-time labor for retail businesses and providing service to schools, museums, hospitals and other community agencies. They can become aware of the contributions of particular ethnic groups, of ways these groups may be marginalized in their communities, and of mechanisms that increase these groups' access to all community services, resources and leadership positions.

Exploring Communities' Needs for Services

A strategy that guides eleventh- and twelfth-graders to explore the reasons that community services are essential to society helps them in two ways. First, it helps them analyze their own communities in preparation for particular service-learning projects. When they think about the services that abound in their own communities and connect these to the diverse nature of their communities, they become more fully aware of the nature and structure of those communities. Second, the strategy orients students to their continuing service responsibilities as citizens in a democracy. Juniors and seniors in high school look forward to becoming employees in the larger community or members of further education communities after graduation. Hopefully they can and will make service contributions in both situations. By exploring rationales for service in a democracy they will be more likely to make such contributions.

The basic version of this strategy begins with students exploring the concept of lifestyle and considering the diverse lifestyles in their community of interest. Next, students brainstorm all possible services needed and available in that community and categorize these as safety-net, educational, health, recreational, transportation and emergency services. Students now discuss ways people who serve in these areas may need to understand and accept the different lifestyles— both constructive and challenging—of the people who use the services. For example, certain kinds of service bring those who serve into contact with people who confront the challenges of poverty, illness, substance abuse, aggression and violence. Other kinds of service bring those who serve into contact with people who have wide-ranging interests, aspirations, and belief systems, who live in a variety of family arrangements, have differing sexual orientations and physical and mental capacities. The strategy concludes with the challenge to students to think about two things: 1) ways they may be able to use up-coming service-learning experiences to serve in situations where people have different lifestyles than their own and 2) the categories of citizen service—safety-net, educational, health, recreational, transportation and emergency services—they would like to explore in greater detail. Students can be encouraged to share their ideas or keep their thinking private, whatever seems appropriate.

The basic version of this strategy can be carried out in a class period discussion which should be lead by a non-judgmental facilitator—teacher or counselor—who has the following group leadership skills identified by Popham (1993, p. 209).

- ability to express self clearly
- good listening skills
- ability to quickly read participants' verbal and nonverbal responses
- spontaneity and liveliness
- ability to convey empathy with participants' feelings
- ability to keep groups on task
- flexibility in response to the unexpected

Teachers can amplify the exploring community needs strategy by having students interview individuals who are community leaders in the six services categories identified on page 144. They can invite these leaders to engage in a panel discussion in which they describe both the constructive as well as the challenging lifestyle issues of people who use their services and the kinds of skills for diversity that those who serve these people need to have.

As descriptions here suggest, strategies that help students analyze the communities in which they are likely to use service-learning form a continuum from simple to complex. For younger and less socially and cognitively mature students, the strategies lead to basic awareness of the internal structure of the community as it is revealed in its physical layout. For older students the strategies lead progressively toward consideration of the dynamic influence of diversity on community function. The strategies can be used in brief to help students develop sufficient understanding of their communities-of-interest for meaningful service-learning projects, and they can be used in more extensive ways to help students build cognitive structures for the concept of community and relate their own lives to the community-service ethos so important in a democracy.

Gathering Needs and Issues Information

Three strategies can help students and their teachers gather information about the actual service needs and issues in the communities they identify as arenas for service-learning. These strategies include 1) finding service-learning success stories, 2) contacting umbrella agencies and 3) using formal needs assessment. As with strategies for analyzing communities, teachers and students can use these strategies in basic forms to accelerate subject-area-based service-learning projects and in amplified forms as part of education-for-democracy units and courses.

*146 * CHAPTER VIII*

Finding Service-Learning Success Stories

This is a starter strategy that helps students use service-learning examples from other communities to develop a list of possible agencies to contact about service needs and issues within their own communities. By learning about the service-learning successes of learners like themselves, students begin to think confidently and creatively about service needs possibilities they might not otherwise considered. For example, seventh-graders in an art class might never think of themselves as being able to contribute through art to their communities. Then they read an article about middle-school students in another state who responded to their local hospital's call for student art to decorate pediatric waiting and examining rooms. This energizes them to explore possibilities not only with their local hospital, but with a number of other service centers used by children and families. Or when tenth-graders read success stories about high-school students who provided math, reading and English tutoring services to recent immigrants, they decide to search out tutoring needs of a variety groups in their own community.

Students can find success stories about students like themselves by using their school and public library resources. The Internet, however, offers the most rapidly accessible wealth of examples of effective service-learning projects and programs. As interest in service-learning grows across the country, groups supporting its use are relying especially on websites to increase their outreach and to interest teachers, students, community agencies, parents and others in the method. Students can use the addresses below as a gateway to a vast network of electronic service-learning resources. Once at these sites, students may need to explore various resource tabs, buttons and hyperlinks to find service-learning examples, but by taking just a little time they will soon find information about what students like themselves across the country are doing to learn and serve.

America's Promise: The Alliance for Youth - http://www.americaspromise.org
Center for Youth as Resources - http://www.ysa.org
Grantmaker Forum on Community and National Service - http://www.gfcns.org
Home of Service Learning on the World Wide Web - http://csf.colorado.edu
National Service-Learning Clearinghouse – http://www.servicelearning.org
National Youth Leadership Council - http://www.nylc.org
Phi Delta Kappa, International - http://www.pdkintl.org
Youth Service America - http://www.ysa.org

The younger-student basic form of the finding success stories strategies has each student devote homework time to finding at least one service-learning success story in the library or on the Internet. Students summarize their stories by answering the five-part question "Who did What and Why, and Where, and When did they do it?" In class, students add their summaries to a class compendium on the board, a classroom computer file or large poster. They then identify service agencies in the success story summaries that might have counterparts in their own communities. They list these local counterparts, and with teacher guidance identify one or more among them to contact via a letter such as the one shown in Figure 8.1.

Figure 8.1 Sample Letter Requesting Service Needs Information From a Potential Community Partner

---

Ms. Marylin Ruskin
Director, Lighthouse Senior Center
1432 MacDonald St
Washburn, Ohio 54321

Dear Ms. Ruskin

Our sixth-grade language arts class at Washburn Middle School wants to use service-learning. We and our teacher, Mr. Jacobs, want to work with community partners to improve our community. Are there ways that we could help you at the Lighthouse Center? Could you send us a list of your center's service needs so that we can explore the possibility for a service-learning project with you.

Please call Mr. Jacobs at 555-1234 if you have questions, and thank you for your help.

Sincerely,

(Class Signatures)

Students now wait for responses to their letters and when they eventually receive service-needs information, they can use it to identify a limited number of potential community partners whose needs seem to match what they are studying. They then move forward in the process of collaboratively outlining and committing with the agency to a service-learning project in way described in Chapter IV.

An amplified version of the finding-success-stories strategy involves students in the same activities up to the point where they use their compendium of story summaries to identify potential partners in their own communities. Instead of writing letters to these potential partners, they visit them personally to gather information about service needs. Students can make these visits as individuals, in pairs or in small groups, and they can prepare for them by simulating in advance how they will conduct their visits. At the actual meetings they emphasize collecting service-needs information from the agency in terms of direct, indirect and advocacy service possibilities. They record service-needs information, return to class to share and discuss what they have found, then select the agencies with needs that seem most promising for future service-learning collaborations and projects. For example, students in an eleventh-grade physics class use success stories to identify their board of education's tutoring office, a city children's science center and a state seniors' independent living program as potential partners in their own communities. They divide into three groups, and one group meets with their board of education, one with the science center director and the third with the coordinator of the senior's program. They summarize the needs information they gather as shown in Table 8.1.

Table 8.1 Needs Information Eleventh-Grade Physics Students Gather from Potential Partners Suggested by Service-Learning Success Stories

Potential Partner	Service Needs
Board of Education – Springfield City Schools	1. Tutor low SES, underachieving students who want to go to college (direct service) 2. Tutor home-bound students (direct service) 3. Locate and prepare instructional materials for tutors. (indirect service)
Springfield Children's Science Center	1. Help make models and displays (indirect service) 2. Guide center tours (direct service) 3. Teach mini-sessions to visiting students (direct service) 4. Publicize science center.(advocacy)
Springfield Senior Independence Program	1. Assist in analysis of seniors' homes for improved insulation, soundproofing, electricity conservation, personal safety (indirect service) 2. Assist in designing and implementing improvement plans for insulation, soundproofing, electricity conservation and personal safety (indirect and direct service)

The service needs recorded in Table 8.1 are not service-learning projects. Rather, they are the services that the contacted agencies told the eleventh-graders they need help delivering. As the class discusses these service needs, students can speculate on which agency's needs might relate in some way to physics. In this case, they decide that service-learning linked to physics may be possible with all three agencies and are thus ready to invite the agencies to meet with them to explore possibilities and ultimately, to collaboratively outline and commit to whole-class, small-group or individual service-learning projects.

Contacting Umbrella Agencies

Teachers and students can develop lists of potential community partners and determine their service needs by contacting three types of umbrella agencies: social services agencies, religious organizations, and civic groups. Students can use local-phone-book government and business listings and community agency directories to assemble contact information for umbrella agency directors. In a basic version of this strategy teachers and students invite an umbrella agency director to come to their classroom, identify the agencies or groups they work with and suggest which among these might have service needs that could be integrated in collaborative service-learning projects. Students then list agency possibilities and contact them for more specific information using the letters or personal visits described in the success-stories strategies.

In an amplified version of the strategy, students integrate the information they gather from umbrella agencies and subsequent letters or visits into a service-learning directory for their school or school system. They create the directory as a computer file that can be published on demand at any time and continually added to by other service-learners in the school or school system who identify additional agencies and groups willing to collaborate. Agencies included in the directory can be categorized as providing safety-net, educational, health, recreational, transportation and emergency services. For each service category, students write a general description of its role in the community. Within categories students include information about the name and location of each agency, its mission, principal service, related direct service, indirect service and advocacy needs, any special training requirements for people who serve, and the person to contact to explore service-learning possibilities. As this brief explanation suggests, extension of the umbrella-agencies strategy to developing a directory can be, in and of itself, a service-learning project. Students collaborate in a general sense with agencies in their community to create an information base that will help increasing numbers of students use service-learning, and help agencies accomplish their missions as they play a role in educating young people both academically and as future citizens.

Formal Needs Assessment

Formal needs assessment provides another technique that teachers and students can use within a low-resource context to gather needs and issues information for a service-learning project. It can be a relatively simple initial step for younger students, or it can become a more comprehensive activity in which students learn a great deal about their own communities and about needs assessment itself. When students conduct formal needs assessments they facilitate development of collaborative service-learning projects, and they also contribute to community building. With respect to service-learning, they gather information about perceived needs and issues in their communities, then draw conclusions from the information to use in proposing collaborative service responses. With respect to community building, the activity of planning, conducting and analyzing a needs assessment is itself, a collaborative activity and one that increases a community's awareness of itself as community.

Students in middle and high schools will be most successful using needs assessment as a lead-in to service-learning if they use it within a formally delimited community that has an administrative structure. By working within such a setting they will be able to carry out the critical tasks of needs assessment: identifying needs that are pervasive in the community and determining strengths and resources available across the community. Thus, sixth-grade English students will be more successful using needs assessment in their own school with its defined population, resources and administration than using it with mall shoppers whose only connection is that they identify themselves as pet owners. Similarly, twelfth-grade civics students will be more successful assessing needs of a community that has a community association supported by member dues and an elected governing board than one that consists of 350 houses built by a developer in geographic area. Teachers help students understand these caveats when they consider using formal needs assessment to gather service needs and issues information.

A short form of needs assessment will take as many as three class sessions and some after-school and homework time to complete. Steps involved include the following:

- Meet with community administration to propose needs assessment, identify community strengths and resources, and agree on a needs assessment focus
- Cooperatively create the needs assessment instrument
- Cooperatively administer the needs assessment instrument
- Analyze and share information gathered

The sixth-grade English class noted above uses these steps in their own, 500-student rural middle school. They meet with the principal who identifies the schools' most important resource as students, teachers and parents who are willing to work together to solve school problems. The principal also explains that the school can request funds for special projects from the Board of Education and suggests that students focus their needs assessment on the school's recreation area. Students then interview 30 students from each grade level in the school, asking them what is best and worst about the recreation area and what the area needs. Results indicate that extra recreation periods are best, wet days with poorly drained playing fields are worst, and the area needs an additional softball field. Students share these results with the principal and a newly formed Recreation Area Committee that includes two teachers, two parents and five students. The stage is set for collaborative service-learning projects.

The twelfth-grade civics students become involved with their neighborhood's community association through hearing parent complaints that the association's activities building is not often used. Students' discussions with the association board suggests that intergenerational activity across the community may strengthen community interest that will, in turn, increase memberships and revenues. Discussion also reveals that there is some funding for community activities and a core of residents willing to work on projects. Students and the board decide to design a survey that asks residents to suggest community needs in the areas of sports and recreation, social activities, and communication. Students conduct the survey and results suggest that a community field day and a little league baseball team, monthly potluck suppers and weekly teen coffee houses, a community bulletin board and a newsletter would all be welcome. Again, the stage is set for collaborative service-learning projects.

Older students in classes oriented to democratic foundations may want to use long-form, comprehensive approaches to needs assessment as they embark on service-learning. The Department of Juvenile Justice website provides a framework they and their teachers can use to do this in a systematic way that leads directly to a service-learning project. The website is located at http://www.ojjdp.ncjrs.org/pubs/youthbulletin/9804/step1.html, and guides students through identifying their community in terms of its boundaries, its population make-up, needs and concerns of sub-populations, and its leaders' backgrounds and perspectives. Next the website lists community information sources students can consult to fill out their picture of their community. It then guides students through the construction, administration and analysis of a community survey and helps them identify community assets. Finally, the website shows students how to integrate the information they collect for use in identifying a problem, i.e., a need that they wish to address in a service-learning project.

Formal needs assessment whether simple or comprehensive is time-consuming. It is a step for initiating service-learning that can be skipped when coordinating groups, community agencies or teachers and students themselves gather and make available ample needs and issues information. But when it can be used, needs assessment carried out by a class will involve students in high levels of decision-making, problem-solving and collaboration from the outset of their service-learning experiences, and it will equip them with skills and understandings essential to democratic citizenship.

Motivating Potential Community Partners

Teachers and students who are in situations where support networks for service learning are not well developed can use one of three strategies to help potential community partners understand service-learning itself and feel confident that students are willing and able to work collaboratively with them. They can use these strategies to help partners conceive of students as people who share with them a vision of community improvement and who are capable of finding ways to make that vision a reality. Students use the strategies once they have narrowed their list of possible community partners to those they believe may be willing to commit with them to a service-learning project. They prepare and send to these potential partners three kinds of materials that explain service-learning as an instructional method and introduce students themselves and their capacities for assisting these potential partners: These strategies include 1) class introductions, 2) resource group descriptions and 3) class member directories.

Class Introductions

This strategy involves students in preparing three components: 1) a letter that explains service-learning and confirms students' already scheduled introductory meeting with a potential partner, 2) information about students and their commitment to skills for collaboration and 3) one or more relevant annotated success stories. Students send these materials to the partner in advance of the introductory meeting and at the meeting, they review the materials. They write the explanatory confirmation letter as a class, and assemble information about themselves and their commitment by preparing a poster that contains a class photo and a list of service-learning competencies, which they identify, discuss and commit to by their signatures on the poster. Finally, students find service-learning success stories to send to potential partners by using libraries and the Internet in ways described earlier in this chapter. The explanatory letter exemplified in Figure 8.2 advances a potential partner's understanding of service-learning by linking the method directly to the partner's service need. Students' commitment on their posters to collaboration skills such as team work, independent work, sticking to tasks, and meeting deadlines builds a potential partner's confidence in students' reliability. Success stories about students similar in age and experience show that service-learning actually works.

Figure 8.2 Sample Meeting Confirmation Letter for Motivating a Potential Community Partner

---

Marvin Tolish, Director
Dinner-at-Home for Seniors
47 West Butler Blvd
Camberton, Oregon 09002

Dear Mr. Tolish:

    Thank you for agreeing to meet with us on October 14 at 3:00 p.m. to talk about developing a service-learning project that will help you deliver meals to old people and help us learn about nutrition. At the meeting, our teacher, Ms. Holcroft and three student representatives will explain service-learning and answer any questions you have.

    Enclosed with this letter is information about our class and about successful service-learning projects completed by middle-school students. We hope you will have time to look over them before the meeting. Please call Ms. Holcroft at 555-0002 or send us an e-mail at holcroftpe@bluebird.net if you need additional information.

    Thank you very much,

    Gena Markowitz,
    For Ms. Holcroft's Seventh-Grade Physical Education Class

---

Teachers can amplify the class introductions strategy by varying ways students describe service-learning and ways they identify, discuss and commit to collaboration skills. Younger students can develop service-learning definitions and personal commitment by talking with their teacher, while older students can develop these concepts through systematic analysis of a group of service-learning success stories, from research on skills essential to team development and maintenance, and by questioning people who work in successful teams.

Resource Group Descriptions

This strategy involves students in assembling a package that contains the basic service-learning definition, meeting confirmation letter and the success stories described in the class introductions strategy and additionally provides information about students, themselves, using the concept of resource groups. The class divides itself into groups in terms of abilities and preferences such as those identified in Gardner's multiple intelligences theory (1983, 1999). For example, students nominate themselves as members of class groups that have strong language, mathematic, artistic, physical, musical, social, personal reflection or nature awareness skills. Once groups form, they make a statement about what their resource group is especially good at doing and how this might help in a service situation. They write this statement beneath a picture of their group. The class then sends sets of resource group information sheets together with letters and success stories to potential community partners. Teachers amplify this strategy by increasing the depth with which students explore the concept of multiple intelligences and their own intelligences profiles. Table 8.2 provides an example of the names students in a twelfth-grade community foundations class might give to their class's multiple intelligence resource groups and the service-learning related skills they identify within group as having. In the table, groups explain their special skills in terms of the potential relationship of those skills to service and in this way help potential partners enrich their understanding of service-learning.

Table 8.2 Example of Multiple Intelligences Resource Group Profiles for Twelfth-Grade Community Foundations Class

Resource Group	Special Skills for Service-Learning
Communicators	Write and speak to obtain support for service needs; prepare educational materials to support service
Number Crunchers	Use mathematical procedures to measure, determine costs, analyze information as necessary to help service projects
Artists	Use media to publicize service needs and prepare relevant educational materials
Sport Jocks	Help people develop positive lifestyles
The Band	Help people use rhythm and music to improve their environments
People Lovers	Help people identify interests and needs and explore ways to meet them
Mediators	Explore walking in others' shoes
The Green Team	Help people interact responsibly with their natural surroundings

Class Directories

A class uses this strategy by creating a volume that contains information about each class member and including this with the service-learning definition and meeting confirmation letter and the success stories they send to a potential community partner. With younger students or students who plan to use service-learning in a particular subject area, this volume can be a simple three-ring binder which contains common-format, individual sheets for each class member. Older students who plan to use service-learning as part of courses in democratic living can develop more elaborate photo-type albums or design a website with a unique page for each class member. In either case, class members' pages include pictures of themselves, descriptions of their service experiences, lists of 3-5 skills they have for service-learning, and personal statements of commitment to learning through service. Students can generate material for their pages by working in pairs and interviewing each other and can construct pages in class and as homework assignments. When students conclude their service-learning projects, they can save their directory pages and other project artifacts for inclusion in personal portfolios that will eventually aid them in applying for acceptance to programs and schools, requesting aid and scholarships, and applying for jobs.

Selecting Strategies for Use

Teachers and students need to consider students' academic goals, capacities and interests when they select strategies that students will use to identify community partners and propose collaborative, service-learning commitments to those partners. They also need to determine the overall amount of time available for designing and implementing their service-learning projects and decide how much of that time can be allotted to the use of strategies for obtaining commitment.

Table 8.3 provides a summary array of the commitment strategies discussed in this chapter that teachers and students can use to select the strategies most appropriate for their use. In the table, 1 class period refers to the typical 45- to 50-minute class period in middle and high schools, and a week refers to 1 week of five class periods. As teachers and students select among the strategies summarized in Table 8.3, they need to recognize that for almost all of them, students will probably need to invest some homework or after-school time.

In Conclusion

The commitment phase of the collaborative service-learning model helps students identify and delimit a community arena for service-learning projects. It then helps them determine the agencies in that community that have service needs and with whom they may use their unique capacities and interests to serve and learn. When students use particular commitment strategies with potential community partners, they prepare themselves and motivate their partners to engage in a commitment meeting that will produce an outline for a service-learning project.

Table 8.3 Summary of Strategies for Commitment Phase of Collaborative Service-Learning Model

Strategy	Examples	Basic Version - Student Activities	Amplified Version - Student Activities
Analyzing Communities	Mapping	Locate primary service agencies on teacher-provided community map. 1 class period	Create large wall or blacktop map. Locate agencies and invite representatives to describe. 1-2 weeks
	Fact Sheets	Identify services needed and used by own family and friends using teacher-prepared fact sheet. 1 class period	Create fact sheet using own research and agency contacts and design community website. 1-3 weeks
	Exploring Needs for Service	Explore concept of lifestyle, brainstorm safety-net, education, recreation, transportation, emergency services in community-of-interest, discuss ways servers in areas may need to accept different lifestyles. 1 class period.	Interview panel of representatives from service agencies that deliver safety-net, education, health, recreation, transportation and emergency services about constructive and challenging lifestyle issues they face in their work. 1-2 weeks
Gathering Service Needs Information	Success Stories	Use libraries and Internet to find service-learning success stories, find counterpart service agencies and write to them for service-needs information. 2 class periods	Use success stories to identify own community service agency possibilities, visit these as individuals, pair or groups after role playing visits. 1-2 weeks
	Umbrella Agencies	Use phone books and community directories to identify social service, religious and civic umbrella agencies. Invite representatives to come to class and identify constituent agencies that may have needs relevant to service-learning. 2-3 class periods	Integrate gathered information in computer-file service-learning directory. Group potential partners in safety-net, education, health, recreation, transportation, emergency services categories. Provide informative and contact information for each agency. 2-4 weeks
	Formal Needs Assessment	Meet with community administrator, identify community strengths and resources select focus, and develop instrument. Analyze and share results and use to initiate collaborative service-learning projects. 2-5 class periods	Use process such as that described at Department of Juvenile Justice website to systematically analyze own community and create service project proposals. 2-6 weeks
Motivating Potential Partners	Class Introductions	Prepare meeting confirmation letter, discuss and commit to skills on class poster and send with success stories about similar students to pre-contacted potential community partners. 2-3 class periods	Prepare letter and poster, but explore and commit to service-learning skills by analyzing many success stories, researching team development and maintenance skills and questioning people on successful teams. 1-3 weeks
	Resource Groups	Form special ability resource groups, photograph, and describe special talents, send group profiles to pre-contacted potential community partners. 2-3 class periods	Form and profile resource groups, but explore multiple intelligences and own intelligences in greater depth. 1 week
	Class Directories	Profile own service experience, service-learning skills and personal commitment, add photos, and send with confirmation letter and success stories to pre-contacted potential community partners. 2 class periods	Create complete personal profiles, present in class album or post with photos on personal pages of class website, then make available to pre-contacted potential community partners. 1-3 class weeks

Activities for Increasing Understanding

1. Describe how you might implement the commitment phase of the collaborative service-learning model with your students by carrying out the following steps.
   a. In a brief paragraph, describe the students you will be working with.
   b. Select a commitment strategy associated with each area in the first column of Table 8.3 and write a condensed lesson plan that shows how you would use each strategy with your students. Include information about your objective for each lesson, the activities in which students will engage, your method of assessing their success and the time you will allot to each lesson.
   c. Describe how you will facilitate actual student and community partner commitment to a service-learning project outline referring back to Chapter IV as necessary.
2. Enrich one of the commitment strategies you selected in exercise 1 above by extending it in ways that help students think about diversity issues related to service-learning. Tailor the strategy so that it helps them think about ways people are different from them and how to reach across differences toward mutual growth and community contribution.
3. Think about your own concerns about relating to people with backgrounds, values and lifestyles different than yours. Talk about these in a small group in your class. Summarize effects on your thinking in a paper of one page or less.

Chapter IX: Strategies for Measuring Student Outcomes

"We've come up with a single form for observing students' service competence and their interactions with clients." Tyrell Jones from the public library passes copies to the others at the table. *"It's adapted from the different forms we use at the library, the hospital and the senior center."*

"We decided to use only the items that relate to skills students need for communicating with people," adds Chris Warlin from the senior center.

"And it's all on one page, you'll notice," says Mac Hill from the hospital.

Twelfth-grade English teacher Hardy Offenbach nods. *"Good. I've created a one-pager for us to take a look at, too. A criterion-referenced, essay test to assess the kids' mastery of the standard we're working on—creating fictional characters in writing."* Hardy turns to guidance counselor Elizabeth Rules. *What about the personal growth piece?"*

"I got a conflict management problem—out of a program we use when we work with groups. I'm going to see what kinds of problem-solving skills students can bring to bear on it."

"So. We've got three specific assessments. I'd like to add a couple more— a survey to see if the project benefits your agencies, and interviews to see how the people the kids work with feel about their service. What do you think?" Hardy looks around the table.

Mac nods. *" We need some time to work up those pieces, but let's try it."*

Chapter Focus

The project team in the scenario is assembling specific instruments to determine how service-learning benefits the students they are working with, i.e. to carry out their student outcomes plan. Their discussion suggests two key ideas related to successful outcomes measurement. First, project teams are aware of and use a range of strategies to determine student outcomes. Second, teams can implement the strategies using instruments that already exist and fit their student outcomes plans as well as instruments they develop themselves. In addition, the scenario notes that, as explained in Chapter V, teams can use several of the student-outcomes measurement strategies to determine outcomes for other project participants. The purpose of this chapter is to explore the range of measurement strategies useful to project teams, describe how to use them and provide realistic and workable examples of their use.

A Framework for Student Outcomes Measurement

Chapter V identifies eight strategies that project teams can use to determine the impact of service-learning: state standards tests, teacher's criterion-referenced tests, rating scales, anecdotal observation, experience analysis, surveys, interviews, and focus groups. The discussion provided here in Chapter IX looks at these eight strategies in three categories: criterion-reference strategies, observational strategies and self-report strategies. The intent of the discussion is to help project teams become familiar with and use these strategies in simple ways to develop a sense of service-learning's contributions to students' academic growth, their abilities to provide genuine service and their personal growth. Teams just beginning to use the strategies will postpone concerns about classical measurement considerations. Their primary concern will be the content validity of the strategies they use. This means that they will do all they can to make sure their measurement strategies call upon students to demonstrate the behaviors which the team has decided are indicators of their outcome expectations for students. As project teams become increasingly experienced in service-learning, they can deepen their understanding of the strategies themselves and of techniques for making inferences from results of strategy use by taking courses in educational evaluation and by referring to the wealth of useful texts on the subject. Among these, Popham's (1993) *Educational Evaluation* and Anderson and Bourke's (2000) *Assessing Affective Characteristics in the Schools* provide practical, yet detailed, lucid and engaging explorations of assessment that can easily be applied to service-learning. These books also contain many references to other helpful publications.

Criterion-Referenced Strategies for Measuring Academic and Problem-Solving Outcome Indicators

Criterion-referenced tests determine the degree to which people can accomplish tasks that indicate they possess particular skills and abilities. These tests are particularly helpful in measuring indicators of students' academic learning—of their abilities to remember, explain and apply the information and processes they have studied. For example, students who have learned division of three-digit numbers by two-digit numbers with remainders can be asked to divide three-digit numbers by two-digit numbers to show how well they have learned the skill of 3x2 long division. The ability to correctly carry out each of the necessary steps in this process is the "criterion" for the test. The level of students' learning is judged by the number of the criterion steps which they can absolutely demonstrate. The "cut score" for the test is set by the test's developer who decides if students must demonstrate all or only some of the long division steps to "pass."

Measurement and evaluation specialists have been refining the knowledge base and technology of criterion-referenced test construction for over forty years. The widespread use of state standards tests has given this effort a tremendous boost as states have developed rigorous and complex procedures to ensure they measure students' abilities to meet specific criteria—state standards—and do so consistently over time. Teachers, too, can confidently develop and use a form of criterion-referenced tests with which they are very familiar—constructed-response tests. They can use these tests to measure student indicators of service-learning academic expectations. The following explains these two types of tests and their use in service-learning.

State Standards Tests

State standards tests are developed, administered and analyzed by the states themselves. They "focus on students' cognitive development with an emphasis on subject matter knowledge, critical thinking skills and problem solving abilities" (Cumbo & Vandeboncoeur, 1999, p. 95). When service-learning teams shape students' service-learning experiences in terms of particular state standards, they can use selected results from state standards tests to answer two questions: 1) To what degree did students reach the standards? and 2) How effective was service-learning in helping them reach the standards? Teams answer the first question by working with their school system testing coordinators to identify the particular test items that relate to a standard to which they have linked service-learning. Then they determine the degree to which students' scores on those items indicate that they have achieved the established cut score on the standard as individuals and as a group. Teams answer the second question by comparing relevant test item scores for their service-learning students with the same scores of the total population of students who responded to the items related to the standard. From this, teams can determine if service-learning is more, less, or equally effective as a method than other instruction for helping their students meet state standards.

Service-learning project teams can facilitate their use of selected data from state standards test results by setting up a spreadsheet along the lines shown in Table 9.1. The spreadsheet shows item and total score averages on three items that test a particular standard for students in a service-learning group and in the total population of students who responded to the three items.

Table 9.1 Results of Service-Learning Taught Students and All Students on a State Test of An Information-Synthesizing Standard

	Service-Learning Group (n = 11)			
	Item 17	Item 18	Item 21	Combined Item Average
Possible Score	0-4	0-4	0-4	0-4
Average	3.27	3.09	2.91	3.09
	Total Tested Population (n = 900)			
	Item 17	Item 18	Item 21	Combined Item Average
Possible Score	0-4	0-4	0-4	0-4
Average	3.11	2.11	2.67	2.63

Reading Standard: synthesizing information from multiple sources
Items: 17, 18, 21 on reading portion of XCAT
Points Possible on Combined Items: 12, **Cut score**: 7

The spreadsheet in Table 9.1 makes it possible for project teams to use selected, state-standards-test results to answer questions about students' achievement of the X state standard, "synthesizing information from multiple sources," and the efficacy of service-learning as a method for teaching to this standard. With respect to overall achievement, visual inspection of the sheet makes clear that students in the service-learning group reached the target standard well above the cut score and at a higher level overall, and on each item than the total group of students who responded to the test. From this a project team is justified in inferring that the service-learning in which students participated was an effective instructional approach for this standard and that for this group, it was as effective as other instructional approaches were for the total population who took the test.

The group performance information that project teams derive from their own analysis of relevant items in state standards tests can be widely and usefully shared with the people who have been directly and indirectly involved in the service-learning project, and with others whose interests may range from general community concern to specific readiness to support service-learning in a variety of ways. This information will have a special authenticity for many who receive it because it arises from state testing based on standards which have broad consensus and because the state criterion-referenced tests have been rigorously developed and implemented.

Teacher-Developed Criterion-Referenced Tests

Teachers, themselves, create criterion-referenced tests that call upon students to construct responses indicating whether or not they can actually do something they have learned to do such as calculating, writing, or performing. Teachers and their project teams can develop constructed-response tests that measure what they intend to measure—have content validity—by following Popham's (1993, pp. 137-8, 144-6) guidelines for " domain specification," and "mid-level test item specification." This means teachers and teams 1) describe the collection or domain of specific behaviors that make up an outcome expectation, 2) develop stimulus material that can elicit these behaviors, 3) write test items that engage students in using the stimulus material to produce the desired behaviors, and 4) establish rules for judging if student-produced behaviors indicate their achievement of the expectation. Because constructed-response tests may call for students to respond in writing or through some kind of performance, it is customary to classify them as either paper-pencil or performance tests. The following explains how to use these four steps to create these two kinds of tests as well as tests in which students demonstrate problem-solving.

Tests in Which Students Construct Paper-Pencil Responses

Describing the Domain of Behaviors That Make Up an Expectation – Teachers who use service-learning expect that it will improve students' knowledge and comprehension of academic material and their ability to apply that material in real-life contexts. To determine if students meet these expectations, teachers create tests that measure indicators of knowledge, comprehension and application. These indicators involve cognitive processes such as reproducing facts, ideas, principles and skills, expressing and explaining learnings, and using learnings to propose best answers to concrete problems. As cognitive processes, reproducing facts, explaining learnings and so forth can only be measured when they are applied to some material—typically the academic material students are studying. Thus teachers develop constructed-response tests of these process that will engage students in reproducing particular subject-matter facts, ideas, skills they have learned and, explaining and applying these facts, ideas and skills in situations related to the specific material they are studying. In other words, for testing purposes, teachers particularize general indicators of service-learning academic expectations in terms of their own subject areas.

To create criterion-referenced, constructed-response tests of the indicators of an outcome expectation, teachers and project teams first describe in a moderately broad way the domain of the expectation—the information and skills students must remember, explain and use, or the performances they must carry out. Moderately broad description is very important here because if the specification of an expectation domain is too narrow, test items based on that domain will also be narrow—even trivial—and will elicit student behaviors adequate only for the limited situation of the test itself. When the specification of an expectation's domain is moderately broad, items based on that domain will engage students in behaviors that can generalize beyond the test situation to other aspects of their lives. An extension of the long-division example mentioned earlier helps make these distinctions clear. Figure 9.1 shows two, domain specifications for the expectation that students can divide three-digit by two-digit numbers with remainders. The first is narrow and the second broader.

Figure 9.1 Alternate Domain Specification for Long Division of Three-Digit by Two-Digit Numbers with Remainders

---

Expectation: Divide three-digit numbers by two-digit numbers with remainders

Narrow Domain Specification
Use the division, multiplication, subtraction and addition steps in long division with given examples to express quotients and remainders in fractional or decimal form.

Broad Domain Specification
Find, format in a long-division framework, and calculate correct answers for 3x2 long division problems embedded in a life-like situation that contain text and numerical information. Calculation includes correctly ordered and accurate use of division, multiplication, subtraction and addition steps. Some of the problems to be solved result in remainders and some do not. Where present, remainders are expressed as fractions or decimals.

The chances are that when students are able to set up 3x2 long division problems based on text and numerical information presented in a life-like context they will be more likely to be able to set up and use this type of long division in their own real-life situations—situations varied in the kinds of information they contain and situations in which the issue is problem-solving with division, rather than a narrow demonstration of the long-division algorithm.

Designing Stimulus Materials - When the domain specifications for a criterion-referenced test are moderately broad, and call for demonstration of an expectation in life-like situations, design of stimulus material poses a special challenge. Often, teams may not find existing classroom materials that are life-like enough to elicit students' life-like applications of what they have learned. Thus teachers and teams may have to create stimulus materials themselves. They will be much aided by the fact that service-learning, itself, is a real-life activity, and they can design stimulus materials that echo or are similar to students' service-learning experiences. Moreover, as students respond to such items during testing, they will bridge between academic learning and described life applications. It is reasonable to infer that this will make them more likely to be able to apply the particular academic learnings being tested to later actual life situations.

Again, an example is helpful. In Chapter V, the Blue Mesa project expects seventh-grade students to develop skill in expressing numbers in equivalent forms as an outcome of gathering and presenting traffic data in a pro-traffic light presentation to the county council. Mr. Vishinsky, their math teacher, specifies the domain of this expectation as the ability to convert numerical information from life-like situations into whole numbers, fractions, decimals and percents. He decides that in order to echo students' service experiences with numbers, the stimulus material for his test will describe a school food drive. The description will contain text and numerical information expressed as one and two-digit whole numbers, simple fractions and dollar amounts less than $100.00. Students will demonstrate their abilities to express numbers in equivalent forms using this material. Mr. Vishinsky writes the domain specification and stimulus material for his test as shown in Figure 9.2.

Figure 9.2 Service-Learning Relevant Stimulus Material for Expression-of-Numbers-in Equivalent-Forms Tests

---

Expectation: Apply mathematical processes necessary to express numbers in equivalent forms.

Domain Specification: Convert numerical information from life-like situations into whole numbers, fractions, decimals and percents. Information represents one- and two-digit whole numbers, simple fractions, and dollar amounts less than $100.00.

Stimulus Material: On its first day, the Maxwell Middle School Food Drive brought in 13 cans of meat products, 43 cans of vegetables, 6 cans of fruit and $3.57 in cash. On the second day, 7 cans of meat products arrived with 25 cans of vegetables, 5 cans of fruit and $10.43. On the closing day of the drive, donations included no cans of meat, 32 cans of vegetables, 9 cans of fruit and $16.00 in cash.

The situation described in the stimulus material for Figure 9.3 differs from the Blue Mesa students' service experience, but it echoes that experience and imitates a real-life context. Hopefully, when students engage in life experience where they have to report numerical information in equivalent forms, they can reach back to their service experience in which they used learned math skills with traffic data, to the information in this stimulus material and most important to the number-transformation skills reinforced by the test items which Mr. Vishinsky develops for this stimulus material. If students are helped to integrate service and learning in this way, their learning is more likely to generalize.

Constructing Test Items - In the Blue Mesa example, Mr. Vishinsky and the project team are interested in students' rich achievement of the equivalent-forms standard. They are not satisfied to write test items that simply instruct students to pick a number from the stimulus material and express it as an equivalent form. Rather, they want to see if students can move back and forth across a variety of numbers and forms embedded in a life-like context. To facilitate this flexible behavior, Mr. Vishinsky writes the explanation, instructions and items shown in Figure 9.3.

Figure 9.3 Items and Test Format for Seventh-Grade Equivalent Forms of Numbers Test

Explanation of This Test: The purpose of this test is to determine how well your service experience—making a pro-traffic light report to the county council—helped you achieve our seventh grade state standard "expressing numbers as equivalent forms." In seventh grade, this means expressing numbers as whole numbers, fractions, decimals, and percents. Your job is to show that you can transform any number from one of these forms to any other of these forms.

Instructions: To demonstrate your ability to use equivalent forms, please read the following report of a food drive. Then carry out the steps necessary to make the transformations requested below the report. Show your work for each transformation.

The Report: On its first day, the Maxwell Middle School Food Drive brought in 13 cans of meat products, 43 cans of vegetables, 6 cans of fruit and $3.57 in cash. On the second day, 7 cans of meat products arrived with 25 cans of vegetables, 5 cans of fruit and $10.43. On the closing day of the drive, donations included no cans of meat, 32 cans of vegetables, 9 cans of fruit and $16.00 in cash.

1. Convert all food donation numbers into whole numbers, then set up three columns labeled "meats," "vegetables," and "fruits" and show the total in cans for each type of food at the end of the three days of the drive.
2. Calculate what percent of all cans donated the total of each type of food represents.
3. Use an equation for each food-type to express as a whole number, a fraction and a percent the amount of that food- type brought in by the drive.
4. Determine the total amount of cash brought in by the drive and identify the day on which just over half of the total cash came in.
5. Assume that the cost of meat averages $3.19 per can, of vegetables $.59 per can and of fruit, $.79 per can and determine the cash value of food donated.
6. Determine how many additional, whole cans of each type of food you could buy if the cash that was donated were spent on that type of food.
7. Determine how much cash you would allot to purchase each type of food if you wanted to buy each in accord with the percentage of all food received that the food type represents.

The seven test items in Figure 9.3 have several important characteristics. First, they are not an exhaustive list. Many more items could be written on the basis of this stimulus material. For example additional items could ask for percentage of food types for each day's type total, or the percentage of cash brought in each day. Second, there is a progression across the items from simple to the more complex. It is simpler to calculate percents that food types represent when they are expressed as whole numbers (item 2) than it is to determine how much cash to allot to new food purchase in terms of existing food type percentages (item 7). Third, depending on the intentions of the project team, students may not need to respond to all the items. It is possible that a team might decide that students' correct responses to items 1-4 would provide sufficient evidence of standard achievement. Whatever items Mr. Vishinsky and his team decide to use, they are now ready to establish the rules they will use to judge what appropriate response to the items will entail.

Establishing Rules for Judging Responses - Teachers and their teams describe how students get credit for test item responses and concomitantly how the items will be scored by making clear the rules or rubrics they will use to judge students' responses. Essentially, for each item they construct, they answer the question, "How will we know when students have correctly done with the stimulus material what the item has asked them to do?" Sometimes the answer to this question will be that students need to complete only one task, but more often the answer will be that students need to carry out several tasks. Thus teachers and those working with them need to clearly list the tasks students must complete to correctly respond to each item. A continuation of the Blue Mesa example in Table 9.2 shows how Mr. Vishinsky establishes a scoring rubric for his criterion-referenced test on expressing numbers in equivalent forms.

Table 9.2 Scoring Rubric for Seventh-Grade Equivalent-Forms-of-Numbers Test

Item One		
Tasks	Task Points	Total Points
Convert food types to whole numbers	1	3
Set up food-type additions	1	
Total columns	1	
Item Two		
Tasks	Task Points	Total Points
Calculate percent of each food type given overall	3	3
Item Three		
Tasks	Task Points	Total Points
Express food type quantities in equations containing equivalent whole numbers, fractions, percents	3	3
Item Four		
Tasks	Task Points	Total Points
Total all cash received	1	2
Identify day when half of total brought in	1	
Item Five		
Tasks	Task Points	Total Points
Convert whole number value of each food-type to cash value	3	4
Calculate total cash value of all food donated	1	
Item Six		
Tasks	Task Points	Total Points
Determine amount of each food-type purchasable with all cash	3	3
Item Seven		
Tasks	Task Points	Total Points
Calculate percent of cash to allot to new food-type purchase in terms of percent of food-type donated	3	3
All Items		
Tasks	Task Points	Total Points
Number work space for each item	1	3
Show calculations for each item	1	
Label answer for each item	1	
Total Points All Items		24

With the scoring rubric shown in Table 9.2 in hand, Mr. Vishinsky and his team can now administer a criterion-referenced test that will tell them how well students meet the equivalent-forms standard with respect to whole numbers, fractions, decimals and percents. If students' pro-traffic-light project activities involved them in expressing numbers in the same equivalent forms, and if they are reasonably successful on the test, the team can infer that service-learning was an effective instructional method for this standard. Because the rubric identifies each task within each item, students' responses can be analyzed on an item-by-item basis to see which equivalent forms translation gave them difficulty. With this information, teacher and team can speculate on ways to modify future service-learning and class-room instruction to increase the likelihood that students will learn to express numbers in the full range of required equivalent numerical forms.

Tests in Which Students Construct Performance Responses

Comparison with Paper-Pencil Tests - Teachers and project teams often determine academic outcomes of service learning by having students perform in some way—in dramatic presentations, reports, speeches, panel discussions—or by having them assemble portfolios that contain artifacts and representations of their growing understanding. Teams specify the domains for these performances and products using much the same approach as with paper-pencil tests and this helps ensure these tests' content validity. Stimulus materials, too, are usually presented in written form. Item specification for performance tests, however, is slightly different. To develop performance tests, teachers and teams also create items, but for each item, they create a scoring guide that explains to students—specifies for them—what they must do to completely respond to the item, and thus across items, to fully demonstrate the desired outcome expectation. This information is then shared with students who use it as a guide in the construction of their performances or products and as a clear description of how what they do or create will be evaluated.

Domain Specification and Preparation of Stimulus Material - The Chapter V example of drama students working with nursing home patients can be helpful in explaining how project teams can specify domains and prepare stimulus materials for performance tests. In that project, the team's outcomes plan expects students to apply their knowledge of monologue as a dramatic form in their own personally developed and performed monologues that identify issues in aging. Because these students' performances will integrate classroom learning (elements of monologue) and nursing-home service (knowledge of issues confronting aging patients), the teacher, Ms. LaBelle, and the staff director at the nursing home, Ms. Barak, decide to specify the performance domain and prepare stimulus material for the test together. This is shown in Figure 9.4.

Figure 9.4 Service-Learning Based Domain Specification and Stimulus Material for Monologue on Aging Issues Test

Expectation: Apply knowledge of monologue elements and understanding of problem situations and aging issues that nursing home patients face in own monologue performance.

Domain Specification: Frame issues related to aging within a monologue spoken directly to an audience by an aging character in a specific situation. Issues include putting concerns to rest, finding a mental comfort zone to live in, accepting death. Situations include but are not limited to upcoming medical procedures, presence or lack of visitors, overwhelmingly sad or happy memories, key interaction with staff or other patients.

Stimulus Material: Use your class notes, service journal and experiences working with patients to create and perform a dramatic monologue in which you portray an aging patient in a typical nursing home situation and in this role, tell your audience about the issues that you and others like you face as people who are growing old.

Item Specification and Scoring Guide Preparation - Ms. LaBelle and Ms. Barak now use their domain specification and stimulus materials to write three test items accompanied by rules for judging the items. They combine all of this in the framework for their performance test shown in Figure 9.5. The top section of the framework restates the outcome expectation for students and the stimulus material students are to draw upon to demonstrate their meeting of that expectation. This section also adds instructions that explain how students are to prepare for their demonstrations. Beneath this, the first column on the left shows the three behaviors that make up the domain of the outcome expectation as the three components that students' monologues must include. Succeeding columns convert the three components into specified test items by describing the performance levels for judging the degree to which students can demonstrate each. Ms. LaBelle and Ms. Barak agree upon the performance levels for each item by first describing the highest and lowest levels as shown in the figure, then describing the performances that range between these levels which are not shown.

The performance assessment framework shown in Figure 9.5 can also be used when teachers and project teams want students to demonstrate project outcomes in portfolios. In this case, the expectation is that students will document their knowledge, comprehension and/or application of specified academic learning through a collection of service-related artifacts. A statement of the expectation is repeated in the frame together with information about stimulus materials and instructions on how students are to use these to develop their portfolios. The standard components column of the frame lists the particular pieces that students are to include in their portfolios, and the performance level columns specify how they are to relate each piece to course learnings. For instance, for math students expected to improve their own math knowledge, understanding and skill through peer tutoring, one portfolio component might be a photo essay. The teacher sets the "outstanding" level for this essay as "snapshots of tutors and peers working on target mathematical processes with captions explaining the process and its importance." The "unacceptable" level might be "unexplained snapshots showing no clear relationship to tutoring target math processes."

Figure 9.5 Framework for Performance Tests

Expectation: Apply knowledge of monologue elements and understanding of problem situations and issues that nursing home patients face in own performance.

Stimulus Material: Use your class notes, service journal and experiences working with patients to create and perform a dramatic monologue in which you portray an aging patient in a typical nursing home situation. In this role, tell your audience about the issues that you and others like you face as people who are growing old.

Instructions: Use the guidelines below to compose your monologue in full text or with notes. Memorize it and present it to at least two other students for critique. Make adjustments accordingly, then sign up to perform your monologue on the scheduling sheet in the classroom.

Standard Components	Performance Levels				
	Outstanding (5)	Good (4)	Fair (3)	Poor (2)	Unacceptable (1)
Portrayal of Aging Character	Vividly portrays believable man or woman through facial expression, language and gesture.				Wooden, lifeless recitation.
Indication of Situation Character Confronts	Produces tension via subtle but consistent reference to difficult situation.				No clear presentation of a typical problem situation for nursing home patients.
Identification of Aging Issue	Refers naturally, and spontaneously to each issue more than once. Reveals positive, negative or ambivalent emotional stance toward issues more than once.				Little or no reference to issues. No emotional stance revealed.

Students can also use the framework shown in Figure 9.5 for portfolios in which they, themselves, select the artifacts to be included. The outcome expectation in this case would be for students to show through the items they choose to include how their service has related to particular academic learnings. Typically, the components of this expectation would be students' abilities to state for each item they include 1) their expressed "purposes" for including the item, 2) their "reflection on linkages" the item has to their academic work and their service-learning experience and 3) the "quality" with which they present each item and its justification. With these components identified, students then work with their teachers to develop scoring guides that describe the range from ideal to unacceptable for each component. Whether portfolio contents are teacher- or student-selected, performance frameworks let students know in advance what is expected of them. Teachers and project teams also avoid over specification of expectations in portfolios by making sure their own and students performance assessment frameworks call for artifacts that help students most fully recall, comprehend and apply classroom and service learnings.

In addition to the framework approach presented here, a number of references explain and demonstrate construction of performance tests. Purdy's (1996) "How Do You Assess Service-Learning?" offers guidelines for a community service portfolio. The *Service Learning and Standards Toolkit* contains extensive examples of teacher-produced criterion-referenced assessments specifically useful in service-learning. Johnson's (1996) *Performance Assessment Handbook: Volume I and Volume II* offers many examples of domain and item specification, stimulus material and scoring rubrics for criterion-referenced tests that are adaptable to service-learning across the disciplines.

Tests in Which Students Demonstrate Problem Solving

Teachers and project teams can use the steps for developing criterion-referenced paper-pencil or performance tests to design tests in which students demonstrate problem-solving skills either in writing or through performance. For beginning teams, however, it is logistically more feasible to use paper-pencil tests. They can do this by using problem-solving indicators such as those proposed in Chapter V. The example shown in Figure 9.6 is based on the senior-year civics project also included in Chapter V and demonstrates how a project team lays out the domain and item specification, the stimulus material and the scoring guide for a test of problem-solving. With the specifications shown in Figure 9.6, the team goes on to design the actual test students will take. This test, like the Blue Mesa math test in Figure 9.3, includes an explanation of the standard to which the test relates, instructions for student use of the problem-solving steps, the stimulus material and the scoring guide.

Collection and Use of Criterion-Referenced, Constructed-Response Test Data

Teachers can use students' individual results on constructed-response tests as part of their normal classroom grading procedures and they can use group results with their project teams as part of their overall service-learning project evaluations. Setting up spreadsheets that array average scores of the group on the items of a particular criterion referenced test and the group's average total scores on the test, helps teams develop a sense of the ways in which service-learning may or may not have contributed to students' abilities to recall, comprehend and apply specific academic material. Because this information is for the group and no individual students are identified, teams can usually share it with appropriate others as part of their dissemination activities.

Figure 9.6 Domain and Item Specification for Test of Ability to Use Problem-Solving Skills to Create Public Policy Awareness Media

Expectation: Demonstrate use of systematic problem-solving skills.

Domain Specification: Use of problem-solving skills to identify civic awareness needs in a life-like situation and to propose media presentations to address these needs. Civic awareness needs include low voter registration, political complacence, lack of inclusion of diverse opinions.

Item Specification: Student teams respond to a stimulus situation by doing all of the following:
- identifying a civic awareness need not easily defined or solved
- determining what more should be learned about the need
- determining how to find resources to increase knowledge and understanding of the need
- using service experience to propose media projects to address the need
- evaluating team use of systematic problem-solving

Teams summarize outcomes of steps in a written report that labels and documents the outcome of each step and acknowledges each team member's participation with his or her signature.

Stimulus Situation: At last year's Fourth of July picnic, citizens of Flagsville wildly cheered the mayor's speech which concluded with the following statement. "Our town is made up of solid Americans who contribute to our community, state and the country. We're a good place to live and like it that way. We have the lowest crime rate of any city in the state, 80% of our high school graduates go on to further education, and we don't fall for the mudslinging that goes on in political campaigns. In the last Presidential election, nearly 50% of registered voters cast ballots, and most people here feel that the country's in good hands and going in the right direction. We have strong neighborhoods, we have good schools and we emphasize neighborliness and cooperation!"

What civic awareness needs might these citizens have, and how might your team use media to increase their awareness?

Scoring Rubric:
Completing each step with steps and outcomes labeled – 20 points
Group members' signatures attesting to participation – 20 points
Identifying one possible civic awareness need of the people in the stimulus situation - 10 points
Identifying 2 or more kinds of additional information needed to explore the need – 10 points
Identifying 2 or more resources for this exploration – 10 points
Describing 2 or more presentations to address the identified civic-awareness need – 10 points
Evaluating team use of each of the first four steps by stating at least one strength and one weakness in use of each step. Strengths and weaknesses must be unique to each step - 20 points

Observational Strategies for Measuring Service Outcome Indicators

Direct observation is widely used to determine if people can or cannot perform target skills. Because observation is particularly popular in education and the helping professions, its use in service-learning seems clearly indicated. It makes good sense to judge the nature and quality of students' interactions with people in their service settings by watching what students do and how they act. Research and experience suggest, however, that results of observation can be problematic because what people do is heavily influenced by who watches them do it, and because observers can interpret what they see in many ways. To counter these problems, project teams need to use a consensus process to specify what they will observe for, observe several times over the course of a project and use multiple observers wherever possible. Finally, they need to treat results of observation as indications of growth trends and as support to other student outcomes information rather than as stand-alone conclusions.

Two types of observation can provide supportive student outcomes information for service-learning projects: rating scales and anecdotal observation. Rating scales are structured to permit observers to quantify their perceptions of the degree to which students demonstrate target behaviors, while anecdotal observations permit observers to record an entire sample of behavior, then from it determine what appear to be the dynamics at play in the observed situation.

Rating Scales

Rating scales are most useful for observing students who are interacting with service clients—working helpfully with people in some way. Typically, these will be older students who can work directly with clients because of their age and experience. Preparation for scale use is essential. Teachers, community partners and students try out the scales in a simulated setting before using them on site, assuring students that observations are confidential and results will be used to evaluate the project and not individuals. They describe and demonstrate the behaviors to be observed, then help students understand scale use through role playing in which students, themselves, play the parts of clients, students and observers. Follow-up discussion helps clarify the match between observed behavior and ratings that student observers assigned.

The most frequent format for rating scales is a series of statements that describe behavioral dimensions agreed upon to comprise the outcome indicator of interest. The numbers 1 (low) through 4 or 5 (high) follow or are positioned beside each statement, and observers circle or check the number that represents their perception of the level of behavior they observe. Where there is no evidence of a particular behavior, the observer makes no mark. Figure 9.7 provides a sample of a rating scale used by a team whose eleventh-graders are helping at a soup kitchen as part of their study of nutrition.

Figure 9.7 Sample Rating Scale to Observe Student's Abilities to Work Dependably Under Supervision

Outcome Indicator of Interest: Working dependably under supervision	
Behavioral Dimensions:	**Ratings:**
1. Works cheerfully without stopping to socialize	1 2 3 4 5
2. Asks clients for their food choice preferences in a courteous and friendly way	1 2 3 4 5
3. Follows portion guidelines when preparing servings	1 2 3 4 5
4. Answers client questions about food knowledgeably and courteously	1 2 3 4 5

In Figure 9.7, the indicator of interest comes directly from the Ferrari and Worrall indicators of service competence proposed in Chapter V, "works dependably under supervision." The behavioral dimensions shown for this indicator in Figure 9.7 may have come from an existing rating scale used by the soup kitchen director to assess competence of personnel there, or the dimensions may have been created by the project team. When project teams can use dimensions from existing scales their observations will benefit. These dimensions have a measure of content validity because they were probably developed through a consensus process by professionals related to the site, and are likely to be site-accepted descriptors of the behavior of interest. They are also likely to have been used for some time so that site staff interpret them similarly and can explain interpretations to project team members in ways that help them form a mental picture of what it means, for example, to "work cheerfully without stopping to socialize." Also site-related scales may be accompanied by validity and reliability information. Teams that decide to use existing site-specific scales can use them to gather reasonably good observation-based information by doing the following.

1. Selecting no more than three indicators to use with students and specifying each with at least three behavioral dimensions
2. Making sure all team members can envision the behavioral dimensions described for selected indicators
3. Making sure all team members agree that the envisioned behavioral dimensions are part of the indicator
4. Restating indicators and dimensions in language that students will understand while retaining their original meaning
5. Keeping the instrument to a single page

When rating scales are not available at service sites, project teams can often find appropriate instruments by consulting resources such as the National Service Learning Clearing House or The Compendium of Assessment and Research Tools for Measuring Youth Development Outcomes (CART), and other groups and organizations listed and described in Chapter XII. Again, teams may adapt instruments to suit their own observational needs and should follow the steps above as they do so.

Finally, teams may construct their own rating scales. To do this they follow the steps for integrating a scale from other sources with one change. After they have identified the 1-3 outcome indicators they will observe (step 1), they work for content validity by brainstorming as many dimensions of each indicator as they can. From this large pool, which may contain as many as 20 behavioral dimensions for a single indicator, they select the best 3-5 to use. Whatever rating scale a team uses, they should make every effort to increase the validity of the information they gather by doing three things. First, they should set up an "observation pair" consisting of two members of the project team—typically the site representative and one other member. Second, the pair should practice using the scale in a trial observation (resulting data is not used in the project) and discuss their ratings to come to agreement on how they will interpret observed behavior. Third, they should together observe each student with whom they use the scale on at least three separate occasions for a 10- to 30-minute time period. Where these procedures are not possible, teams need to recognize the limitations on conclusions they can draw from observation-based assessment.

Anecdotal Observation

This kind of observation involves writing a running description of what happens in a situation. The observer is not attempting to record instances of predetermined behaviors, but rather notes what people say and do in a given period of time without interpretation. Observers develop their own codes and shorthand in order to record as much as possible of what transpires, then analyze their records afterward. This analysis can include but is not limited to determining if observed behaviors relate in some way to outcome expectations, identifying events and actions that seem to trigger particular behaviors, and speculating on the nature of people's interactions in the observed situation.

The results of anecdotal observation are particularly useful for providing feedback to students about the dynamics of their situations and ways they, themselves, may be contributing to those dynamics. Feedback discussions can often help students gain perspective on what they do and identify ways to change their actions so that they can function more effectively. This formative use of anecdotal observation can be combined with its summative or project-evaluation use in a sequence that contributes to service-learning by creating bridges for students between abstract outcome targets and real behavior. A look at a seventh-grade supportive communication project provides a helpful example.

In the project, students are asked to present mini-workshops on supportive communication at the elementary schools that feed to their middle school. The project team identifies "sensitivity to diversity" as a community expectation indicator for the seventh-graders, and the guidance counselor on the team uses three anecdotal observations to assess their growth toward this indicator. As part of the first observation, the counselor notes that students regularly ignore input from disabled elementary-school children in their workshops. She engages students in a reflective discussion of reasons for this, and together they explore understandings, attitudes and behaviors that can help them feel more confident with disabled children. Students continue their workshops, and the counselor completes second and third anecdotal observations, which reveal that the seventh-graders are increasingly inclusive of disabled children. She summarizes this finding for the team's student outcomes report in a brief narrative which reviews the outcome expectation, describes when and how she observed and concludes by stating that "Over the course of the project students' growing sensitivity to diversity was revealed in their increasingly unbiased inclusion of disabled children in workshop activities." [1]

The counselor could have assumed that during the regular reflective learning activities incorporated in the project, seventh-graders would discuss their discomfort with disabled children and therefore decided not to share results of her first observation with them. But she saw the opportunity to act as a mirror-on-the-spot too good to pass up educationally. She chose to use anecdotal observation to enact the learning-for-all values associated with service-learning. She learned that her service-learning students needed immediate reflective instruction in order to meet the needs of their clients. Her students learned something about their own biases and how to change them. And because the seventh-graders changed their behavior, their elementary-school clients may have had more opportunities to learn.

The critical features of anecdotal observation are completeness and accuracy of records. Users of the strategy benefit from paired practice in which observers record a ten-minute sample of regular activity by a friend or family member, analyze the resulting record for patterns, and interpret these in discussion with each other. For instance, two project team members can record a ten-minute sequence in which someone prepares a meal. They might record among other behaviors that the cook rinsed and dried his hands three times, mislaid a cooking tool four times, checked a recipe book once, then closed it. As they discuss their records, observers focus on the cook's clear attempts at sanitary practice, his need for a standard place to put tools in use and his independence from recipes. During actual service-learning observation, only a single team member is necessary. That person can contribute to completeness and accuracy of records by using the first ten minutes to blend into the situation, quietly observing and recording for the next ten minutes, then either leaving as appropriate or waiting for the service episode to end.

Self-Report Strategies for Measuring Personal Growth Indicators

Self-reports invite respondents' to express their attitudes and values and seem to make good sense as a strategy for assessing students' personal growth

---

[1] This example is based upon insights gained from "Service-Learning: A Disservice to People with Disabilities?" by Pamela J. Gent and Louis E. Guerecka which appeared in the Fall 2001 issue of the *Michigan Journal of Community Service Learning*. The authors who teach a course in service-learning pedagogy for in-service teachers note that in a study of high-school students providing service, "Many students without disabilities expressed embarrassment and unease when working with their classmates with disabilities. For some, these feelings were so intense that they permeated the service experience and resulted in bitterness toward the assignment and the people with whom they were working. This common type of discomfort or emotional strain must be addressed through structured reflection activities" (p. 40).

through service learning. If students' expressed attitudes related to personal growth expectations change over the course of a service-learning project, perhaps those changes have been influenced by the widening arena of experience that service-learning makes possible. Just as with observation, however, research and experience suggest that information gathered through self-report can be problematic. This is because self-report instruments may not actually elicit information about attitudes and values of interest, and because people who respond to them may provide the wrong information either intentionally or inadvertently. As with observation, however, the use of self-report in service-learning outcomes measurement is warranted if project teams work together to identify and specify the attitudes and values they want to assess, follow basic guidelines for instrument design, use instruments at appropriate points within service-learning projects, and treat results as indications of growth trends and as support to other outcomes information rather than as stand-alone conclusions.

Four self-report strategies can help provide information about students' personal growth in service-learning: surveys, interviews, focus groups and experience analysis. Surveys are structured sets of statements that represent attitudes or values of interest to those collecting outcomes information followed by response choices that range from disagreement to agreement. Respondents are asked to indicate how strongly they feel about these statements by marking the response choice closest to their own feelings or beliefs. Interviews range from individually administered surveys to open-ended questioning that encourages respondents to provide free-flowing, oral information. Focus groups are interactive group interviews in which respondents engage in guided and interactive discussion of their attitudes and values with respect to a set of experiences. Experience analysis involves respondents in recalling and analyzing in writing specific experiences in terms of their own attitudes and values.

Surveys

Anderson and Bourke, who are experts in measuring affective characteristics in schools, advise educators to select surveys for use from among existing instruments (2000, pp. 106). They base this advice on the time, expertise and expense involved in developing a new instrument. But for those situations in which educators want to design their own surveys, these authors suggest six steps: developing a blueprint, writing survey items, preparing survey directions, having the draft survey reviewed, piloting the survey and preparing the survey for administration (pp. 112-115). The following introduces and summarizes the Anderson and Bourke steps in terms of designing surveys to assess service-learning outcome expectations in middle and high schools. Project teams can use the steps as presented here to design surveys for use within their initial, learning-phase implementations of service learning. As teams become more skilled with service-learning they can strengthen the surveys they design and improve the quality of the information they collect through surveys by learning about and using the Anderson and Bourke steps in detail.

Developing a Survey Blueprint

This plan identifies who the survey is for, lists and defines the attitudes and values—the scales—that will be assessed, enumerates the number of items per scale and the number of responses per item, and provides a sample item with sample response options. Surveys should be limited to 1-3 scales with each scale on the final form having no fewer than four items, although through the development process many more items will be proposed and tried out. Observing the three-scale, four- item limit helps teams keep the survey as short as possible and no more than a page in length. Figure 9.8 suggests a format for a blueprint based on a project in which twelfth-graders worked with Habitat for Humanity as part of their Living in Democracy course.

Figure 9.8 Sample Blueprint for Survey of Twelfth-Graders' Service Attitudes and Values

---

Survey Population: Twelfth-grade students in Living in Democracy, Section Four

Attitudes and Values to Be Assessed:
1. Attitudes toward service (5 items)
2. Confidence in abilities to provide service (4 items)
3. Plans for future service (4 items)

Responses per Item: 4

Sample Item:

Service is an essential element in democratic society.

strongly agree   agree   disagree   strongly disagree

The blueprint in Figure 9.8 shows that there are three attitudes and values to be assessed, the number of items that will be used to assess each and thus the total number of items on the survey. It also shows in its sample item that each item on the survey will have four response categories. This may represent a departure for some project teams who are familiar with five-response items. But as Anderson and Bourke state, "There is clear and increasing evidence that having an even number of categories produces a more reliable scale than having an odd number" (p. 94). They believe that this is because the "odd" category which is often stated as "no opinion" or "don't know" may be selected by respondents who do not want to state their positions or beliefs as well as respondents who truly do not have an answer for the item.

Writing Survey Items

This activity brings the service-learning team—including students—together to generate as many statements as possible related to each attitude or value to be assessed. A team member can function as leader for each target attitude/value and for each asks the question, "What are all the statements we can make about _____?" Brainstorming is essential here so that team members push beyond their first and immediate reactions and produce as many statements as possible. Once the team is satisfied that they have a sizable pool of items perhaps four or five times as many as will appear on the final survey) they need to edit items using the Anderson and Bourke guidelines (p.113) reproduced in Figure 9.9.

Figure 9.9 Anderson and Bourke Guidelines for Editing Survey Items

1. Write statements that cover the entire range of the affective characteristic. (Plus its target).
2. Ensure each item involves feeling and affect and not a statement of fact (or a statement that can be interpreted as a factual).
3. Keep the language of statements simple, clear and direct.
4. Write statements in the present tense.
5. Each statement should contain only one, complete thought.
6. Avoid statements likely to be endorsed by everyone or almost no one.
7. Avoid words that are vague modifiers or words that may not be understood by those who are asked to respond to the scale
8. Avoid statements that involve double negatives.

(Reproduced with Permission from Anderson, L. W., & Bourke, S. F. (2000). *Assessing affective characteristics in the schools* (2nd ed.). Mahwah, NJ: Lawrence Erlbaum Associates, p. 113)

Teams that follow the Anderson and Bourke editing guidelines substantially increase the likelihood that their surveys will be understood by respondents and elicit thoughtful and honest responses that provide meaningful information about achievement of outcome expectations.

Writing Survey Directions

Project teams need to make sure their surveys contain clear written directions. When the survey is actually administered, it will be useful to read over these directions aloud and answer any questions respondents may have about any part of the survey. Nonetheless, the directions need to be in writing first, and the team needs to carefully check through them to make sure they convey the following information:

- the general purpose of the survey
- the meaning of target attitudes/values if necessary
- the optional nature of participation
- the way to respond to items (circle, check, etc.)
- the fact that there are no right or wrong answers and opinions are being sought

The project team that is designing the twelfth-grade survey blueprinted in Figure 9.8 uses these guidelines to state the following directions:

> The purpose of this survey is to learn about ways our Habitat for Humanity project has influenced your attitudes toward providing service now and in the future. Your participation is optional, and you may answer all or some of the items, or you may choose not to participate. If you do respond to the survey, please circle the response beneath each item that is closest to the way you feel about the statement the item makes. There are no right or wrong answers; your honest opinions are what count. Your responses are anonymous and nothing you say on this survey will be used in any way in your grade for our Living in Democracy course.

Reviewing the Draft Instrument

Two groups help a project team review a draft of their survey and thereby strengthen its content validity: people who understand the attitudes and values being assessed, and students similar to the ones who will eventually respond to the survey. In the case of service-learning, guidance counselors and human services personnel not associated with the project might be asked to review the pool of survey items to answer questions such as the following:

- Do the items relate clearly in some degree of strength and direction to the target attitudes/values?
- Are there items that do not relate to the targets?
- Are items too similar or redundant?
- Are there aspects of the targets for which there are no items?

The team uses information from expert review to narrow its instrument to those items which seem to best relate to the attitudes and values it is seeking information about. Now the team can give the survey to students not in the project for the purposes of determining its communication effectiveness. The team encourages these students to look closely at the language of the survey and to determine if they can understand what it is asking respondents to do, if items make sense and are clear, and if changes could be made to improve the communicability of the survey. Again, the team revises the survey on the basis of this review.

Pilot Testing the Survey

At this point the survey is in draft form and can be pilot tested with at least a small sample of the students who will eventually complete it. In the case of a service-learning project, trying out the survey with 5 of 25 students who have actually performed service, then revising it accordingly can increase the likelihood that the remaining 20 will be able to respond more effectively to the final draft. As the 5 pilot students take the survey, project team members will want to observe them at work to see if parts of it are giving them difficulty and to talk with them afterward about what they didn't understand and how the survey could be improved. As with other trials, the team revises the survey in terms of information it receives from pilot students.

Preparing the Final Survey

Students who receive a survey that is grammatically and typographically correct and professional in appearance from paper used to type font are more likely to believe that their opinions are respected and thus more likely to respond thoughtfully and honestly. Computerized word processing ensures that professional presentation is well within the capacities of project teams, but even here, proofreading and checking by a non-team member will catch the little errors that often slip by. The use of underlines and bold-face type can be very helpful, but teams need to avoid a cluttered and confusing appearance as well.

Teams that carry out these six steps will construct surveys that help them gather information about students' attitudinal and value outcomes of service-learning. As teams begin using service-learning it is likely that they will be doing so with small numbers of students, perhaps a single class, perhaps three or four. According to Anderson and Bourke (p. 115), these small numbers generally mean that it is not possible to make meaningful statistical comparisons between results of service-learning groups and other groups. However, teams can analyze results by determining the level of students' responses as a group to each attitude/value of interest as well as their levels of response as a group to individual items. As projects become larger—across grade levels or school wide—and student sample sizes increase toward 500 and more, teams may use a variety of statistical procedures to test the technical qualities of a survey or to compare survey responses by various groups.

Interviews

As stated earlier, interviews range in form from structured, individually administered surveys to open-ended questioning. If a project team intends to conduct interviews as individually administered surveys, they can carry out the steps in survey design, then simply read the resulting survey to each respondent and mark the answer the respondent provides. Teams that wish to use open-ended interviews can design them through adaptive use of the survey design steps. This means they develop a blueprint that contains interview questions, prepare directions for interviewers and respondents, have interview questions reviewed, and pilot test the interview. A brief review of these steps shows how they can be carried out.

Writing an Open-ended Interview Blueprint

This blueprint identifies who will be interviewed—in cases of small service-learning projects, perhaps all students, but where this is not feasible, perhaps only a quarter or a third of the group. The blueprint also identifies the attitudes and values of interest in the interview, indicates the number of questions to be asked, lists the question to be asked and suggests probes to encourage respondents to expand on their answers. Figure 9.10 shows an interview blueprint that the Greenmount High School Advisory Board and the City Service-Learning Council outcomes measurement coordinator develop together for the senior-year civics project on ways citizens can influence public policy. This team plans to interview a random sample of the many students involved in the project. They are interested in determining these representative students' community commitment as they express it in statements that show recognition of the needs in their community and orientation toward helping to meet those needs.

Figure 9.10 Blueprint for Open-Ended Interview of Students in Senior-Year Civics Cross-Disciplinary Program, Knowing Ways Citizens Can Influence Public Policy

---

Interview Respondents:
30 twelfth-grade students chosen at random from the GHS service-learning civics projects on public opinion influence strategies

Attitudes and Values of Interest:
Expressing community commitment through recognizing and orienting to community needs

Number of Interview Questions: 5
1. What major problems in our community has service-learning helped you recognize?
2. Which of these is most important to the life of our community and why?
3. In what ways will work on this problem improve community life?
4. How confident are you that you can help work on this problem in a way suitable to your age and experience?
5. How committed are you to working on this problem?

Probes to encourage expansion of responses: (for flexible use by interviewer)
1. Can you add to that?
2. Are there other possibilities?
3. Is there more you want to say?

Writing Directions for Interviewers and Respondents

The most useful way for service-learning project teams to support the content validity of interviews is to prepare an interview booklet that will be consistently completed by an interviewer for each student respondent. The booklet is limited to four pages, keeps the interview to 30 minutes or less in length, and contains the following elements:

- Explanation and directions for interviewers
- Interview questions and probes
- Labeled space for recording answers to each question
- Labeled space for recording interview notes and concerns

Interview booklets prepared in a fully professional way to make it easy for interviewers to use them and to imply to interviewers that their work is valued and counted on to be professional as well. As with other forms, word processing and copying technology make this kind of booklet presentation well within the reach of project teams. Once booklets are designed, interviewers should have an opportunity to review them in advance so that they understand booklet contents and how they are to record responses. Figure 9.11 suggests a workable arrangement of the basic components in typical four-page interview booklet.

Figure 9.11 Layout for Open-ended Interview Booklet

Page 1 - Explanations and Directions for Interviewers :
States purpose of the interview and reminds user to review interview booklet, practice reading questions silently, then aloud, and set up a suitable time and quiet location for the interview. Explains that interview is coded with student number and no other identification is needed. Reminds interviewer to tell students participation is optional and anonymous and has no bearing on grades.

Page 2 – Interview Questions and Probes:
Includes student code at top right. Lists reviewed and pilot-tested questions and expansion probes.

Pages 3 and Top Half of Page 4:
Requests interviwers to review answers they write down so they are clear to those who will summarize interviews. Restates each interview question followed by sufficient space to write answers.

Page 4- Second Half :
Begins with a request that interviewers make note of information pertinent to the interview content and process. Provides the remainder of the page for this purpose. Concludes with spaces for interviewer's signature and date.

Reviewing Interview Questions

As with review of survey items, it is important that people who understand the attitude/value being assessed look carefully at the interview questions to determine if they effectively elicit expressions of those targets. These people, again perhaps guidance counselors and human service personnel from community agencies, can use questions such as the following to determine the match between interview questions and attitudes or values to be assessed.

- Are there booklet revisions that will help interviewers?
- Do set-up questions elicit information relevant to target attitude/values?
- Do attitude-eliciting questions relate clearly in some degree of strength and direction to the target attitudes/values?
- Are there questions that do not relate to the targets?
- Are questions too similar or redundant?
- Are there aspects of the targets for which there are no items?
- Are there other useful probes?

Pilot Testing Interview Questions

Interview questions should also be pilot tested with the kinds of students who will ultimately be interviewed. In projects where only a sample of students will be interviewed for outcomes measurement, those not included as assessment subjects can serve as pilot students and provide information that may result in the revision and improvement of the interview instrument. What is important here is to determine if students understand the questions and can respond to them with the kind of opinions and ideas being sought.

Analyzing Interview Results

Again, by using careful preparation project teams can develop interviews that provide them with useful results. Analyzing these results involves assembling all answers to each question, then looking at the patterns and relationships that appear in the answers. For example, after grouping answers to questions in the sample interview in Figure 9.10, project teams can ask questions such as, "Are there similarities in the strength of students' confidence in and commitment to work on community needs?" "How do response patterns relate to the major and primary needs students identify?" "Are there relationships between response patterns and the media services where students engaged in service-learning (newspaper, radio and TV)?" Answers about response and relationship patterns such as these can be summarized in a narrative to provide useful student outcomes information and support information for the overall evaluation of a service-learning project.

Focus Groups

Popham (1993, p. 195) defines a focus group as a "relatively small number of homogeneous individuals who provide qualitative data during a moderated, small group interview." His description of the use of focus groups in program evaluation clearly implies their potential as a technique for service-learning outcomes measurement. The following summarizes Popham's focus-group basics (pp. 204-214) in terms of planning, set up, implementation and analysis of results, and demonstrates ways middle- and high-school project teams can use this strategy to gather qualitative information about service-learning outcome expectations for students.

Planning a Focus Group

Project teams can plan focus groups using the blueprint procedure for interviews described in the preceding section. As with interviews, the blueprint identifies who will participate in the focus group, from one to three attitudes/values the strategy will collect information about, and three to five questions the group will discuss. The focus group blueprint differs from that of the interview in an important way, however, and that is with respect to the probes. These need to be designed to promote the focus group's special, interactive character, so that the group is not a question-and-answer session between facilitator and individual participants, but is instead, "a lively and illuminating discussion among those present." (Popham, p. 196). Focus group probes build upon answers offered by one participant in ways that invite other participants into a discussion that may then go back and forth across the group for several minutes without intrusion by the facilitator. To stimulate this kind of interaction, probes such as the following appear on the focus group blueprint:

- What more can others add to that?
- What are some examples from others experiences?
- In what ways do others feel the same or different?
- What is the range of possibilities here?
- What are some alternative views?
- What other ideas does that bring to mind?
- What are some inferences you might make?

These probes seek divergent responses and work to include the perspectives of all in the group. Because probes are so important to the open-ended inclusiveness in an effective focus group, project teams need to take the time to develop them carefully. They can do this by avoiding probes that seek one and only one right answer and constructing probes that call for a range of possible answers.

Setting up a Focus Group

Effective focus groups take place in a relaxed and comfortable environment that encourages participants to express their ideas and opinions in an open and honest way. Thus project teams need to select facilitators who can make young people feel comfortable and at the same time move discussion forward over planned questions. These facilitators may be members of the team, or outsiders chosen particularly for their interpersonal and group management skills. In either case, the team works together to select these individuals on the basis of the following personal qualities identified by Popham (p. 209).

- ability to express self clearly
- good listening skills
- ability to quickly read participants' verbal and nonverbal responses
- spontaneity and liveliness
- ability to convey empathy with participants' feelings
- ability to keep groups on task
- flexibility in response to the unexpected

It is especially helpful to have co-facilitators for a focus group: one to ask the questions and one to record answers. Once selected, facilitators can arrange the time and location of the group, issue invitations to potential student participants until seven to ten have agreed to take part, and decide on how to record what participants say. Traditionally this means using a tape recorder with a back-up written record, but increasingly, use of a laptop by a person who can touch type while watching and listening to the discussion can substantially reduce the labor of data collection and analysis. Facilitators need to visit the area in which the focus group will take place in advance and decide on how to arrange tables and chairs in a pattern that maximizes group interaction and discussion. They also need to make sure recording equipment works, that other mechanical noise such as that caused by heaters or air conditioners will not interfere with sound recording and that interruptions will not take place during the group meeting. Finally, the facilitator who will ask questions memorizes their substance and their order.

Implementing a Focus Group

Co-facilitators begin by greeting participants and talking with them informally for five or ten minutes about topics that are not part of the focus group discussion. During this time the person who will serve as recorder can collect information about where students provided service if that will be a factor in data analysis. This person can also decide who should sit where to best support group interaction if that seems appropriate. Usually this means seating those who seem shy in the middle and front with more expressive students on the sides. Seats can be assigned using previously prepared 5 x 8 cards folded to stand in front of each student and showing his or her first name.

The facilitator who will ask the questions introduces that activity by welcoming the group and explaining its purpose. He or she explains that the information students will provide will be used to determine group achievement of outcome expectations and for program evaluation purposes, and will not be used to evaluate the work or service of individual students. He or she also explains any guidelines the group will use during discussion such as having the right to pass on questions they do not want to answer. The facilitator invites students to introduce themselves, then often involves all in a very brief "ice breaker," that gets them into a participation mode. When this is complete, the facilitator begins the session.

As the facilitator questions the group, he or she does so without notes and adheres to the order of questions insofar as possible. The facilitator makes every effort not to influence responses, does not engage in head nodding for example, or express personal opinions. If asked to give an opinion, the facilitator deflects by explaining that it is the group's ideas and perspectives that are essential. The facilitator may occasionally rephrase what students say to bring clarity to the discussion, but more often pauses after answers are given to allow others to contribute. Probes as explained earlier help increase the scope of the discussion and can also be used to increase the specificity of responses.

The recording facilitator can help the group process by giving the questioning facilitator an unobtrusive five-minute warning and can then announce conclusion when the time allotted for the group has elapsed. At that point both facilitators thank participants again and answer questions they may have about how the outcomes of their discussion will be shared with them. As participants leave, facilitators make sure that all the notes they have kept are in hand, then leave themselves without discussion of or comment on what happened during the meeting. As soon as possible after leaving the meeting, facilitators review and organize their records of what transpired to ready them for analysis

Analyzing Focus Group Results

Almost invariably, project teams find that the focus groups produce a great deal of information for them to make sense of in terms of outcomes assessment and project evaluation. They can do this within a reasonable amount of time by creating a single, overall written transcript of the group discussion then reducing the information it contains using the codes and themes technique described by Root (1998). An example based on the Chapter V project in which students learn about aging shows how this technique works.

In the monologues-on-aging project, the team's career counselor member and a representative from the commission on aging conduct a focus group to gather information about students' increased understanding of aging as a community issue. The career counselor asks students two questions: "How has your view of aging changed?" and "In what ways do you see aging as an important community issue?" The commission representative serves as recorder and produces a five-page transcript of students' discussion of these two questions. The co-facilitators then identify each student statement related to these questions and code those related to the view-of-aging question with "V" and those related to the community issue question with "C." Next they look at each set of statements to determine themes in them. In V statements they find and code responses addressing the importance of family and friends to older people (V-ff), their pleasure in recreational activities (V-r), and their high incidence of illness (V-i). In C statements they find and code responses addressing the cost of care for the aging (C-cc) and the obligation of a healthy and compassionate society to care for all its members (C–com).

At this point, facilitators and the project team need to pull coded information together in a way that permits them to draw to conclusions about students' perspectives as revealed in the focus group. They can do this in a reasonable amount of time by using a matrix technique adapted from Frechtling and Sharp (1997) which organizes the themes which emerge from the group's discussion. An example of the use of this technique is shown in Table 9.3.

Table 9.3 Matrix of Themes in Focus Group Discussion of Views on and Importance to Community of Aging

Questions	Themes			
Changed view of aging	Importance of family and friends (7)	Pleasure in recreational activities (5)	High incidence of illness (11)	
Importance as a community concern	Cost of Care (13)	Obligation of healthy, compassionate society (10)		

Table 9.3 shows the frequency of student responses for each question-related theme in parentheses. These numbers are not an attempt to convert the qualitative statements students made into quantitative data, rather, they are recorded in order to indicate the relative emphasis students as a group gave to each theme as a contributor to their understanding of aging issues. Their display permits the project team to draw conclusions. In this example, the team concludes that above all, students became aware of the fact that age is often accompanied by illness. At the same time they gained insight on the human dimension of older people's lives—their need to be with family and friends and enjoy recreation. In terms of the importance of aging to the community, students recognized that the cost of care is a major issue, but almost equally that providing that care is the mark of a healthy and compassionate community.

When project teams analyze focus groups using the codes and themes technique, they gain a sense of the impact of service-learning on students' personal growth. Together with other types of outcomes information, focus group results help paint a full picture of the outcomes of service-learning as a comprehensive teaching method.

Experience Analysis

This essay-test strategy helps students become conscious of and reveal their maturing attitudes and values as indicators of their affective development. Project teams use the strategy by asking students to write about service-learning experiences in terms of the framework for affective development provided by Krathwhol, Bloom and Masia (1999). In brief, that framework proposes that people internalize values by identifying life situations that have value potential, exploring their own value stances with respect to these situations, and integrating these stances in their own behavior. When used for measuring affective outcomes of service-learning, the strategy asks students to complete three writing tasks: 1) identify and describe service-learning experiences related to an outcome expectation, 2) explore their own attitudes and values related to the experiences and 3) suggest how they can integrate the results of this exploration in their own future actions.

Project teams can use experience analysis to fruitfully explore relationships between students' service-learning experiences and their maturing sense of caring, self-awareness, career awareness and community commitment. By asking students to recall significant experiences related to these outcome areas and to relate these experiences to their own values in their own words, teams can get a sense of how service-learning may be contributing to students' development as individuals and as members of their communities. In a typical project, a team assesses only one or perhaps two of these outcome expectations via experience analysis then combines resulting information with information gained through surveys, interviews or focus groups.

Table 9.4 shows templates for experience-analysis prompts for the three writing tasks in the outcome areas of caring, self-awareness, career awareness and community commitment. Teams use the outlines these templates provide to create prompts, but they adjust the prompts to their own projects in two ways. In their prompts, they ask students to recall experiences related to a particular aspect of service-learning that they believe had potential for nurturing values related to caring, self-awareness, career awareness and community awareness, and they state their prompts in language appropriate to students' ages and reading and writing skills. By using prompts in this way, teams steer clear of "values education" and instead, help students become aware of and focus their own values on their service-learning experiences. As students respond to the prompts, they recall—without coaching from their teachers or other team members—their own experiences related to caring, self-awareness, career awareness and community awareness, and what they, themselves, value about those experiences. They then explore how they will make these memories and values part of their own lives. And as students explore and analyze self-chosen experiences they become more fully aware of their own emerging values while they are at the same time providing evidence of their affective development.

Table 9.4 Prompt Templates for Experience-Analysis Assessments of Students' Affective Outcomes of Service-Learning

Outcome Area	Identification Writing Task	Value Exploration Writing Task	Value Integration Writing Task
Caring	Describe a need of the clients in the agency where you served	Describe and explain your feelings about this need	Describe how your feelings about this need will make you act in the future
Self-awareness	Describe a service you provided for the agency or its clients	Describe and explain your feelings about what you did	Describe how what you did will make you act in the future
Career Awareness	Describe the occupation you found most interesting at the agency where you served	Explain why this occupation is interesting to you and why it is important to society	Describe how your interest in this occupation will make you act in the future
Community Commitment Through Service	Describe a moment in your service when you were "fired" to help	Describe and explain what it was that made you want to help	Describe how this "fire to help" will make you act in the future

In order to help students succeed with experience analysis, teams make sure that from the outset students have opportunities to record the experiences that they will eventually use to respond to their prompts. Teams do this by having students keep journals throughout service-learning in which they record brief accounts of experience related to the outcome areas of interest. For example, in the Blue Mesa traffic light project, in the outcome area of self-awareness, the team will look for evidence that students increasingly value personal responsibility in group work and can hold themselves to standards as they work in groups. The team creates the following prompt to assess the degree to which service-learning group work helped them do this.

> Write a sentence or two describing how we used groups in our traffic light project. Then tell in two or three sentences your feelings about your own work in the group and explain the reasons for these feelings. Finally, write two or three sentences to suggest how you can use what you learned about working in groups in future group work.

The team ensures that students have group-work information to refer to in their experience-analysis essays by having them keep brief, daily journal records of their group traffic-data collection and preparations for presenting to the county council. In their journals, students identify group tasks worked on, rate their own group contributions on a 1-5 scale, and comment on positive or negative aspects of their own and the group's work. When they write their experience-analysis essays, they use their own journal records as resource material. The actual writing requires them to produce essays of five to eight sentences or 150-200 words—a writing task within the capacities of most seventh-graders.

Project teams can judge experience-analysis essays in terms of students' expressed progress toward integration of values related to the outcome indicators of interest. A progress-toward-integration judgment can be made on the basis of the richness of students' responses to the three writing tasks. Thus with respect to the identification writing task, teams look for students' clear description of experiences that relate to the attitude/or value of interest. With respect to the exploration writing task, teams look for students' in-depth explanation of one or more personal attitudes related to the experience, and with respect to the integration task, they look for realistic and thought-out proposals for living the personally identified and explored values. In the Blue Mesa project, for example, one student faithfully records all instances of group work, states that she likes it as long as everyone does a fair share, but does not address how to use this value in her own future group work. Another student describes group work in two sentences, discusses mixed feelings of elation and frustration in group work, and asserts the critical importance of participating in the development of group rules and holding himself and other group members personally accountable. The team judges the first student at low to mid range on self-awareness gained from the project, and the second student as a more self-aware internalizer of a group-work ethic. Across all students in the project, experience-analysis essays indicate to the team that students are approaching a more self-aware understanding of group work which the teacher endorses as substantial progress in terms of his experience to date with these seventh-graders.

Teams can also judge experience-analysis essays on their inclusion of statements that reflect indicators of target outcome expectations. When determining students' caring attitudes and values for instance, teams can look for the number and quality of statements that indicate students' concern to promote least pain and harm, maintain positive relationships and respond in terms of the situations they shared with those they served. Results for a group can be coded then summed in a narrative. For example in the nursing-home project described in Chapter V, students' experience-analysis essays contain many accounts of how their own feelings when they were confined to bed due to illness or injury, helped them understand their patients' feelings and needs. The team sees this as an important indicator of students' growth in caring.

Experience-analysis has much to offer as a service-learning assessment. It engages teams in identifying aspects of their projects that have the potential to aid students' development in the outcome areas of caring, self-awareness, career awareness and community commitment. It helps teams think clearly about how to elicit student's exploration of their development in these areas. It helps students reflect upon and discover how they feel about what they did during service-learning, and encourages them to speculate on how these feelings and actions will be integrated in their lives. In these ways it supports the personal and social outcomes that research suggests are fruits of service-learning.

In Conclusion

Service-learning project teams use a range of strategies to measure student outcomes of service-learning. These include state standards tests and locally developed criterion-referenced tests that assess academic and problem-solving expectations. They also include rating scales and anecdotal observations that assess service competence; and surveys, interviews, focus groups and experience-analysis essays that reveal attitudes and values related to caring, self-awareness, career awareness and community commitment. With the exception of state standards tests, teams can design their own instruments to implement these strategies, although experts in outcomes measurement suggest that with respect to reliability, validity, time and expense, the use of existing instruments usually has advantages over locally developed instruments. When teams elect to construct their own instruments, they need to obtain evidence of the content-related validity of those instruments, and as Popham points out, evidence of content-related validity comes from informed, qualitative judgment of "the degree to which a test is consonant with the content, skills or objectives it is supposed to measure" (p. 123). Teams can lend content-related validity to their instruments by developing them through thoughtful, collaborative discussion and by asking knowledgeable others to review what they create in light of their outcomes measurement purposes.

Beginning project teams need to develop their outcomes measurement skills. They do this by using two or three of the strategies with small groups or samples of students. As teams become more experienced, and as the school systems and communities within which they work become are more able to provide outcomes measurement assistance, they can explore the classical considerations of outcomes measurement in greater detail and adjust their own work accordingly.

Activities for Increasing Understanding

1. Talk with your school system's state standards test coordinator to determine the feasibility of comparing your students' achievement on service-learning linked items with the population of students who complete the items. Prepare a brief written explanation of why comparisons are or are not possible and comment on your reactions to this.
2. Write the domain specifications, stimulus material, test items and scoring rubric for a criterion-referenced paper-pencil test of your students' abilities to recall and apply knowledge or skill that you expect as an outcome from the project you are designing. Ask a teacher with the same teaching assignment as yours to comment on the content validity of your instrument.
3. Use Figure 9.5 as a model for constructing a criterion-referenced performance test of your students' abilities to demonstrate knowledge or skill that you expect as an outcome from the service-learning plan you are designing. Again, ask a teacher with the same teaching assignment as yours to comment on the content validity of your instrument
4. Select an indicator of one service outcome expectations you have for students in your service-learning project. Work with at least one other educator and one relevant community partner to write five observation-scale items an observer could use to determine the degree to which a student is demonstrating the indicator as he or she provides service. Use the format in Figure 9.7 to present your items.
5. Prepare a blueprint for a survey you could design to assess students' attitudes/values related to an outcome expectation in your service-learning project. Use the survey blueprint format provided in Figure 9.8.
6. Use Figure 9.10 as a model to prepare an open-ended interview blueprint for use in assessing students' attitudes/values related to an outcome expectation in your service-learning project. Add a brief description of how you could also use this blueprint as the basis for a focus-group plan.
7. Develop an experience-analysis prompt to assess attitudes/values related to an outcome expectation in your project. Plan the prompt using Table 9.4 as a guide, then write out your prompt in the form that it will be given to students. Make sure the prompt encourages students to recall and analyze their own experiences related to your outcome area of interest.

Chapter X: Strategies for Designing Reflective Learning Experiences

"This year's County Student Arts Festival will be the best ever because your students answered our call for help and linked the festival to service-learning. It'll be sold out, and that means we can award ten summer arts camp scholarships!" Festival coordinator Gleason James beams at teachers Jack Porteus, and LaDonna Mills from Tremont High School, advertising executive and parent Kip Tolenger, Mel Smith from the County Arts League and student Leontine Perry.

Kip nods vigorously. "We're excited about our piece—helping students focus on and reach their marketing audiences. And those cooperative learning strategies are great. We're going to use some of them with our own professionals."

"The project's a natural for multiple intelligences too—art and music activities for sure," says Jack. "LaDonna and I've also mapped out verbal, mathematic and interpersonal activities that are real elements in the project."

"Don't forget the sound system. Kids working on that'll use a big mix of intelligence." Leontine says.

"But what about this reflection and conceptualization we're all trying to help with?" Mel leans back with crossed arms.

"I see it two ways, Mel," says LaDonna. "We need to help students connect their honors program courses to their service to the Festival. And we need to help them think about the arts in life—what they mean to all our students, the people who come to the concerts and exhibits, and to our community."

Chapter Focus

The project team in this scenario has nearly completed its instructional plan—one that will help their high-school students use arts honors course experiences and other school learnings as foundational material for supporting a major arts event in their community. Things seem to be going well. Members are sharing instructional responsibilities, using cooperative learning and multiple intelligences approaches, and they are exploring uses of reflection and conceptualization activities. To get to this point, however, the team had to work through a three-stage process. They had to come up with instructional goals and objectives, integrate reflective learning experiences and accept responsibility for individual assignments. The purpose of this chapter is to describe the possibilities open to project teams in each of these three stages of the service-learning instructional planning process and to show in examples how teams might use these possibilities.

Stating Instructional Goals and Objectives

Chapter VI introduces a service-learning instructional planning process that begins with project teams using the outcome expectations and indicators in their student outcomes plans to state instructional goals and objectives. This is a straightforward process in which teams simply repeat their expectations and indicators as goals and objectives. As teams do this, however, they may realize that connections between a particular expectation and its related indicators are not clear when these two components are stated as an instructional goal and related objectives. When this happens, the team revisits its outcomes plan and adjusts the expectation and indicator accordingly. An example helps explain this somewhat confusing but not unusual situation. Chapter V describes an outcomes plan in which high-school drama students link study of dramatic monologues to service to patients in a nursing home. A service outcome expectation of that plan is that students will relate competently to patients and will indicate this competence by selecting appropriate materials to read to them. Table 10.1 shows the team's initial work with this outcome and its indicator.

Table 10.1   Restating Outcomes and Indicators as Goals and Objectives

Expectation (Becomes Goal)	Indicators (Becomes Objective)	Measurement Strategy	Data Source	Person Responsible
Relate competently to patients	Select appropriate reading materials for patients	Interviews	Patients	Ms. Barak (nursing home staff director)

When the team restates the expectation and indicator above as a goal and related objective, they realize that students' selection of appropriate reading materials will not necessarily help them relate competently to patients. There is, a disconnect between the expectation and its indicator and between the instructional goal and its related objective. The team discusses the disconnect and decides that students will more clearly show they can relate to patients when they talk in a confident, friendly and cheerful manner with them. The team restates this component of its outcomes plan as shown in italics in Table 10.2.

Table 10.2   Revised Outcomes Plan as a Result of Instructional Planning

Expectation (Becomes Goal)	Indictors (Become Objective)	Assessment Strategy	Data Source	Person Responsible
Relate competently to patients	*Talk with patients in a confident, friendly and cheerful manner*	Interviews	Patients	Ms. Barak (nursing home staff director)

This revision has two benefits. The team now has specific criteria to use in developing the interview questions patients will answer about their perceptions of students' abilities to relate to them. The team can also design reflective learning experiences that help students focus on these qualities—perhaps can have them observe and analyze the behavior of competent nursing home staff acting in a confident, friendly and cheerful manner with bedridden patients. Students can then practice ways to incorporate confidence, friendliness and cheerfulness in their own interactions before actually talking with patients.

The second look at the connections between expectations/goals and indicators/objectives that occurs during instructional planning may turn up other insights. It may, for example, reveal that limited personnel or material resources will constrain the team's abilities to actually provide the academic or service experience necessary for students to achieve a particular objective. Or a team may realize that an expectation/goal is inappropriate in terms of students' age or experience. Whatever the case, teams benefit from using the lens of instructional planning to look back on their student outcomes plans and adjust them where necessary. When teams are willing to revise backward as they go forward, the result is a stronger project overall.

Selecting Activities for Reflective Learning Experiences

Reflective learning experiences "have a threefold purpose: to focus attention, create opportunity for experiencing varying perspectives and elicit insights" (England & Spence, 2001, p. 2). Three kinds of learning activities help project teams and students accomplish this three-fold purpose: focusing activities, reflection activities and conceptualizing activities. Project teams design reflective learning experiences by linking focusing, reflection and conceptualizing activities together. They can choose from a wide range of these three types of activities. They can also integrate activities within reflective learning experiences in a variety of ways in order to address students needs, interests and abilities, targeted service-learning outcome expectations and the interests and needs partners in their project. The following describes each of these types of activities separately and explains their use, then provides several examples of their use together within reflective learning experiences.

Focusing Activities

Service-learning projects are extraordinarily rich in learning opportunities for students. Planned and unplanned events unfold, and students are often caught up in new experiences from moment to moment. Often, too, they are called upon to apply in real and demanding situations academic learnings which they may have viewed as "school stuff." Sorting through these dynamics can pose a challenge. What will be important in a particular project? What deserves attention? Where will learning begin? Focusing activities help students meet this challenge by directing their attention to relevant material from their academic study, service activity and personal knowledge and perspectives. And as they help students attend to this material, focusing activities use multiple intelligences approaches and engage students in cooperative learning.

Material for Focusing Activities

To help students move through the complex and often messy experiences of service-learning projects in ways that result in learning, project teams focus them on particular kinds of material in the academic, service and personal growth service-learning outcome areas. Teams design focusing activities that call students' attention to 1) material they are learning or have already learned that will be useful to their service and to their personal growth, 2) aspects of their service that will help them understand their service, school work and themselves better and 3) personal perspectives they may need to expand or modify as they meaningfully integrate academic, service and personal growth_elements. Table 10.3 summarizes these kinds of material for focusing activities as they relate to the three, service-learning outcome areas.

Table 10.3 Material for Focusing Activities Related to Service-Learning Outcome Areas

Outcome Area	Material for Focusing Activities
Academic	facts, ideas, principles, propositions, skills, procedures needed to understand , act and reflect in service situations
Service	missions, goals, objectives, interactions, events, organizational features that reveal the nature and function of a service agency or a service initiative
Personal Growth	emotions, perceptions, opinions, thoughts, questions that can contribute to new and enlarged personal perspectives

Table 10.3 implies that students' focus on academic material they need for successful service enables them to connect classroom learning to service. It

implies that their understanding of the philosophical and organizational features of a service agency or service initiative readies them to make caring and competent service contributions. It also implies that relating their own feelings to service-learning orients them to personal growth. To help students make these connections in the three outcome areas, project teams carefully select the material that will become the content of students' focusing activities in each area. Then they design focusing activities that activate students' use of their multiple intelligences and engage them in cooperative learning.

Activating Students' Multiple Intelligences

As explained in Chapter VI, multiple intelligences (MI) theory implies that learning activities which call upon students' varied capacities and abilities are likely to increase the depth and scope of their learning and to strengthen the range of their capacities and abilities. Further, service-learning as an instructional method that involves students in life-related and life-based experiences is ripe with possibilities for multiple-intelligences learning. Project teams can create focusing activities that guide students to the material they need for service-learning and at the same time activate and strengthen students' multiple intelligences by becoming familiar with and using guidelines for multiple intelligences activity design such as those proposed by Armstrong (2000) and cited in full in Figure 10.1.

Figure 10.1 makes clear that team members new to MI theory will need some time to become familiar enough with the eight multiple intelligences to use them in designing focus activities as described in Chapter VI. Teacher leaders of project teams can help team members gain understanding here in two ways. The first of these is to conduct a multiple-intelligences mini-workshop of no more than an hour with team members. In this session, team members read and discuss the Armstrong descriptions. Next they analyze a list of learning activities of any kind that are regularly used by the teacher and his or her colleagues and identify the intelligences that the activities call upon. As they do this, the teacher makes clear that these activities may each involve several intelligences. Finally, team members think about a simple but substantive school learning task such as describing democracy, then suggest eight ways to involve students in the task using the eight different intelligences. A second way to help team members learn about MI theory is to ask them to use the Internet and go to www.thirteen.org/edonline/concept2class/month1/ which is a website entitled "Tapping into Multiple Intelligences." At this website, MI theory is explained in simple and interesting terms and video clips show students involved in multiple-intelligence learning activities. Team members who use either of these strategies will develop sufficient understanding of multiple intelligences to contribute to the design of multiple-intelligence focusing activities

Figure 10.1 The Seven Intelligences Described

Linguistic Intelligence: The capacity to use words effectively, whether orally (e.g., as a storyteller, orator, or politician) or in writing (e.g., as a poet, playwright, editor or journalist). This intelligence includes the ability to manipulate the syntax or structure of language, the phonology or sounds of language, the semantics or meanings of language, and the pragmatic dimensions or practical uses of language. Some of these uses include rhetoric (using language to convince others to take a specific course of action), mnemonics (using language to remember information), explanation (using language to inform), and metalanguage (using language to talk about itself).

Logical-Mathematical Intelligence: The capacity to use numbers effectively (e.g., as a mathematician, tax accountant or statistician) and to reason well (e.g. as a scientist, computer programmer, or logician). This intelligence includes sensitivity to logical patterns and relationships, statements and propositions (if-then, cause-effect), functions, and other related abstractions. The kinds of processes used in the service of logical-mathematical intelligence include: categorization, classification, inference, generalization, calculation and hypothesis testing.

Spatial Intelligence: The ability to perceive the visual-spatial world accurately (e.g., as a hunter, scout or guide) and to perform transformation upon those perceptions (e.g. as an interior decorator, architect, artist or inventor). This intelligence involves sensitivity to color, line, shape, form, space and the relationships that exist between these elements. It includes the capacity to visualize, to graphically represent visual or spatial ideas, and to orient oneself appropriately in a spatial matrix.

Bodily-Kinesthetic Intelligence: Expertise in using one's whole body to express ideas and feelings (e.g., as an actor, a mime, an athlete, or a dancer) and facility in using one's hands to produce or transform things (e.g., as a craftsperson, sculptor, mechanic, or surgeon). This intelligence includes specific physical skills such as coordination, balance, dexterity, strength, flexibility, and speed as well as proprioceptive, tactile and haptic capacities.

Musical Intelligence: The capacity to perceive (e.g., as a music aficionado), discriminate (e.g., as a music critic), transform (e.g., as a composer), and express (e.g., as a performer) musical forms. This intelligence includes sensitivity to the rhythm, pitch or melody, and timbre or tone color of a musical piece. One can have a figural or "top down" understanding of music (global, intuitive), a formal or "bottom-up" understanding (analytical, technical), or both.

Interpersonal Intelligence: The ability to perceive and make distinctions in the moods, intentions, motivations, and feelings of other people. This can include sensitivity to facial expressions, voice and gestures; the capacity for discriminating among many different kinds of interpersonal cues; and the ability to respond effectively to those cues in some pragmatic way (e.g., to influence a group of people to follow a certain line of action).

Intrapersonal Intelligence: Self-knowledge and the ability to act adaptively on the basis of that knowledge. This intelligence includes having an accurate picture of oneself (one's strengths and limitations); awareness of inner moods, intentions, motivations, temperaments, and desires; and the capacity for self-discipline, self-understanding and self-esteem.

Naturalist Intelligence: Expertise in the recognition and classification of the numerous species—the flora and fauna—of an individual's environment. This also includes sensitivity to other natural phenomena (e.g. cloud formations and mountains) and in the case of those growing up in an urban environment, the capacity to discriminate among nonliving forms such as cars, sneakers and music CD covers.

(From *Multiple Intelligences in the Classroom, 2nd Edition* by Thomas Armstrong, Alexandria, VA: Association for Supervision and Curriculum Development: Copyright 2000. Reprinted by Permission. All rights reserved.)

Empowering Focus Activities With Cooperative Learning

Johnson, Johnson and Smith (1995) cite extensive research evidence of the positive effect of cooperative learning on student achievement and identify the elements that mediate this effect. As they point out, "Any assignment in any curriculum for any age student may be done cooperatively" (p. 40). Service-learning project teams can empower their multiple-intelligences focus activities with cooperative learning by structuring what students and teachers do together within these activities in terms of the mediating elements Johnson, Johnson and Smith identify. The following discussion summarizes these elements in two groups: those related to what students do as cooperative learners and those related to what teachers and team members do as facilitators of cooperative learning.

Students as Cooperative Learners - Focusing activities become cooperative-learning activities when project teams structure them so that students use positive interdependence, promotive interactive, individual accountability, social skills and cooperative processing. (p. 31) This means that in pairs and groups, students depend upon each other to successfully complete learning tasks, interact to help one another accomplish the tasks, take individual responsibility for their work, use interpersonal and social skills, and mindfully evaluate the processes they are using. (pp. 32-38) These five elements and the learning structures that Johnson, Johnson and Smith believe help students use the elements are summarized in the first two columns of Table 10.4. In the third column of the table, sample focusing activities from the tenth-grade drama project demonstrate use of the structures that are underlined in the second column.

Table 10.4 calls attention to three ideas important to project teams' use of cooperative learning with focusing activities. First, as Johnson, Johnson and Smith assert, cooperative learning can be used with any activity. Thus in the case of service-learning, it can be used with activities intended to help students accomplish objectives in the academic, service and personal growth areas. Second, teams need not use all possible cooperative learning structures with any given focusing activity. For instance, in the student activity example related to positive interdependence (row 1), students have the mutual goal of finding monologue characteristics in a piece of literature, and they earn joint rewards for finding numerous examples of each characteristic, but the activity does not require them to divide resources or take on complementary roles. Third, most focusing activities use more than one cooperative learning element. Although the focusing activities in Table 10.4 are aligned with and primarily evidence use of one element, they often incorporate two of these elements. For instance, the activity in which students role play, critique and improve patient interaction behaviors (row 3) involves the cooperative learning element of individual accountability in its analysis and critique features, and the element of promotive interaction in the improvement that team members are expected to help each other make in their monologues. Similarly in the final activity (row 6), members keep journals to use in the element of group processing, but keeping these journals also promotes the element of individual accountability.

Table 10.4 Cooperative Learning Elements, Facilitating Structures and Examples of Use in Tenth-Grade Drama Prototype Focusing Activities

Cooperative-Learning Student Element	Structures for Promoting	Examples of Use with Focusing Activities from Monologue Project
Positive Interdependence	Mutual Learning Goals Joint Rewards Divided Resources Complementary Roles	**Objective:** Find monologue characteristics in example **CL Activity:** Small groups. Teacher describes characteristics, students discuss in pairs then find characteristics in Truman Capote's "A Christmas Memory." Pairs earn score points for correct examples.
Face-to-face Promotive Interaction	Seating Arrangements Discussion Guides Assistance Expectations	**Objective:** Create and perform own monologue **CL Activity:** Small Groups. Each student describes a character to be portrayed. Group members use discussion guide to help each other identify character's interests, concerns, views on aging, then suggest statements and gestures for character.
Individual Accountability	Personal Reporting Individual Assessment Group Reporting	**Objectives:** Talk with patients in a confident, friendly and cheerful manner. Respond in a caring manner to patients as persons. **CL Activity:** Small Groups. Members discuss similarities and differences in objectives' target behaviors Each member offers one indicator of each target behavior. Individuals round-robin role play talking and responding to patients Other members analyze and critique, then individual reperform accordingly.
Social Skills	Democratic Process Recognition of Strengths Social Skills Instruction	**Objective:** Understanding aging as community concern **CL Activity:** Group elects task leader who helps group identify types of information needed to support the idea that communities' concern about aging is justified. Individuals commit in writing to gather types of information and to format it using own strengths.
Group Processing	Time Allotment Reflection Framework	**Objectives:** All of the above **CL Activity:** Group timelines activities for each objective and includes 15-30 minutes processing time for each. Assigns one member as leader for processing of each objective. Members keep journal record of daily group work accomplished, personal contributions and feelings for use in group processing sessions.

Team Members as Cooperative Learning Facilitators - The nature of cooperative learning makes it possible for project team members other than teachers to take appropriate and effective instructional responsibility within a service-learning project. The central dynamic of cooperative learning is that students increasingly take responsibility for their own learning and that teachers play a consultative and expert assistance role. Students who have been prepared for

Figure 10.5 Instructional Plan for Tenth-Grade Drama, Prototype Project

Session I: At Nursing Home, Teacher with Team Members Present and Assisting

Introductory Activities: Teacher

1. Introduces team members and areas of expertise.
2. Explains logistics of service: schedule, transportation, orientation, patient assignments, mentors, journal requirements.
3. Provides overview of project flow, initiation to and provision of service, classroom connection of service to state English standard in drama as service continues and concludes, analysis of outcomes and celebration.
4. Explains centrality of cooperative learning to project, announces group assignments and names consulting team facilitator for each group.
5. Asks students and consulting team facilitators to meet in groups.
6. Distributes instructional schedule showing individual sessions organized around specific objectives, learning activities, and group processing activities.
7. Has team facilitators help student groups review cooperative learning elements, evaluate their social skills and establish guidelines for future group interaction.
8. Has nursing home director review and justify service outcome objectives for all groups:
   - Talk with patients in a confident, friendly and cheerful manner
   - Respond in a caring manner to patients as persons

Facilitator Activities: Team Members as Facilitators for Student Cooperative Learning Groups

1. Help students identify similarities and differences in target behaviors in the two service objectives and asks each to offer one indicator of each target behavior.
2. Provide scenarios relevant to each outcome objective and guide student pairs in role-plays of talking with and responding to patients.

Student Cooperative Learning Activities

1. Role play scenarios in pairs then analyze and critique role-plays as a group
2. Role play again in pairs in light of critiques, reflect, conceptualize and analyze own group process.

Students Begin Service in the Nursing Home

Session II – In Classroom, Teacher with Team Members Present and Assisting

Introductory Activities: Teacher

1. Reviews project as linking needed service to creating monologues and developing understanding of aging as a community concern.
2. Explains upcoming use of pairs and continued use of already formed cooperative-learning groups and distributes group assignments.
3. Presents illustrated lecture on monologue characteristics.

Facilitator Activities: Team Members as Facilitators for Student Cooperative Learning Groups

1. Call cooperative learning groups together.
2. Review session objective: find monologue characteristics in monologue example.
3. Read excerpt from Capote's "A Christmas Memory" aloud and distribute copy to each student.

Student Cooperative Learning Activities

1. Work in pairs to discuss excerpt and use lecture notes to find numerous examples of monologue characteristics. (Team facilitator assists by helping students check proposed examples against definitions of characteristics and records points for each pair.)
2. Decide which is best example of each characteristic and elect representative to share this at conclusion of session with class.
3. Reflect, conceptualize and analyze own group processes.

Figure 10.5 Instructional Plan for Tenth-Grade Drama, Prototype Project

Session I: At Nursing Home, Teacher with Team Members Present and Assisting
Introductory Activities: Teacher 1. Introduces team members and areas of expertise. 2. Explains logistics of service: schedule, transportation, orientation, patient assignments, mentors, journal requirements. 3. Provides overview of project flow, initiation to and provision of service, classroom connection of service to state English standard in drama as service continues and concludes, analysis of outcomes and celebration. 4. Explains centrality of cooperative learning to project, announces group assignments and names consulting team facilitator for each group. 5. Asks students and consulting team facilitators to meet in groups. 6. Distributes instructional schedule showing individual sessions organized around specific objectives, learning activities, and group processing activities. 7. Has team facilitators help student groups review cooperative learning elements, evaluate their social skills and establish guidelines for future group interaction. 8. Has nursing home director review and justify service outcome objectives for all groups: 　▫ Talk with patients in a confident, friendly and cheerful manner　▫ Respond in a caring manner to patients as persons **Facilitator Activities: Team Members as Facilitators for Student Cooperative Learning Groups** 1. Help students identify similarities and differences in target behaviors in the two service objectives and asks each to offer one indicator of each target behavior. 2. Provide scenarios relevant to each outcome objective and guide student pairs in role-plays of talking with and responding to patients. **Student Cooperative Learning Activities** 1. Role play scenarios in pairs then analyze and critique role-plays as a group 2. Role play again in pairs in light of critiques, reflect, conceptualize and analyze own group process.
Students Begin Service in the Nursing Home
Session II – In Classroom, Teacher with Team Members Present and Assisting
Introductory Activities: Teacher 1. Reviews project as linking needed service to creating monologues and developing understanding of aging as a community concern. 2. Explains upcoming use of pairs and continued use of already formed cooperative-learning groups and distributes group assignments. 3. Presents illustrated lecture on monologue characteristics. **Facilitator Activities: Team Members as Facilitators for Student Cooperative Learning Groups** 1. Call cooperative learning groups together. 2. Review session objective: find monologue characteristics in monologue example. 3. Read excerpt from Capote's "A Christmas Memory" aloud and distribute copy to each student. **Student Cooperative Learning Activities** 1. Work in pairs to discuss excerpt and use lecture notes to find numerous examples of monologue characteristics. (Team facilitator assists by helping students check proposed examples against definitions of characteristics and records points for each pair.) 2. Decide which is best example of each characteristic and elect representative to share this at conclusion of session with class. 3. Reflect, conceptualize and analyze own group processes.

Figure 10.5 continued

Students Learn in Classroom as They Continue Nursing Home Service

Session III – In Classroom with Teacher and Team Member Consulting with Student Groups

Introductory Activities: Teacher
1. Explores ways authors create fictional characters that reflect characteristics of real people.
2. Helps students suggest ways they can imbue their monologue characters with interests, concerns and views of patients they are working with in service experience, yet keep their characters fictional.
3. Asks students to record techniques in journals.

Facilitator Activities: Team Members as Facilitators for Student Cooperative Learning Groups
1. Call groups together.
2. Review session task: create a one-minute monologue for later performance that reveals character's interests, concerns, views of aging.
3. Ask each student to word web a character with interests, concerns, views in five minutes.

Student Cooperative Learning Activities
1. Present own created character.
2. Use discussion guide to help presenting student refine character's interests, concerns, views on aging.
3. Suggest statements and gestures that could be used by presenting student to dramatize his/her character to within monologue.
4. Schedule monologue presentations meeting as part of future outcomes measurement.
5. Reflect, conceptualize and analyze own group processes.

Students Complete Service in Nursing Home

Session IV: In Classroom Led by Commission on Aging Team Member with Teacher Assisting

Introductory Activities: Commission on Aging Team Member
1. Talks briefly about aging, then raises the question "Why should a community be concerned about aging?"
2. Invites students to use existing cooperative-learning groups to answer this question through group investigation.

Student Cooperative Learning Activities
1. Elect student leader for cooperative learning group.
2. Identify types of information needed to support idea that communities' concerns about aging are justified.
3. Commit in writing to gather types of information and to format it according to particular interests and intelligences.
4. Schedule summation and presentation of ideas about community concern for aging as part of future project assessment phase.
5. Reflect, conceptualize and analyze own group processes.

Students and Project Team Assess and Celebrate New Learnings and Perspectives

Students work through these activities in pairs and continuing cooperative-learning work groups to learn, reflect and conceptualize. Their team-member teachers organize them in groups, explain objectives, provide necessary information and help students work toward the objectives as they function effectively in their groups.

More generally, analysis of Figure 10.2 suggests three guidelines for project teams as they integrate focusing activities into instructional plans. The first relates to sequencing. When teams develop student outcomes plans, they are not concerned about the order of learning experiences students will have; their interest is in identifying and measuring expected outcomes for students. As teams develop instructional plans, however, the order of students' learning experiences becomes very important. Teams have to think about what students need to learn first, next and last in order to assure that they make the most meaningful connections between service and learning and their own personal growth. In some cases, students will need to begin with their own attitudes, assumptions and understandings—their personal growth status quos. For example, it may be very important for students who will eventually serve developmentally disabled adults to begin with instructional activities that help them explore their own anxieties about these clients.

In other cases students may need to begin with academic focusing activities. For example, students who will be helping a church soup kitchen set up its revenue and expense records may need to begin with direct academic instruction in relevant accounting principles and practices. In the example in Figure 10.2, the project team believes that students need to interact first with older people in order to gain a psychological understanding of them, so the team begins its instructional plan at the nursing home with a focus on students' service there. In essence, as teams develop instructional plans they need to consider how to most effectively sequence the activities in those plans

A second guideline suggested by the Figure 10.2 example relates to consistent facilitation by team members. In the plan, all activity facilitators, whether teacher or team members, call cooperative learning groups together, help students relate the work they will do in the group to their outcome objectives and provide the information groups need to work. All of these facilitators are on hand to provide consultative assistance and intervene when group skills need to be strengthened. This consistency of facilitation gives collaborative service-learning its power for enhancing student outcomes and also works to build the project team itself as a cooperative learning group.

A third guideline suggested by the example relates to students' progression toward learning independence. Use of cooperative learning in service-learning projects results in "an open, high-participation system that emphasizes personal relationships among students, the flow of information between them, their use of diverse talents and skills to contribute to each other's learning and their use of feedback to improve function and plan new approaches" (Sharan, 1994, p. 323). This kind of system encourages students to develop and use decision-making skills for learning. The sample project's creation of an open, high-participation system can be seen in the shifting balance between facilitator and student control of learning within each session. In the first session, the balance is largely in favor of facilitator control with students beginning to participate in groups near the end of the session. By the last session, students direct their own group investigation. The "teacher" is a team member who facilitates students management of their own learning by raising a question, then letting students take charge as he or she assumes a consultative role. In this important way, cooperative learning is an essential component in effective service-learning.

The example in Figure 10.2 refers to the use of reflection and conceptualization in each of its sessions, but does not specify particular reflection and conceptualizing activities. This is in part because these kinds of activities have yet to be detailed, but it is also because real instructional plans allow for spontaneity in the selection of reflection and conceptualization activities. Teams can plan the overall design of reflective learning experiences and detail their specific focus activity components, but they cannot be sure what will happen as student engage in those activities, cannot know with absolute certainty at the outset which reflection and conceptualization activities will be most effective as students work in pair and in groups. If, however, team members become familiar with a range of reflection and conceptualization activities, they can learn to use one or two that apply well in many situations, or choose from among the many available, the particular ones that seem appropriate for situations as they spontaneously arise.

Reflection Activities

Reflection activities are sets of questions that students learn to ask themselves so that they will gain meaning from experiences. In *How We Think* (1933), John Dewey lays the theoretical foundation for reflection as the central process in education, and John Saltmarsh (1996) expert in community service learning, states that "Reflective inquiry is at the core of service-learning, creating meaning out of associational experience." (p.18). But it is teachers, themselves, who make clear the essentiality of reflection to learning, who recognize both the very real challenge of helping students to reflect and the remarkable outcomes it can make possible. One such teacher is Wayne Harvey (1996), who directs a reflection-based experiential education program that has been operating for over 23 years. His thoughts on reflection provide project teams a powerful orientation to this essential service-learning component.

> Through the years of promoting and enculturating reflection at Linworth, our experience has taught us many lessons. What we have experienced is that reflection is a learned process that can be enhanced through practice and that in all probability, very few of us take enough time to reflect on our current experience. We have discovered that putting information and experiences into a broader context gives tremendous personal meaning to what is learned. Reflection takes the learning process to a personal depth far beyond simply accumulating information and experiences.

> Promoting reflection is almost always difficult. In a world geared more and more to immediate gratification, taking the time to reflect is not an instinctive activity for most students. Frustration can get incredibly high for both students who are being pushed to reflect and staff who are trying to take students in that direction. However, when connections are made, when insight is found, when the reflective process works, the benefit of what is learned far outweighs any of the problems encountered along the way. (p. 130)

As project teams select and use reflection activities from those described here or from other sources, they benefit from bearing Harvey's five ideas in mind.

- Reflection unites information and experience in meaning.
- Reflection is a process that can be learned and enhanced by practice.
- Pushing students to reflect can be difficult and frustrating for them and for team members who work with them.
- When the reflection process works, the benefits in deeper learning are truly worthwhile.
- Time is essential for effective reflection.

Use and Types of Reflection Activities

The procedure for using reflection activities is generally the same across activities. The facilitator invites students—in small groups of 5-7 wherever possible—to reflect on particular information, ideas or experiences and asks them to take a minute or two to mentally evoke what they will reflect upon. Next, the facilitator reviews the questions that will be used to reflect, posts them or asks students to note them down, then asks them to think about and answer the first question. If students seem hesitant about getting started, the facilitator may ask them to discuss answers to the question in pairs, possibly to make notes of what they come up with, then share their thinking with the group. As reflection moves from question to question, students may draw blanks, even resist. Here, the facilitator can rephrase reflection questions and ask helping questions that direct students toward areas of recall and perception that may give them material for thoughtful answers. But here, too, the facilitator does not directly answer questions, and he or she uses wait-time—periods of silence after questions—to allow students time to think and to capitalize on their human tendency to fill silence and thus respond.

Because students often are not familiar with reflective learning, it is helpful for facilitators to begin with simple, practice reflection on fairly neutral material, then gradually move to reflection that increasingly focuses on students' own service-learning experiences. For instance, in the dramatic monologue example, students may need to reflect upon their own attitudes toward the unattractive features of aging. Requiring them to admit immediately that they need to confront and overcome an initial distaste for life in a nursing home might turn them away from reflective thinking altogether. To move gradually toward challenging reflection they might begin by reflecting on what they need to take with them on their service assignments and why. They might then reflect on previous experiences with very old people and nursing homes and in this way gradually move to reflecting on their uncomfortable feelings

The following describes questions used to implement specific interrogative, emotion-based, critical-thinking, metaphoric and symbolic reflection activities. As the descriptions reveal, reflection activity questions are brief and limited in number, thus easy for facilitating team members to remember as they teach students to reflect in ways that are continuous, connected, challenging and contextualized. The questions are also easy for students to remember as they accept responsibility for taking the time to reflect on all aspects of their service-learning.

Interrogative Reflection – Students' answers to brief, generic questions help them map and explore experience. Interrogative reflection can be used at any point in a service-learning experience.

Name	Reflection Questions	Thinking Encouraged
Probes	<ul><li>Who?</li><li>What?</li><li>Where?</li><li>When?</li><li>How?</li><li>Why</li></ul>	1. Elicits perceptions and ideas about content, process and people 2. Leads from simple recall through analysis to interpretation
"Cool" Questions	<ul><li>What?</li><li>So What?</li><li>Now What?</li></ul>	1. Focuses on key elements 2. Encourages search for connections 3. Initiates next step planning

Emotion-Based Reflection - Students recognize how they feel and why in order to gain self-awareness, think creatively and think critically. Emotion-based reflection is particularly useful when students' manifest disorientation and discomfort, or condemn new ideas, events, and others' points of view.

Name	Reflection Questions	Thinking Encouraged
Transformative Thinking	<ul><li>What is disturbing here?</li><li>What are our assumptions about people/ things involved?</li><li>What are our assumptions about the processes used?</li><li>What different assumptions can we consider?</li><li>How could we try out these new ways of thinking?</li></ul>	1. Helps lead through immediate emotional reactions to understanding of own perspective 2. Encourages development of mental flexibility, tolerance for ambiguity, and increases capacities to make meaning from experience. (See Mezirow, 1994, and discussions of Rogers and Maslow in Joyce et al. 2000)

Critical-Thinking Reflection – Students' use of formal thinking heuristics helps them reason toward hypotheses, and apply principles and propositions to their experiences.

Name	Reflection Questions	Thinking Encouraged
Inductive Thinking	• What did you see, hear, notice? • How can you group these perceptions, on what basis? • How can you relate groups and why? • What ideas do the relationships between groups suggest?	1. Elicits perceptions and ideas about content, process and people 2. Initiates conceptualization through category justification and naming 3. Encourages exploration of relationships between concepts 4. Leads to formation of propositions and hypotheses (See Bruner and Taba in Joyce et al., 2000)
Deductive Thinking	• What is the idea, principle, proposition, hypothesis we are studying? • What did you see, hear, notice that supports this principle and why? • What did you see, hear, notice that opposes this principle and why?	1. Encourages reference to and validation of advance organizers—propositions and principles provided at the outset of service-learning (See Ausubel, 2000) 2. Requires justified discrimination of experience relevant and not relevant to advance organizer

Metaphoric Reflection – Students compare aspects of their experiences to apparently unrelated things and ideas that their facilitator suggests or that they themselves suggest and in doing so, develop new concepts and perspectives. (See discussion of Synectics in Joyce et al. 2000.)

Name	Questions	Thinking Encouraged
Personal Metaphor	• How does what you are learning or what you are doing to serve make you feel like a computer (or any thing suggested by student or teacher)? • How are parts of your experience like parts of the computer and why?	1. Helps objectify own feelings 2. Encourages flexibility in thinking about own feelings 3. Encourages extended analysis of own feelings
Direct Metaphor	• How is (an aspect of learning or service) like an apple (or any thing suggested by student or teacher)? • Which parts of your experience correspond to which parts of the apple and why?	1. Suggests new frames of reference for perceptions that can promote new integrations of meaning and new perspectives 2. Encourages analytical thinking
Warring Ideas	• How is your experience (academic or service) sadly happy, excitingly boring, untruthfully honest, warmly cold (or any conflicting concepts suggested by student or teacher)?	1. Encourages close analysis of experience to find bridges between opposite descriptors 2. Promotes new integrations of meaning and new perspectives on experiences

Symbolic Reflection – Students use things to represent and explore aspects of their experiences.

Name	Questions	Thinking Encouraged
Personal Icons	• What physical object would you use as an icon to represent this experience? • Why would you choose this icon?	1. Helps identify most personally meaningful features of experience 2. Encourages selection of image that will represent the experience through time and can help share it with others

In closing this discussion of reflection activities, it is essential to state again that reflection activities are sets of questions students learn to ask themselves so that they will gain meaning from academic and service experiences. Project team members begin by helping students learn what questions to ask and how and when to ask them. As they work with students, team members have opportunities to move them toward confident independence as learners by helping them take responsibility for their own reflection. Ideally, as students use the reflection so central to service-learning, they will grow in their capacities to think reflectively about all their school work, all of their interactions with others, their own personal perspectives and about how the meanings they construct from this reflection relate to their own lives and the lives of others.

Conceptualizing Activities

Students bring the new understandings they gain from reflection to the forefront of their thinking by engaging in conceptualizing activities within their cooperative- learning groups. These activities result in oral, written, constructed or performed products that represent and explain students' new understandings both to themselves and to others. They are activities that bring closure to individual reflective learning experiences and are usually brief in nature. Results can often be used as part of larger-scale culminating events that project teams and students use in the fourth and celebratory phase of the collaborative service-learning model.

As with reflection activities, the procedure for using conceptualizing activities is generally the same across activities. Project team members who have worked with students through a reflection activity, ask their cooperative learning groups to express their new understandings using a particular conceptualizing activity. The facilitator allots a specific amount of time to the activity, usually no more than five or ten minutes, and outlines whatever steps are necessary. Students work on the activities independently, recording results in their journals whenever possible, or using simple materials the facilitator provides as necessitated by the nature of the activity. When students complete their products they share them with their groups.

Not every reflective learning experience requires closure with a conceptualization activity. In some cases students gain new insights and understandings in clear and often startling ways as a result of reflection. By recording these directly in their journals, they engage in written conceptualization and thus obviate the need for further activity. In other instances, however, a facilitating project team member may see a particular need for students in a cooperative-learning group to stabilize the results of their reflection and thus helps them sum up with a formal conceptualizing activity. Or, the teacher may want the entire class to make manifest what they have gained from a particular reflective learning experience and asks all students to use one or more formal conceptualizing activities.

Types of Conceptualizing Activities

The following describes ways project team members can help students visibly conceptualize the new ideas and perspectives they gain from reflecting on their academic study and service experience. Use of the activities is predicated on students' keeping of journals that include their notes about academic work, service experience and results of reflection. Descriptions indicate where students can use blank pages in their journals to conceptualize and where facilitators will need to provide handouts or construction materials for the activities. Activities are ordered within categories so that those useful with younger students or students who are less familiar with reflection appear first, and those useful with older students or students who are more skilled with reflection appear last.

Graphic Summarizing and Sharing - Students use graphics to summarize key ideas and processes that unfolded as they progressed through their service-learning experiences. Summaries include ideas and information drawn from academic and service experience and resulting from reflection.

Name	Instructions to Students	Materials Needed
Concept Spins	1. Choose the most important idea from your reflection and write it horizontally in spaced capital letters across the center of your paper. 2. Use each letter in this key-idea word as part of another vertical word or phrase the relates to or expands upon the key-idea word.	Blank journal page and an example that shows how support words and phrases may run vertically through the horizontal key word
Word Webs	1. Choose 3 (or more) key words from your reflection. 2. List 3-5 important features of each key word. 3. Use labeled lines including Cs (causes), RI (results in), TSA (the same as), IPA (is part of) and ST (suggests that) to show how key words relate to each other and to their features.	Blank journal page and list of connecting terms and their initials

STRATEGIES FOR DESIGNING REFLECTIVE LEARNING EXPERIENCES * 209

Name	Instructions to Students	Material Needed
Kolb Wheels	1. Set up or obtain a Kolb wheel that is labeled "Experience" at the 12 o'clock position, "Understandings from Reflection" at the 3 o'clock position, "New Ideas" at the 6 o'clock position and "My Resulting Actions" at the 9 o'clock position. 2. Use journal notes to describe your service-learning experience briefly with words or phrases inside the wheel beneath each label.	Blank journal page or handout of labeled Kolb wheel (See Eyler, Giles & Schmeide, 1996)

Insight Identification and Sharing — These activities use the metaphor of light to help students express and share insights resulting from reflection on their service-learning experiences.

Name	Instructions to Students	Material Needed
Light Bulb	1. Look back over your reflection notes and recall which idea seemed most like a light bulb going on in your head. 2. Draw a light bulb that is about 2" x 2" in size. 3. Inside the light bulb write a phrase explaining the important idea that came to you. 4. Use "shine lines" around the bulb to note what you may do differently because of this idea.	Blank journal page or handout containing light bulb image
Stars	1. Draw a star the way you like to draw it—as a five-pointed, six-pointed or "explosive" irregular shape. 2. Review your reflection notes to identify an "explosive" new understanding you see. 3. Write a word or phrase in the center of your star that explains this idea 4. Write words or phrases that explain what helped you come to this idea in the star's points.	Blank journal page or handout containing star image

Proposition Identification and Sharing — These activities help students frame insights and understandings they gain from reflection on academic learning and service experiences as ideas that they can validate in future experiences.

Name	Instructions to Students	Materials Needed
Sentence Frames	1. Review your reflection ideas and decide which seem most important to tell other people about. 2. Complete the following sentences as a way to share your idea. • The idea I want to share with others is that _____. • I want to share this idea because _____.	Blank page in journal or handout containing sentence frames

210 * CHAPTER X

Microthemes	1. Develop a thesis statement based on your reflection ideas. 2. Write your thesis statement in sentence form on a vertical 5" x 8" card. 3. Support your thesis statement with an idea drawn from class work, an idea drawn from service experience and an idea drawn from your personal value system.	5" x 8" blank file card and samples of thesis statements that might be drawn from reflection on experience other than the one students are working with. (See Bean, Drenk & Lee, 1982)

Problem Identification and Sharing – These activities help students express personal challenges and community problems they become aware of through reflection of service-learning.

Name	Instructions to Students	Materials Needed
Three Wishes	1. Think about needs you learned about during service-learning and reflection on your experiences—others' and your own needs. 2. Identify what you would ask for and why if you had three wishes in a one-page paper.	Blank page in journal or three-section handout
Conversations	1. Recall a community problem you became aware of during service-learning or reflection on your experiences. 2. Write a half-page conversation in which a student helps another person understand your identified community problem.	Blank page in journal
Cartoons and Comic Strips	1. Draw an editorial type cartoon in which you call attention to a community problem you became aware of during service-learning or reflection on your experiences 2. Choose a favorite comic strip character and write a four-frame strip that shows the character recognizing either a community problem or a personal growth need.	Blank page in journal or blank 4-frame comic strip handout

Values Identification and Sharing – These activities help students identify new values resulting from their service-learning experiences and to identify what is important to them in this way of learning.

Name	Instructions to Students	Materials Needed
Talismans	1. Recall your service-learning experience and review your reflection on it to identify 3-5 values that have become clear to you and that you want to remember. 2. Choose a symbol for each value and integrate these in a design on a talisman.	Wooden or paper disk 2-3 inches in diameter
Triangles	1. Think about service-learning as a way to learn, and review your reflections service-learning. 2. Draw an equilateral triangle and label it to show the three qualities you believe are most important about service-learning as a way to learn.	Blank page in journal or handout of equilateral triangle with 5 inch base

STRATEGIES FOR DESIGNING REFLECTIVE LEARNING EXPERIENCES * 211

Commitment Identification and Sharing – These activities help students recognize ways to continue to make service a part of their lives and to share these commitments with others.

Name	Instructions to Students	Materials Needed
Banners	1. Think back on your service-learning experiences and review your reflections on them. 2. Identify a way in which you will continue to commit to service. 3. Create a banner about your commitment that you want to wave for service-learning.	Paper banner shape
Pledges	1. Use your reflections on service-learning experiences to identify the kinds of commitment service-learning can strengthen in all who become involved in this method. 2. Write a one-sentence pledge that a person embarking on service-learning could use to affirm allegiance to these commitments.	Blank page in journal or pledge sheet handout

As stated earlier, conceptualizing activities are brief and students use them to express the ideas, insights and understandings they gain from reflection. They are intended for sharing within cooperative-learning groups or the class, and not meant to be disseminated beyond the project. In some cases, however, students may wish to use the products they develop through conceptualizing activities as part of their end-of-project celebrations. They may want, for example to make displays of graphic organizers, talismans, or pledges. They may want to decorate with banners and symbols. What is important here is that students themselves, decide whether or not to share conceptualizing activity results beyond the project.

Conceptualization activities bring a service-learning project team's reflective learning experiences—the instructional sequences or sessions that comprise the team's instructional plan–to completion. Figure 10.3 reviews the content and process of these sequences as they were introduced in Chapter VI.

Figure 10.3 Content and Process of Reflective Learning Experiences Within Instructional Planning for Service-Learning

(1) Focus Students on Academic, Service and Personal Experience with *Multiple-Intelligence Cooperative Learning Activities*

(2) Guide Students' 4 Cs Reflection on Experience with *Interrogative, Emotion-Based, Critical-Thinking, Metaphoric, and Symbolic Activities*

(3) Help Students Develop Concepts from Reflection with *Activities that Elicit Summaries, Insights, Propositions, Problem Identification, Values, and Commitments*

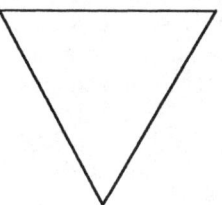

Figure 10.3 shows that reflective learning experiences entail thoughtful design and implementation that is likely to take more time and energy than traditional classroom instruction. But teachers and project teams can meet the challenge of designing reflective instruction in three ways. First, as explained earlier, they can use what they know best to focus students on learning from service: teachers can use their classroom materials and learning activities and other team members can use information and resources from their areas of expertise. Second, project teams can require themselves and their students to use journals. Third, project team members can share responsibility for facilitating reflection and conceptualizing activities just as they share responsibilities for facilitating focusing activities.

Using Journals to Integrate Reflective Learning

Implementation of reflective learning experience through the process described in Figure 10.3 depends upon the use of journals. Students and project team members manage and provide substance for these experience by keeping brief, but regular records of what they do during academic and service aspects of focusing activities, what they think and come to understand through reflection, and how they conceptualize from their reflection. A simple and straightforward approach that captures the three dimensions of reflective learning experiences has students and team members use spiral binders (so no pages are lost). They set aside a page for each reflective learning experience, divide it into three sections entitled "focusing," "reflection," and "conceptualizing" and make brief notes in each section as the overall experience evolves. Keeping the notes related to component activities together in this way helps team members become aware of emerging ideas across the experience that they may want students to especially consider, and it helps students see important aspects of study and service and as they reflect and conceptualize.

Sharing Responsibility for
Reflection and Conceptualizing Activities

Team members can learn how to assist teachers in guiding student reflection and conceptualizing activities by becoming familiar with the activities and practicing their use. They can begin by looking over all the activities and selecting one or two each for reflection and conceptualizing to concentrate on. They memorize the questions or instructions for students, then practice using the activities with friends or other team members. Next they practice with three or four students, making clear that the session is a practice one and asking students to provide feedback about how activity implementation might be improved. Finally when all team members feel confident in their grasp of the activity's use, they can use it as part of a reflective learning experience within the team's overall instructional plan. When project team members learn how to facilitate student reflection and conceptualizing, they add resources to the team and continue to help students learn from many teachers. They can also use the skills they develop in other aspects of their own lives and work. In addition, they are likely to enhance their own capacities to reflect and conceptualize, particularly about learning itself and the many opportunities today's students have to learn. From this their citizen awareness can increase.

In Conclusion

Service-learning project teams sequence their instructional plans as reflective learning experiences that consist of focusing, reflection and conceptualizing activities. Focusing activities help students attend to particular aspects of the academic, service and personal experiences that provide content for their service learning. Teams shape focusing activities to appeal to and activate students' multiple intelligences and engage them in cooperative learning. Reflection activities help students analyze academic and service experiences in ways that lead to new ideas, insights and understandings. They help students reflect from emotional, cognitive and metaphoric perspectives. Conceptualizing activities help students stabilize the meanings they gain from reflection by expressing and sharing those meanings in written and visual products. These activities are brief and intimate in nature. Teams strengthen their capacities to integrate reflective learning experiences by requiring themselves and students to keep journals throughout service-learning projects and by sharing responsibility for the design and implementation of focusing, reflection and conceptualizing activities.

Activities for Increasing Understanding

1. Continue working on the practice instructional plan you began in Chapter VI activities by doing the following:
   a. Shape each focusing activity in terms of a different intelligence.
   b. Structure each focusing activity so that it uses at least one of the five cooperative-learning elements.
   c. Select one reflection activity to use with each focusing activity.
   d. Select a conceptualizing activity to use with each focusing activity.
2. Integrate your activities into an instructional plan that uses Figure 10.2 as a model. Describe the activities that you and your imaginary team members will facilitate, what students will do as they focus, reflect and conceptualize, and how service will integrate with classroom activity throughout the plan.
3. Write a half-page explanation of how you plan to help students and team members in your project use journals throughout the project. Include explanation of how you will introduce and monitor journal use.

Chapter XI: Strategies for Evaluating Projects and Celebrating Growth

"Here's our piece for getting feedback from the administrators and staff at the Family Services Center. We're not sure we did it right, and I don't see how you're going to make sense of all this—let alone share it all with anyone else." Fatigue edges student Rachel Killing's voice.

Juliana Baxter, state university education professor and project evaluator reads over the sheet Rachel hands her. "This is solid, Rachel. Right on target. I could implement your part of our evaluation plan myself if you weren't able to." Juliana squares Rachel's sheet on the pile in front of her and addresses the team. "All your pieces look good, and you'll have them implemented by the end of next week. Then next Monday, you, Holly, can help us use inductive thinking to make some judgments about information we've collected."

"I hope I can." Social Studies teacher Holly Martinez grimaces. "I want to practice using inductive thinking at least once more with my fifth-period class before we actually use it with the team."

Rachel, now relieved, jumps in. "It was great when we tried it last week with the biographies of famous women. You'll do fine with our evaluation results, Ms. Martinez. I just hope Cheryl and I will do as well helping the class decide on a culminating activity and good dissemination strategies. Will you help us, Mr. Zorn?"

"You bet! And I found some good ideas for us on the Internet. We can look at them after this meeting," says parent Tucker Zorn.

Chapter Focus

This project team is in the final phase of the collaborative service-learning model. Members are assembling the team's evaluation plan and preparing to analyze and interpret the information that implementation of that plan produces. They are also looking ahead to sharing outcomes of their project. As the scenario suggests, in order to reach this point and move a project forward to conclusion, members of a service-learning project team take responsibility for carrying out several tasks. Each member creates and carries out a part of the team's overall evaluation plan. At least one member of the team learns how to lead the rest of the team in using inductive thinking to analyze evaluation results, and some or all team members help students who engaged in service-learning celebrate the growth that evaluation reveals. The purpose of this chapter is to detail ways team members individually and as a group contribute to evaluation plan development and implementation, explain how they use inductive thinking to analyze and interpret the information they gather, and describe a range of activities and strategies they and students can use to celebrate and share results.

Team Members' Responsibilities for Evaluation Planning

Service-learning project teams collaboratively construct and implement project evaluation plans. To do this, individual team members agree to find or develop instruments the team will use to gather student-outcomes, project-impact and team-effectiveness information and to describe in writing how they will administer the instruments, score them and summarize results. Team members then assemble results of individual work in an overall project evaluation plan.

The Blue Mesa project evaluation plan presented in Chapter VII and repeated in Table 11.1 provides a model for collaborative evaluation-plan development. In this event-design example, students learned how to express numbers in alternate forms in the classroom, used these learnings to collect data about traffic at a busy intersection, then organized their data in a presentation to their county council that supports installation of a traffic light at the intersection. As a model, the Blue Mesa team's collaboratively developed evaluation plan shows the three areas in which project teams need to gather information in order to fully evaluate their projects, and it shows that teams systematically gather this information. It also highlights examples of team members' areas of individual responsibility within the overall plan via shaded rows in each of these information-gathering areas. In each area, individual team members contribute to the overall plan by identifying particular instruments that will be used and laying out procedures for administering, scoring or coding, and summarizing the information the instruments produce. The discussion which follows Table 11.1 describes how service-learning project team members use the evaluation model it represents to develop individual components for their own project evaluation plans.

Table 11.1 Evaluation Plan for Seventh-Grade Pro-Traffic-Light Service-Learning Project

Instrument and Team Member Responsible	Logistics	Materials	Scoring and or Coding	Summary Format
Academic Area				
State Standards Test – Items 33, 34, 45 – expressing numbers in equivalent forms Mr. Vishinsky	School staff administers state test three months after project completion. Obtain results for use next year in seeking new SL project support	State test forms	Each SL student's total score on 3 relevant items using state test-item score values: Item 33 - Percents, value = 3 Item 34 – Fractions, value = 4 Item 45 – Decimals, value = 3	Array of item scores and total scores for SL students vs. item and total scores for all students tested on items 33, 34, and 45
Criterion Referenced Test of ability to express numbers in food drive example in equivalent forms Mr. Vishinsky	Administer in regular class period to all students. Allow 30 min. after 10 min. for review – Week 3, Day 3.	Seven-item printed CRT based on stimulus material describing food and money collected in a food drive	24 points total score based on 14 number-conversion related tasks that range from 1 to 3 points each in value	Summary showing students' scores by task with class average for each task; total on all tasks for each student with average score on all tasks for class
Service Area				
Anecdotal Observation of students' dress at council meeting, re CL group dress guidelines Student CL group reps and Ms. Selkirk	Ms. Selkirk takes photographs as appropriate throughout 2 hour council meeting. Student reps evaluate – Week 3, Day 1	Camera and film or disk for at least 5 photographs of students arriving at and presenting to council meeting	5 photographs scored for evidence of 3 CL group dress criteria, each instance receives 1 point	Summary showing criteria score for each photo, summary of all points for each criteria and statement ranking criteria in photos from most to least evident
Rating of student use of data collection and checking process Sgt. Pandars	Implement as each group completes data collection on site daily Week 2, Days 1-5	Printed traffic record sheet sectioned for cars, trucks, motorcycles with columns for whole number total of each and, fractions and percents of all vehicles	Student data sheets scored 1 point each, for correct record of traffic; counts in whole numbers, fractions and percents; and partner's accuracy certification	Summary showing students' scores by task with class average for each task; total on all tasks for each student with average score on all tasks for class

Table 11.1 Continued

			Personal Growth Area
Experience Analysis of students' perceived best CL group contribution Mr. Vishinsky & Sgt. Penders	Administer in regular class period to all students. Allow 30 min. after 10 min. for student review and questions – Week 3, Day 2	Printed prompt: Use your journal to review CL group work. Identify your best CL contribution, explain why it was best, suggest ways you can build on this kind of contribution in future group work.	Papers rated on identification of CL elements (3 points each), number of justifications (1 point each) and ways to build on contributions (1 point each)	Summary describing elements identified and their frequency, kinds of justifications and their frequency and kinds of contributions and their frequency

			Project Impact	
Client Feedback – Council's perceptions of students' contributions Students	Distribute to all council members at beginning of council meeting, collect at end - Week 3, Day 1	Printed 5"x 8" cards asking council members to list student contributions to meeting, rate overall service and willingness to invite future student input	Contributions categorized and coded excellent, good, fair, poor ratings tallied, yes/no for inviting future student input tallied	Summary of contributions most/least frequently identified, percent of total for each, percent yes/no for inviting future student input
Community Partner Feedback – Traffic Division's perceptions of students' potential as future project partners Sgt. Penders	Complete in own office during Week 3 by end of Day 2	Form asking Sgt. Penders to list student contributions, rate overall service and possibility of student partnering in appropriate future projects	Number and types of contributions, rating 4-1 excellent, good, fair, poor, yes/no for future work with students.	Summary listing student services, rating overall service and describing division's willingness to involve students in future appropriate projects

			Project-Team Self-Evaluation	
Process Evaluation – Team rankings of use of cooperative learning elements All team members	Complete in 1-hour, after- school meeting – Week 3, Day 2	Form for team collaborative ranking of use of positive interdependence, face-to-face interaction, accountability, group skills, group processing	Evidence of use of elements found in journals coded by element and tallied	Summary ranking of use of process with anonymous interpretive comment from team members
Product Evaluation – Team rating of selected plans and activities on three efficacy criteria All Team Members	Complete in 1-hour, after- school meeting – Week 3, Day 3	Form for team collaborative rating of instructional plan & materials re CL group guidelines of collaborative development, clarity and coherence, use	Rating of 4-1 for excellent, good, fair, poor tallied	Group rating of instructional plan and materials with anonymous interpretive comment from team members

Identifying Instruments Used to Collect Evaluation Information

The first task of a team member who is contributing to construction of a service-learning project evaluation plan is to identify the instrument he or she will use to collect data and information for his or her area of responsibility. In some cases team members can find already developed instruments for collecting student outcomes, project-impact and team process/product evaluation information by reviewing the service-learning literature or turning to Internet resources such as the Compendium of Assessment and Research Tools for Measuring Education and Youth Development Outcomes (CART) and the National Service-learning Clearinghouse. In other cases, teams decide to create their own instruments for these three evaluation areas. This book can help them do that.

Team members can obtain information for creating instruments to measure student outcomes from Chapter V and Chapter IX. Chapter V provides a general summary of eight strategies that can be used to create instruments that measure student outcomes of service-learning. The chapter also suggests the time and value considerations associated with the use of each strategy. Chapter IX details ways team members can operationalize the eight strategies as measurement instruments to use in their own projects.

Team members can obtain initial information about ways to determine the impact of their projects on community partners and service clients and about engaging their own project teams in self-evaluation from Chapter VII. Additionally, they can find more detailed suggestions about how to create feedback collection instruments in the following discussion.

Collecting Feedback About Project Impact

Collecting feedback is different from measuring student outcomes or outcomes of other project constituents. When teams want to know if their projects contribute to student outcomes, they decide—in advance—what students will be able to do at projects' end. Then they use measurement instruments to determine if students can, in, fact, do those things. When project teams want to know if their projects are valuable to service partners and their clients, they ask them—after the fact—to describe project benefits and their attitudes toward those benefits. Collecting feedback about project impact is a more direct activity than outcomes measurement, and feedback instruments are relatively direct and simple in nature. Members responsible for gathering feedback can create instruments using the three questions suggested in Chapter VII.

- What services did students provide?
- Do you rate the overall service experience as excellent, good, fair or poor?
- Would you like to participate in a service-learning project/receive student services again?

Feedback Collection Forms

Team members can create feedback collection forms by printing the three questions above on a card or sheet in a professional way as shown in Figure 11.1. The form can be used to obtain feedback from service clients or community partners depending on the wording of the first feedback request.

Figure 11.1 Forms for Collecting Service-Learning Project Impact Feedback from Service Partners and Service Clients

---

Service-Learning Participant Feedback Form

1. Please list below the services that students in this project provided to you or to your organization. Include services originally intended as part of the project as well as services that evolved as the project took place.

2. Beside each service you list, please indicate your rating of student performance of that service.

    E=Excellent   G=Good   F=Fair   P=Poor

3. Please circle yes or no to indicate your willingness to be involved with students in future service-learning projects.

    Yes   No

4. Please use the reverse side of this sheet provide below other comments or information that you believe is important to this project or to service-learning itself.

Figure 11.1 shows that though simple, a feedback collection form can gather a good deal of important information. Its request that respondents list the many services students provided, whether these were the intended services or not, helps provide a full picture of what students actually did. Its request that respondents state their positions on the two attitudinal questions encourages respondents to make clear, unequivocal judgments about their own experience with service-learning. Its request for open-ended comment helps generate contextual information that may be useful as the project team integrates feedback results from the first three sections of the form.

Feedback Information Summaries

Team members can summarize results from feedback forms such as the one in Figure 11.1 by creating summary sheets that parallel the form. The first section of such a sheet lists all intended services that students provided in one column and all the project-evolved services students provided in another. Services under each heading can then be categorized, and categories can be ranked in terms of greatest to least number of instances in the category. The second section of the sheet shows the percent of responses at each of the four rating levels for each service noted, and the third section records the percent of respondents willing and unwilling to be involved in future service-learning projects. The fourth section then categorizes all the open-ended responses elicited by the form. The team member who has responsibility for collecting feedback information describes this summary in the team's evaluation plan. When the team member has collected and summarized feedback, he or she uses the summary in a whole-team inductive-thinking analysis session that examines all of evaluation information team members collect for patterns and relationships and integrates findings in positive and needs-improvement judgments about the project overall.

Collecting Project Team Self-Evaluation Information

Chapter VII introduces project-team self-evaluation as team analysis of ways its processes and products contributed to the overall success of the project. The chapter proposes that teams use the elements of cooperative learning as criteria for evaluating their own processes, and service-learning context criteria for evaluating their products. Explanation of how to use these two sets of criteria continues here based on the following understandings. Team self-evaluation is similar to outcomes measurement in that it compares actual team processes and products to pre-determined goals. Self-evaluation goals, however, are not specific outcome objectives. They are ideals rather than performance expectations, and when teams engage in self-evaluation, they seek information about their progress toward these ideals and about ways that they can improve that progress. Thus, in evaluating their own group processes, teams use the five elements of cooperative learning as ideal criteria and determine with evidence from their journals and project experiences the degree to which they as a team approached these ideals. To evaluate their instructional products, teams rate the materials they produced in terms of their appropriateness within the context of service-learning: their collaborative development, clarity and coherence, and their usefulness to project participants.

Team Process Evaluation Strategy

Project teams can evaluate their own processes by coming together for about an hour and using three steps. The team member responsible for gathering team process information acts as a facilitator and lists the five cooperative-learning elements as ideals on individual sections of the board or sheets of news print: face-to-face promotive interaction, positive interdependence, individual accountability, interpersonal and small group skills, and group process reflection. Next team members use material from their journals and experiences they remember to list specific instances of the team's use of each element on the appropriate sheet. The team discusses all postings to arrive at a team rating for each cooperative-learning element using a 1-4, low to high scale. The team member facilitator then expresses these ratings by cooperative learning element in a summary for use in inductive analysis of all project evaluation information.

Team Product Evaluation Strategy

The same three process-evaluation steps help teams judge the quality of their instructional products. To use the steps for this aspect of self-evaluation, the facilitator lists the three service-learning efficacy ideals—collaborative product development, clarity and coherence, and usefulness to those for whom the product was designed—on the board or on sheets of newsprint. Now the team examines the instructional products they created and recalls use of those products to find evidence of meeting the three ideals. Each piece of evidence gains credibility as it is offered and discussed, then validated by the team as an indication of meeting the criteria. For instance, a team evaluating the reflective learning activity sequences it used to orient students to their service site accepts a team member's suggestion that these sequences are clear and coherent because they list student and facilitator activities in steps and arrange activities so that students learn basics first, then move to applications. The same team also accepts another team member's suggestion that library-reserved readings developed to teach students an academic principle relevant to their service experiences were not useful because only three of 28 students checked them out. The responsible team member who is acting as facilitator summarizes findings for each of the three instructional product ideals on a single sheet for use in upcoming inductive analysis of all evaluation information.

In summary, team members who take responsibility for helping construct their project evaluation plans, can use guidelines in this book to create instruments for gathering evaluation information about student outcomes, project impact and team process and products. Table 11.2 summarizes information that will help them in their work. It identifies the three sources of evaluation information for service-learning projects, names strategies/instruments useful for collecting information from these sources, notes service-learning-related considerations associated with strategy/instrument use and indicates the chapters in this book where information on creating each instrument can be found.

Developing Guides for Instrument Use

Once individual team members have in hand the instruments they intend to use to collect evaluation information, they construct the guides for instrument use that will fill out the overall evaluation plan for their project. The format shown in Table 11.3 facilitates construction of these components and their integration in the evaluation plan.

Table 11.2 Summary of Resources for Creating Service-Learning Project Evaluation Instruments in *Serve and Learn: Implementing and Evaluating Service-Learning in Middle and High Schools*

Evaluation Plan Component	Strategies/Instruments	Service-Learning Considerations	Chapter Location
Student Outcomes Measurement			
• Academic Area	State Standards Tests	Identify "subtest" for service-learning standards-based academic outcome using items from state test related to the standard	Chapter V and Chapter VIII
• Service Area	Teacher Constructed CRTs: Paper-Pencil, Performance, Problem-Solving Tests	Write domain specifications to make clear what students are to do as indicators of meeting academic expectations	
	Rating Scales Anecdotal Observation	Recognize effects of observers on behavior, make several observations with several observers, use results in conjunction with other indicators of competent and caring service	
• Personal Growth Area	Survey Forms Interview Questions Focus Group Questions Experience Analysis Prompts	Develop using CRT design steps Develop with six-step design process Develop with four-step design process Avoid facilitator influence during sessions Have students keep journals to prepare for essay test	
Project Impact			
• Community Partner Impact	Feedback Forms and Questionnaires	Allow space for listing services, rating overall service, indicating yes/no for future service-learning participation and open ended comments on particular service and service-learning in general	Chapter VII and Chapter X
• Service Client Impact			
Team Self-Evaluation			
• Process	Cooperative Learning Ideals Evidence Sheets Form	Keep team member journal to prepare for rating or ranking of team use of 5 cooperative learning elements	Chapter VII and Chapter X
• Products	Service-learning Context Ideals Rating Sheet	Examine master instructional plan and reflective learning experience sequences for collaborative development, clarity/coherence, usefulness	

Table 11.3 Format for Describing Student Outcomes, Project Impact and Team Self-Evaluation Components

	Evaluation Information Area			
Instrument and Team Member Responsible	**Logistics**	**Materials**	**Scoring and/or Coding**	**Data Summary Format**

As team members select or create instruments to gather evaluation information, they identify the evaluation areas to which these instruments relate. Next, in the first column of the format they name the instruments they will be using together with their own names as responsible administrators. They then determine how the named instrument will be administered and in doing this develop information to record in the "logistics" and "materials" columns of the profile. Next they describe how the instrument is to be scored or coded and how results of instruments use will be displayed. They record this information in the "scoring and/or coding" and "data summary format" columns of their profiles.

Determining How Instruments Will Be Administered

Team members responsible for administering instruments attend to two features of that administration: the unique conditions necessary to use each instrument effectively, and the common conditions associated with effective administration of all instruments. The unique conditions associated with an instrument are essentially self-evident in the instrument's purpose. If, for example, a team member is responsible for giving students a criterion-referenced test of their abilities to identify and name plants that do well in shady locations, and if students will be looking at actual plant samples, the test administrator must make sure that the right kinds of plants are available for students to see. Or if a team member is responsible for conducting interviews with elementary-school students who have received service from a high-school class's math-tutoring project, the interviewer must make sure that there is a private and comfortable place in which to conduct interviews. Team members with instrument-administration responsibilities make sure they determine and specify the procedures for administering their instruments as unique information collection tools by asking and answering the question. "What scheduling, physical arrangements, materials and other conditions must be available to correctly administer this instrument?" As they answer this question they will specify the major part of the administration information they need for the logistics and materials columns in their section of the project evaluation plan.

The common conditions associated with instruments' administration relate generally to the way in which they are presented as printed documents.

Guidelines summarized earlier (p. 177) are worth repeating in full here because they affect both the quantity and quality of information an instrument can collect. These guidelines are as follows:

- Instruments should be presented in a professional manner with respect to paper quality, print font, visual and graphic components, layout of parts, spelling, punctuation and capitalization.
- Instrument components should be adjusted to meet needs of particular respondents such as very young children, non-English speaking or older people.
- Instruments should include clear directions for their use and all stimulus and reference materials that respondents will need.
- Instruments should not contain information that does not relate to their purpose or use.
- Instruments should make clear whether or not respondents are required to participate and how responses will be used.
- Instruments should assure respondents that results will be treated with appropriate confidentiality and should be packaged to protect confidentiality as appropriate.

Team members indicate that these guidelines will pertain to the formal presentation of the instruments for which they are responsible when they state in the materials column of the Blue Mesa plan that materials will include "5 x 8 cards asking council members to list student contributions," a "printed writing prompt," or "printed traffic record sheet." In effect, the use of the word "printed" (and also the word "form") in the instrument administration guide indicates that the instrument will be presented in terms of the six guidelines for formal presentation stated above. Team members can do much to ensure that their instruments follow these guidelines by asking a teacher or friend or colleague with good editing skills to review and proofread the instruments for which they are responsible well before they are to be used.

Summarizing Collection and Display of Information

Evaluation instruments produce either quantitative data or qualitative data. Quantitative data appears in the form of scores that result either from the number of times a response occurs, or from values assigned to the occurrence of particular responses. In the Blue Mesa evaluation plan, for example, students will complete an experience-analysis essay in which they identify their best cooperative-learning group contributions, explain why they are best and suggest ways they can build on these contributions in future group work. The team member responsible for this instrument decides that remembered contributions will be awarded three points each, one point will be awarded for each justification and one point will be awarded for each potential future use of the contribution. This assignment of points helps the team member weight scores according to what the full team thinks is most important for students to have learned about cooperative learning, in this instance, students' own ability to use it. Weights here, could be changed however, by assigning more points to justifications or future uses—depending on what the team member and team believe is most important to find out about students' growth in cooperative learning.

Surveys with their scaled responses also produce quantitative data as do observational rating scales and state standards tests. What is important is that team members make clear the meanings of the numbers and scores their instruments produce. As they enter information in the scoring/coding section of their evaluation plan rows, they need to make statements such as this one from the Blue Mesa evaluation plan, "Student data sheets scored 1 point each for: correct record of traffic, counts shown as whole numbers, fractions and percents, and partner's accuracy certification." The plan then specifies that scores for the group will be arrayed in a manner almost invariably used with quantitative data—in a summary showing students' scores on each task with the class average for the task and showing students' total test scores with the average test score for the class. An evaluation plan row that specifies the meaning of the scores its instrument produces and calls for summary of the central tendencies in these scores facilitates analysis and interpretation of score result during the inductive thinking phase of evaluation.

Qualitative data results are usually expressed in descriptive statements such as "Students identified their courage to ask questions as critical to their success at service sites." or "Students were only moderately interested in serving again during the community clean-up day." Interestingly, quantitative techniques often help produce qualitative descriptive statements such as these. While team members who are analyzing information and ideas expressed in interviews and focus groups can use intuition to get a subjective sense of what respondents saw of interest or value, they can get a better sense by coding participants' responses. They can do this using pre-determined codes, or by finding recurring ideas in what respondents say and assigning codes to them, then summarizing ideas offered in terms of their frequency. For example the Blue Mesa evaluation plan includes information from a student focus group. It specifies use of codes in the following way. "Identified needs of parents (np), identified needs of council (nc), conflicts (x) coded. Appropriate codes assigned to other statements." It then specifies data summary as statements based on frequency of needs in each category. Thus, when team members who facilitate the focus group look over their transcripts of the session, they tally the number of statements related to the predetermined codes "np," "nc," and "x." And when they find students referring frequently to council in-fighting, and parent lack of budgetary knowledge, they code these new ideas as "fc" and "bp," respectively. They then tally the number of statements within each of the five codes to make statements such as "Students seemed more aware of parent concerns for safety than of council needs to distribute limited resources," "Students noticed several instances of council in-fighting," and "Students made few clear statements about conflicts between parents' and council needs." Again, an evaluation plan row that specifies how ideas resulting from instrument use are to be coded for meaning and presented in descriptive statements facilitates analysis and interpretation of these descriptions during the inductive thinking phase of evaluation.

In summary, team members contribute to the development of their project's overall evaluation plan by taking responsibility for the identification of particular instruments and by developing administration guides for those instruments that specify the logistics of their use, the materials that will be needed, scoring and/or coding procedures and ways results will be summarized. Team members develop their guides in this consistent way so that the overall project evaluation plan will be consistent when it is assembled. They also use this consistent approach so that, if necessary, someone else can carry out their responsibilities for identifying (selecting or creating) and administering their instruments, assembling data and information produced, and displaying results. This in turn assures that evaluation goes forward, instruments are used, and the information they produce is summarized in ways that promote team analysis and interpretation through inductive thinking.

Using Inductive Thinking as an Analytical and Interpretive Tool

Inductive thinking is a critical-thinking strategy that project teams use with evaluation results to reason from specific information through observed patterns and relationships to generalizations. Chapter VII suggests that team members responsible for particular evaluation instruments can analyze and interpret results of instrument use in this way by working with non-team partners through a five-step inductive-thinking process. The five steps include describing the instrument, summarizing results of its use, observing patterns in the results, determining relationships among patterns and generalizing from these relationships. These five steps are essentially the same ones described in Chapter X for coding and summarizing qualitative information produced by focus groups. When teams use the inductive-thinking steps in the second stage of project evaluation, however, they apply them to both qualitative and quantitative information—to scores generated by tests and observations as well as to perceptions and attitudes generated by surveys, interviews and focus groups. This broader use of the inductive-thinking process is demonstrated in an example related to a tenth-grade biology class's Seeds for Sustenance (SFS) service-learning project that was described in Chapter VII. In that project, students respond to a call for help from an organization that grows and distributes worldwide, seeds suitable for subsistence farming. The record of the team's use of inductive thinking with the results of a variety of instruments the project team used for evaluation is repeated as Table 11.4

Table 11.4 Inductive Thinking About Tenth-Grade Biology Service-Learning Project Evaluation Results

Instrument	Results	Patterns	Relationships	Generalizations
Academic test: Students recall arid-region subsistence farming strategies taught in class and reinforced in service activities	Cut score = 3 strategies Class Av. = 5 strategies 93% of class at or above cut score	Highest reported: Resistant Seeds, Water Management, Mulching, Windbreaks Lowest reported: Interplanting, Shelter, Resistant Animals	Patterns cluster as: Plant Related Strategies Animal Related Strategies	Students recalled more of the strategies reinforced by service (i.e. plant strategies)
Comparison of actual and expected growth rates of 6 types of oat seeds in students' test plots after 2-weeks of drip water, mulching, cultivating. Analysis of student logs.	27 of 30 of student test gardens showed expected growth rate, 3 did not. 27 of 30 student logs show complete, daily cultivation records, 3 did not.	Students with expected growth rates kept logs, used elevated drips and large mulch chunks. Others had gaps in log records, poor drip runs and used mixed mulch.	Patterns cluster as: Competent use of subsistence growth techniques Incomplete use of techniques	Most students understood and used competent practice and were successful in helping SFS with its seed testing work.
Feedback from SFS Mentors re types of student service, service quality, future service	By frequency, students helped with: Sorting seeds for mailing, testing seed type growth, visitor tours, newsletter articles. 7 students showed unusual skill in test work and publicity	Overall Service Rating – Good Future Return – Yes Give special invitations to highly skilled students	Patterns cluster as: Students as a group did what was needed. Some students showed particular skill/interest in test work and publicity	Students directly or indirectly helped SFS subsistence agriculture mission; some showed particular potential as future interns.
Team Evaluation of its Instructional Products Academic: Readings and video about subsistence agriculture Service: Orientation package	(1-4 = low-high) Collab. Dev – 1 Clarity & Coherence – 4 Usefulness to Students – 2 Collab. Dev – 3 Clarity & Coherence – 4 Usefulness to students - 4	Academic material: Little collaboration in producing, is clear and coherent but not usefully related to SFS thrust. Service Material: Good collaboration, material clear and coherent, reflects actual SFS practices.	Patterns cluster as: Collaboratively developed material rated useful Clear and coherent material may or may not be rated useful.	Instructional materials that were collaboratively developed were rated most useful to students.

As was the case in team development of an evaluation plan, the inductive-thinking record shown in Table 11.4 is a composite of the individual records of team members and their non-team partners who analyzed and interpreted the results of a particular instruments. In the figure, the shaded area represents the inductive thinking record of the team/non-team pair that was responsible for assessing students' abilities to effectively test growth rates of plants as part of their service with the SFS group. The pair completed their record by writing the instrument description from their team's evaluation plan in the first column of their row in the record, and the summarized results of instrument administration in the second column. The pair then looked for patterns within these results and found that students who consistently kept records of their plant cultivation activities had test gardens in which plants reached expected growth rates. They noted this in the third column of their record. Next, the pair clustered the patterns noted in the third column and labeled these clusters in the fourth column as "competent use of subsistence growth techniques" and "incomplete use of techniques." Finally the pair looked across the four columns in its record to generalize their findings for the instrument in the statement that "Most students understood and used competent practice and were successful in helping SFS with its seed testing work."

Because it is an example, Table 11.4 represents ideal possibilities inherent in the use of inductive thinking with evaluation information. However, real life is not always so neat and well organized. As service-learning project teams use the five inductive thinking steps offered here to analyze and interpret their evaluation data and record their generalizations, they need to bear several considerations in mind. The first relates to the steps themselves, their nature and use. The second relates to the importance of practice in strengthening use of inductive thinking to analyze and interpret service-learning evaluation information. The third relates to the nature of the generalizations that use of these steps can produce, and the fourth relates to using these generalizations to judge project worth.

The Nature and Use of Inductive Thinking Steps

Although it is easy to describe inductive thinking as reasoning from the particular to the general and from the concrete to the abstract, inductive thinking itself is a very complex and in some measure indescribable process. Some people engage in inductive thinking with such speed and effectiveness that they seem able to derive meaningful generalizations from very little information and are often said to be making "intuitive leaps." In other instances, people need to have a great deal of particular information, minutely examine each feature of each information item, search for similarities and differences—patterns—among items, abandon patterns and search again, then cluster patterns in a variety of ways before they reach generalizations that seem meaningful and satisfy them. Moreover, in either approach the ability to see patterns and relationships and to bring these together in abstract generalizations depends upon a person's perceptual abilities, the care he or she takes to use these abilities, and the relevant experiences the person can bring to bear on material that he or she is working with. Essentially, the five inductive thinking steps proposed in this chapter at best only approximate inductive thinking. They provide a framework that can help move project team members' thinking from the particular and concrete to the more general and abstract, but they are not inductive thinking itself. Project team members need to use the steps as guides, not as laws. And as they use each step they need to rely on careful analysis of the information items they are attempting to bring together into patterns and relationships and to consider those items in the context of other relevant experiences. As they do this they will activate their own natural inductive thinking processes.

Practicing Inductive Thinking

Project teams can strengthen inductive thinking skills through two levels of practice. The first level can be termed a "safe" level because it involves using the five steps to derive generalizations from information items in which team members, themselves, have little if any personal interest or emotional investments. To use safe practice, a team brainstorms as many individual information items as possible about a neutral topic. For example, in step one, a team might choose the neutral topic "libraries," then in step two, brainstorm information items about libraries such as "contain reference books," "contain fiction," "ask people to be quiet," "check out materials," "charge fines for overdue materials," "staffed by trained librarians," and so forth. Once a large pool of such items is generated, the team uses step three to examine items and categorize them in meaningful ways. These categories are patterns and the team examines them in step four to see if any relate to each other. Finally in step five, the team looks back across relationships, patterns and the items themselves to derive one or more generalizations about libraries.

Next the team moves to the second level of practice with inductive thinking. This can be termed a "risky" level because it may involve team members in drawing generalizations from material that relates to them more personally as will the material produced by the instruments for which they are responsible within their service-learning projects. This level begins with the identification of an everyday social behavior in which most people engage. An example here is the situation in which one person invites another to a party, a sporting contest, a dinner or some such event, and the second person while able to accept, does not want to accept. The second person, however, wishes to maintain good relationships with the first, so offers an excuse. When used to practice inductive thinking, the invitation becomes the first step. Next, team members offer many possible ways to refuse the invitation while maintaining good relationships and these become the information items. Team then analyze the character of the refusals, categorize them in patterns, relate patterns to one another and finally derive generalizations about the kinds of excuses people use when they refuse unwanted invitations.

Teams can practice inductive thinking together to develop a shared understanding of the general process. As team members participate they can think about how they, themselves, categorize and find relationships and thus develop a heightened understanding of their own thought process when they generalize. When team members feel reasonably confident with the five steps, they can then work through practices with the non-team partners they choose to assist them in analyzing and interpreting evaluation results. These sessions will be most effective when they use safe and risky practice with new topics and social behaviors as the source of information items with which to use inductive thinking. Finally, when team/non-team member pairs become confident in their use of the steps they can apply them to the instrument results they are responsible for analyzing.

Stating Generalizations

As explained in Chapter VII, educational evaluation differs from educational research. Educational evaluation seeks to determine the worth of a particular educational project, by analyzing outcomes, impact, and processes and products, then using this information to make value judgments about the project. Educational research, on the other hand, seeks to determine if a given educational method can promote learning outcomes in a wide range of settings. It uses quasi-experimental or experimental design to determine the power of a method to affect learning and make statements about the method's correlation with or cause of particular learning outcomes. Accordingly, when service-learning team members and their partners use inductive thinking to generalize from evaluation information, they express their generalizations as descriptive statements relevant to the particular students, community partners and team members involved in their projects, not as statements of correlation or cause and effect. For instance, as the SFS project team looks at the information across the first row in Table 11.4 they may see the hint of a cause and effect relationship—that the SFS service experience apparently reinforced academic learning. If the team states this as a general, cause-effect relationship they may take a natural, but erroneous next step and decide they have evidence of the benefits of using service-learning across the board. Such a conclusion is not justified. At best, the team can hypothesize a possible connection between recall of academic material and service-learning. To determine if service can be consistently counted on to reinforce academic learning, the team would need to test their hypothesis in a future, controlled-design study. For the purposes of evaluating their project, however, the most valid generalization team members can make based on students' test results is that students in this SFS project recalled more of those subsistence farming strategies that were reinforced by their service experience.

Using Generalizations to Judge Project Worth

Teams use the descriptive generalizations from their inductive-thinking record to make positive judgments and needs-improvement judgments about their projects using frames described in Chapter VII. They make these judgments in different ways for each area in their evaluation plans. When they make judgments for the student outcomes component, they do so in terms of the outcome expectations established in their original student outcomes plans. In the case of the SFS project for example, the notation "cut score=3" in the second column of the first row indicates that the original outcome expectation for students was that they recall at least three arid–region subsistence strategies. The results column of this row notes that the average score for the class was 5 and 92% of the class achieved the cut score of 3 or above. On the basis of these results the team states the positive judgment that "The Seeds For Sustenance project was valuable for students because it helped them remember classroom learnings about arid-region subsistence farming." The team does not, however, disregard its generalization about students' better recall of plant than animal subsistence strategies and makes the needs-improvement judgment that "Student outcomes in the Seeds For Sustenance project could be improved by engaging students in additional academic or service opportunities that increase their knowledge of animal-related, arid-region subsistence strategies."

Teams make positive and needs-improvement judgments about project impact in terms of the ideas that underlie the questions included in their feedback collection forms: project impact was positive, students helped in a variety appropriate ways and new service-learning possibilities emerged. Teams determine the positiveness of the project's impact from service-partners' levels of willingness to have students return. Next, they look at partners' lists of the kinds of services students gave to determine if those services related to the missions and goals of partnering agencies. They also look closely at comments service partners offer to see what features and processes of the project were worthwhile and which need improvement. Here, teams may find suggestions about service focuses that should continue in future projects and features that if added might benefit both students and community partners. In the SFS project for example, the special interest and capabilities of some students as revealed in service-partner feedback may lead to a pre-internship dimension in future SFS service-learning projects.

Teams make positive and needs-improvement judgments about their own process and products by considering possible connections between what they did as a team and relevant outcomes of project participants. As explained earlier, they will not be drawing research-type conclusions about the effects of team interactions on student learning or service-partner contribution, rather they will be looking at possible relationships and suggesting that future versions of their projects adjust these relationships in aid of producing different outcomes. For example, the SFS team sees possible relationships between their own collaborative production of materials and the usefulness of those materials to students. They make a needs-improvement judgment in the form of the statement that "Usefulness of learning material to students in future Seeds For Sustenance projects could be improved by ensuring school and SFS collaboration in the design of all instructional activities for the project."

The judgments that project teams make as a result of evaluation are likely to provide them with much to celebrate. They will be ready to share their perceptions with all who help implement their projects and to inform their wider communities about ways they have used service-learning to build bridges between schools and those communities.

Celebrating Service-Learning

The National Youth Leadership Council is among today's foremost advocates and supporters of service-learning as "a new vision of learning" that "helps young people establish the foundation for a lifetime of meaningful community involvement."(http://www.nylc.org/profile.cfm) The Council endorses celebration as vital to this vision and, accordingly, identified its 2003 National Service-learning Conference theme as "Weaving the Fabric of Community: A Celebration of Service-Learning." Conference organizers, presenters and participants saw celebration as a way to explore their emerging understanding that "service-learning creates a cultural commons—a way for diverse peoples to unite around shared community and generational issues." The conference is concluded, but the celebration continues. In a very real sense, each time a project team and its students celebrate their own service-learning engagement, they partake in and share the vision of service-learning as a way of orienting toward life, one that strengthens the fabric of their communities and increases opportunities for people with many different abilities and views to learn and work fruitfully together.

Project teams and students who have engaged in service-learning are almost invariably ready and eager to celebrate. They are proud of what they have done, see it as building bridges between academic learning and providing genuine service and want to tell others about it. Planning culminating activities for themselves and their affiliates brings their projects to a natural and happy conclusion. To some degree, however, project teams and students may be less aware of the equal importance of celebrating their service-learning with their wider community by disseminating information to individuals and groups who may know nothing about what has happened. When teams and their students celebrate with affiliates, they call attention to the power of service-learning, to its challenges and opportunities as a learning method. This builds internal, contextual support for future projects. When teams and students celebrate with the wider community, they call attention to its value to the community. This builds external resources for the future. Thus, both dimensions of celebration work to strengthen the case for service learning and built support for its extended use.

Two Dimensions of Celebration

To help project teams and their students fully share service-learning as a new vision of learning that creates a cultural commons, this section describes two types of celebration—culminating activities and dissemination strategies—

and provides examples of each. The examples are offered as ideas, suggestions, and springboards that teams and students can use to shape their own, unique celebrations in ways that Wells (1996) identifies as "essential for successful closure to service-learning experiences." That is ways that help student "review and discover, encapsulate and decorate, vocalize and enlighten, memorialize and project" (pp. 135-6).

Culminating Activities

Culminating activities usually take place in the classroom itself or in the project team's school, although they can take place at a service site if that is convenient and seems appropriate to all. These activities have two essential goals: to help students communicate new learnings and perspective and to help them acknowledge the many ways collaboration has helped them to learn. Service-learning students, themselves, plan culminating activities to include as many as possible of those who participated in their projects—teachers, parents, administrators, service-partners and clients, community members. And these participants help students share and celebrate individually or in groups the new skills, ideas and perspective they gained from service-learning. Culminating activities capitalize on students' creative use of multiple intelligences and are often expressed in visual or performance modes. Examples of culminating activities described in terms of the multiple intelligences on which they center are offered below.

Verbal-Linguistic Activities - Many of these are familiar "school type" activities that focus on the use of language yet enhance their messages by engaging all the intelligences. For example, students can write essays and papers to bring new personal insights to greater consciousness, and can write poems and books in which they use inter- and intrapersonal intelligences to play with metaphors, analogies and symbols for their service-learning experiences. Students can also conduct panel discussions and symposia that explore issues raised in service-learning through verbal discourse, data and pictorial displays, and deductive and inductive reasoning. They can make computerized presentations that strengthen logical outlining skills as they combine clip art and photographs with text to create celebratory messages.

Perhaps less familiar, but equally attractive as a verbal-linguistic culminating activity for teachers and students is the staff workshop. This kind of workshop seeks to inform others about a particular instructional approach and provide how-to information to those interested in trying it out. This makes staff workshops ideal for celebrating service-learning. Again, a mix of media helps put the message across. Pictures, posters, videos and handouts as well as other graphic materials all support and enhance the verbal messages the workshop is designed to deliver. Central in importance are student's personal accounts of how they planned, implemented and evaluated their service-learning projects.

Visual-Spatial Presentations - Team members and students often spontaneously photograph aspects of their service-learning projects. With advance planning these photos can become the basis for photo essays that provide testaments to the vital human dimension of service-learning as well as documenting key aspects of particular service-learning projects. Cameras and film are inexpensive and widely available. Digital still and video photography, which does not rely on film or developing and can be displayed on and printed from personal computers, opens immense possibilities here. Further, both film-based and digital images can easily be enlarged to poster size. Photo essays, as their name implies, rely essentially on images to communicate and ideally are accompanied by minimal explanatory text. By meeting the challenge of letting the pictures explain as much as possible, students are more likely to enhance their own and others' understanding of the nature and outcomes of their service-learning experiences. Most helpful here is for students and project teams to decide together which people and events during service-learning should be photographed and then to take numerous shots during the event—shots in which people are central and backgrounds meaningful in terms of the project's objectives, activities and outcomes. Students can then select the pictures that best convey what they wish to communicate and emphasize.

Two-dimensional graphic representations of service-learning experiences can play an important role in celebrating who and what were involved and what happened as a result. Drawing upon the service-learning experience itself as well as the reflection and conceptualization associated with it, students can express insights, understandings, disappointments, questions, commitments and more by creating murals, drawings, paintings, cartoons, prints, etchings and the full range of two dimensional art forms using an equally full range of media. If students are willing, this output can be contributed to the service site and/or the agency that partnered in the service project and stand as an acknowledgment of the value of service-learning and as an invitation to support its continuation.

Bulletin board displays combine media and can consist of from one to five or more linked bulletin boards that together explain a process or event in effect provide the chronology of a real-life story. These displays memorably culminate service-learning projects as each panel can be devoted to a particular aspect of the project, and each can incorporate the mix of graphic, text and logical-mathematic information most useful for projecting the central focus of the panel. The construction of a service-learning bulletin board display offers opportunities for students with wide ranging skills from carpentry to visual art to writing prose and poetry.

Sculpture provides students powerful opportunities to express the experiences and insights of service-learning. Students can use artifacts from the service site itself to create expressive forms or can carve, shape and construct in substances including clay, plastic, metal, stone or wood. A sculpting project can be adapted to any age and experience. This three-dimensional art can also be offered to the school or service partner as a contribution that acknowledges the worth of service-learning over the long term and an inspiration to others to become involved in service-learning.

Younger students may find that making buttons and medallions excites and motivates them to fruitfully review their service-learning experiences and to identify key elements of those experience for sharing with other students, parents and friends. Students can give their buttons to others as an invitation to become involved in some way in service-learning and can award their medallions to the full range of participants in service-learning celebratory events. Buttons and medallions can be made from simple materials such as lids, caps and wooden disks, or can be designed as a group project and reproduced commercially at low cost.

Musical-Rhythmic Activities – Until recently, writing music has been seen as the province of particularly gifted students, but as in so many other expressive areas, contemporary technology puts musical production within reach of nearly every student. By using electronic keyboards and inexpensive, readily available software, students can use personal computers to write one or two lines of music that express service-learning experiences, then orchestrate these as full compositions within pre-existing sound and rhythm formats. Younger students are usually quite capable of creating basic sound phrases and can be helped by their teachers to orchestrate these with technology. Older students can create full compositions with minimal guidance. These compositions can be shared as independent pieces with the full range of service-learning participants or function as adjunct support material for dissemination strategies.

Bodily-Kinesthetic Activities - Dance is an expressive medium accessible to students of every age, and it requires no special equipment or technology to create a dance. While it is true that computer software can be used to model dance sequences, students can independently explore and express their service-learning experiences and insights through body motions then combine these to express understandings. They can determine what they wish to share, select music, (or create it as described in the previous paragraph) compose and perform dances. Storyboards are helpful in planning phases and group feedback or videotaping if conveniently available can help teams and students refine their presentations.

Students of any age can also develop dramatic presentations to share their service-learning experiences and understandings. By working together to write, produce, direct and act out a scene or short play based on their experiences and insights, students have opportunities to re-explore and deeply assimilate the meaning of their service. There are so many different tasks to complete in creating dramatic presentations that many students can be involved in ways that capitalize on their multiple intelligences.

Dissemination Strategies

The essential goals of dissemination strategies are to teach about service-learning, gain support for service-learning and reinforce understandings of the social contributions that service-learning can make. These activities are designed to send messages related to these goals to particular audiences. Dissemination strategies centrally enlist students' use of verbal-linguistic and logical-mathematical activities but also incorporate the other multiple intelligences in ways that encourage all students to become involved in their production. While culminating activities have a spontaneous character, dissemination strategies are usually formatted according to standard conventions. They are, in a sense, "packaged" so that they can be sent or delivered to target audiences, and even when they involve performance, that performance, too, is packaged so that it can be given in the same general form on more than one occasions. The following provides examples of these strategies.

Evaluation Reports are probably the most ambitions, and most important dissemination strategies. An evaluation report formally presents the background and justification for a project, describes who was involved and the methods used, and presents findings and recommendations. Data and data arrays amplify report components. Evaluation reports are particularly helpful to school boards, instructional supervisors and administrators and to potential funders. Ideally, too, project teams and student groups who implement service-learning projects will develop and contribute evaluation reports to the National Service-learning Clearinghouse (http://www.servicelearing.org.) and/or the ERIC Clearinghouse (http://askeric@askeric.org). Project teams and students can develop evaluation reports together by dividing responsibility for completing sections, then having one person carry out final integration and editing. Many word-processing programs contain templates for these kind of reports and this helps students know what their particular sections should contain.

Executive Summaries - Project teams and students typically develop executive summaries to place at the beginning of their evaluation reports as advance organizers for readers. These summaries can also serve as independent dissemination strategies that are particularly helpful to administrators and professional groups. Executive summaries are comparable to research article abstracts and include very brief explanations of what was done and who was involved, with the major emphasis on findings. They may also include summary data arrays. Teams and students can develop executive summaries together on the basis of an already constructed evaluation report, or through a discussion that thoroughly reviews and records on the board or overhead projector what occurred during service-learning and what happened as a result.

Popular Articles help students reach a wide range of audiences. These articles focus primarily on results and discuss the implications that results might have for specific groups of other students, parents, administrators and the community. Since all of these groups are potential audiences for the article, it is often helpful to produce several versions, each using language and data that reach particularly to the interests and characteristics of its target group. The project team might develop a first version targeted to administrators and then have students work together to develop versions appropriate for their peers, parents and community members. Local papers, school system and state board newsletters provide important venues for these articles.

Highlights or Brief Papers can be developed from a popular article or independently in much the same way as the executive summary. Project teams and students distill the findings, recommendations and implications from either the pre-written article or a careful, documented summary of the service-learning project and its results. It is fruitful here for team members to challenge students to include vital, service-learning information within a 50- or 100-word limit. Highlights and short papers are very useful to administrators, community groups and newspapers.

Press Releases will include much the same material as highlights or brief papers, but the style is likely to be somewhat more terse and promotional. Perhaps the soundest way to help students write and frame press releases is for the project team to invite a representative of a school system publicity department to explain the nature and purpose of press releases and to provide examples of them. Word processing programs also often provide formats for press releases. Press releases usually target the general community and are important vehicles for raising awareness of school-community collaborative efforts and their outcomes.

Brochures and Flyers engage students in using the full range of their intelligences, and personal computer technology makes these items easy to produce to a professional standard. Most word processing programs include templates and step-by-step guidelines for producing flyers and brochures, and students can work in groups to design and create various versions of them. They can experiment with layout, font size and type as they consider ways to highlight the basic information about what happened during service-learning, why it happened, who was involved, results observed and questions raised. Brochures and flyers can be widely distributed in the community to inform and seek support.

Memos can call effective attention to a service-learning project as it unfolds and after it is complete. Using the basic format of "to," "from," and "subject," project teams and students can select key information about service-learning and direct it to specific individuals and audiences. Memos can also serve to whet appetites for more information about service-learning projects and as invitations to particular audiences to take part in projects as they unfold or in the future. Again, templates for memos exist in most word processing programs and students are often capable of developing their own memos about their service-learning projects and experiences. A series of memos developed over the course of a project can be saved and become the basis for articles, brochures and reports or can stand alone as an historical record of a project.

Newsletters can be as brief as a single, 8.5" by 11" sheet with two columns on each side, or as lengthy as 16 or more pages with two columns per page and can be developed and disseminated in several issues during the course of a service-learning project or in a single issue at the project' s conclusion. The constituent articles of a newsletter and their balance can be determined through student and project team discussion. Individuals and cooperative learning groups can work on components according to their interests and abilities. Articles can range from informative accounts of aspects of service-learning projects to essays on the meaning of those experiences and their personal impact on students.

Source materials for the articles can include but are not limited to notes from reflection discussions, student's journals, experience-analysis papers, interviews with people on site and evaluations of service-learning projects. Because of the scanning capacities of copiers that reproduce newsletters, students can include photographs, diagrams, personal art work, clip art, charts, tables and other graphic information in machine readable copy. In spite of their complexity, students are often highly motivated to produce newsletters and can use readily available word processing templates to insure high quality production.

Video Presentations can range from documentaries to impressionistic pieces. They can use the basic components of the evaluation report to provide a full account of a service-learning project, or can focus on a particular aspect of the project. Students conceive and produce video presentations by using storyboards to design and represent individual scenes with accompanying dialogue, and to arrange and integrate scenes to achieve the effects they want. Video presentations make it possible to include shots of service recipients and other involved community members as well as service sites themselves. Most schools have video equipment and many families own video cameras themselves so making service-learning videos is well within the realm of possibility for most projects. Video presentations can easily be sent to community groups and agencies that are prospects for future service-learning involvement.

Web Pages are among the most popular dissemination strategies in use today. Students can construct and locate them within their school or school system web sites or independently on the Internet by using free space available from many Internet access providers. Most word processing programs contain web page templates; software for web page design is readily available and affordable; and some school systems have personnel who will assist teams and students in creating web pages. In addition to providing information about service-learning projects in a succinct yet comprehensive form, web pages can be set up so that they count the number of visitors to the page and permit interaction between visitors and web page managers. It is also becoming increasingly easy to incorporate sophisticated, high-impact graphics into web pages. In light of today's enthusiasm for Internet communication, a service-learning web page can be vital for networking with the service-learning community and gaining support from a wide range of groups and agencies.

Computerized Presentations can be used as dissemination strategies as well as culminating activities. Today's office management software includes programs for designing slides that can be organized into a wide range of informative and persuasive presentations. Once designed and integrated, the slides can be accompanied by sound and run on a computer or printed in color or black and white or on transparencies for use on an overhead projector. Presentation software is designed to lead a student developer through the selection of slide backgrounds, incorporation of text and images in slides and the creation of special effects in the appearance of text and images. Students can use the software to create highly professional project reports and present these either independently or as part of other strategies such as public meetings and discussion groups.

Press Conferences help students access their communities and generate interest in service-learning. Many school systems regularly schedule press conferences and project teams can help service-learning students take advantage of these opportunities. As with workshops, efficiently prepared graphic materials help send clear messages about what and who service-learning projects involved and resulting outcomes. Handouts in the form of executive summaries and highlight papers are especially helpful to reporters as they provide clear and succinct answers to questions about the projects. Teachers and students who practice with expected questions prior to the press conference can do much to ensure that the clearest possible information reaches reporters and their audiences.

Media Appearances are increasingly within reach of service-learning students and their project teams as National Public Radio, the Public Broadcasting System and other public-access radio and TV channels extend services to communities across the country. As Fertman (1998) points out, "Media coverage conveys a sense of importance about a program, increasing the possibility that evaluation results will be heard and taken seriously." (p. 32) Typically, teachers need to contact representatives of these media to arrange for interviews and then include students as service-learning spokespersons. In order that students present information about service-learning projects in the most effective form, it is a good idea to determine in advance what general types of questions will be asked, make sure students understand the questions and then give them opportunities to practice answering them.

Public Meetings and Discussion Groups provide project teams and students opportunities to disseminate service-learning outcomes information to a wide range of target groups. Parent-teacher associations, community service groups and neighborhood associations are all interested in what is happening in their communities and welcome presentations about community related projects and their impact. Core presentations to such groups need to be focused and succinct, but team members and students also need to be ready to provide information and answer questions in free flow discussions. Again, thought in advance about questions that are likely to be raised and how to answer them helps ensure the best possible presentation. Artfully constructed illustrations and handouts also enhance these presentations.

As these examples of culminating activities and dissemination strategies show, there are many ways to inclusively celebrate service-learning. There is room at the party for students of diverse interests and abilities to share their new vision of learning in ways that will contribute to the building of the cultural commons. And as they use approaches such as these to communicate their new understandings, insights and perspectives within their schools and out into their communities, they will activate and strengthen the full measure of their abilities.

In Conclusion

Project team members individually conceptualize and carry out the evaluation activities that comprise the team's collaborative evaluation plan. They do this by identifying particular instruments for gathering students-outcomes, project-impact, and team process-product information and profiling the logistics, materials, scoring/coding and data summary formats that will be used to administer those instruments. They then administer the instruments and use inductive thinking with non-team partners to analyze results and derive generalizations from them. Team members learn how to use inductive thinking by practicing with information items that are essentially neutral in character, then with items in which they have some emotional investment. They then apply inductive thinking to evaluation results to generalize about project outcomes. Project teams integrate members' evaluation generalizations in positive-value judgments about the benefits of their projects and needs-improvement judgments about ways their projects could be strengthened in future implementations. Celebration ensues as students plan and implement multiple-intelligence culminating activities that acknowledge and communicate their new vision of collaborative, service-enriched learning and multiple-intelligence dissemination strategies that inform and garner support for future projects from the community.

Activities for Increasing Understanding

1. Return to the evaluation plan you developed for your practice service-learning project in activity 1 at the end of Chapter VII. Refine and clarify your plan in light of the Chapter XI discussion of evaluation plan logistics, materials, coding/scoring and data summary format elements.
2. Work with three to five colleagues or friends to practice inductive thinking at safe and risky levels in the manner described in this chapter. With this group, brainstorm information items for a topic selected from each of the two following lists, then use inductive thinking with each topic to find patterns in the brainstormed items and relate patterns together. Derive generalizations about the topic on the basis of the your thinking.

Safe Practice Topics	Risky Practice Topics
Daytime Television	Saying Thanks for an "Awful" Gift
College Basketball	Showing a "Prickly Pear" That You Care
Gourmet Cooking	Asking an "Ogre" for Mercy
Community Service	Inviting a "Luminary" to Speak in a Class
Life-long Learning	Apologizing for an Error in Judgment

Return to your evaluation plan as refined and clarified in activity 1 above. Imagine data or information that would be likely to result from the admini-

stration of each of the three instruments in your evaluation plan. Then analyze these results with inductive thinking. Make a record of the patterns, relationships and generalizations you derive using the format in Table 11.3.
3. State two positive- and one needs-improvement value judgments that could be expressed on the basis of the generalizations you derived from thinking inductively about the results of implementing your practice evaluation plan. Also imagine two new understandings students in your practice project might attain from the service-learning experiences. Then complete the following:
   a. Describe one culminating activity that students within your project might design to share what they have learned with fellow students.
   b. Write a 100-word executive summary of your practice project that includes value-judgment information based about the project's (imagined) outcome, and information about the (imagined) new learning and perspectives students' gained from the project. Prepare your summary in a format you would use to share it with a professional association to which you belong.

Chapter XII: Additional Resources for Service-Learning

"That sums up our project—we learned an awful lot and we believe we helped, too. Now we'd like to answer any questions you have." Twelfth-grader Karina Michaels holds up the portable mike encouraging workshop participants to join in.

How she's grown! teacher Tolly Petranova marvels silently. The poise, the confidence up front like that! She's come a long way.

"I'd like to know how you planned the project. What steps did your team use?" The short, dark-haired young woman in the front row asks with a certain fierceness.

"I'm going to ask Nick to tell you about that," Karina says.

As the questions come and Karina and the other twelfth-graders answer, Tolly looks inward, remembering—the shock on the team's faces when they saw that planning outline, the near-frantic scurrying for help in the community, the kids searching the Internet for resources. There were times when she'd been sure the whole thing would fall apart. Real conflicts—tears, anger, disappointment. But somehow the center had held. They'd gotten through it, found what they needed, healed the scrapes and scratches. And now look at them. Shining! Nick and Timothy, Lakisha, Jerran and Paul, Karina and Jack. Spanish class was alive for them and their classmates as well. And for the rest of us on the team, too!

Questions and answers flow. Tolly smiles at the companionable wink from Hispanic House director Miguel Ramon. Lakisha and Jerran are explaining intently and as she listens, Tolly's happy heart flutters its wings.

Chapter Focus

Service-learning projects are most successful when they are designed to take advantage of but not exceed the resources available to project teams. In situations where support for service-learning is less developed, projects will be simpler. In situations where resources are well developed, teams can often take on the challenge of more complex projects. Across this spectrum, however, project teams have access to a number of important additional resources beyond those in the networks of administrators, parents and potential community partners who consciously support service-learning. These include additional human resources in their school and larger communities, information resources on the Internet and strategic resources in relevant conflict resolution concepts. Teams can selectively draw upon these resources as they plan and carry out their own unique projects whether their projects are simple or complex. The purpose of this chapter is to provide an overview of these resources. The discussion begins by describing an array of human resources that project teams can draw upon within their own settings and situations. Next, the chapter explains how Internet websites maintained by organizations and groups that promote service-learning can provide information that leads to many kinds of resources for service-learning projects. Finally, the chapter suggests strategies teams can use to resolve types of conflicts that normally arise as collaborative groups work together.

Additional Human Resources

Even in the simplest projects, service-learning requires additional human resources for three reasons. First, service-learning asks students and their teachers to function in some degree beyond their classrooms, to visit community partner sites and often to provide direct service within the cultures of their community partners' agencies. Second, service-learning asks teachers, students and community partners to engage with each other in "complex instruction," a form of teaching and learning that depends for energy and success on small-group use of multiple-intelligences, cooperative and reflective learning. Third, service-learning calls for accountability through collaborative project evaluation. When students in classroom-based instruction complete learning activities and pass tests, teachers share results via grades on report cards. When students complete service-learning projects they and their project teams judge the value of what they accomplished—to themselves and to other—and share their findings widely. To fully address these service-learning specific requirements, those who use service-learning need extra human resources.

Project teams can find many extra human resources in their own backyards. Colleagues, school administrators, school workers, parents, school system resource staff, higher education faculty, and community members not directly affiliated with service-learning efforts can often provide unexpected, yet welcome additional resources for teams developing and implementing service-learning projects. People in each of these categories have expertise relevant to service-learning and connections to other people who can help. In many cases, people in these categories may be able to provide funding and materials for projects. Thus it is worthwhile for project teams to brainstorm lists of individuals within each category who might assist with their particular projects. They can then invite potential supporters to a general group meeting to discuss possibilities or contact them individually. In either case the team should have in hand the key project documents that describe the activities for which they will need support and use these to ask for specific kinds of assistance. The following suggest a few examples of the kinds of resources often resident in these "backyard" groups that project teams can use as starters for finding the additional human resources they need.

Same-Subject-Area Teachers

Service-learning projects benefit when their teams call upon teachers in the disciplines relevant to the projects for expertise. These teachers know the standards and the objectives that relate to a team's project. They can review the team's planned academic assessments and reflective learning experiences to make sure they do, in fact, relate clearly to the academic standards of interest and provide opportunities for students to learn specified objectives. These teachers can also make suggestions about other activities the team might want to use. Additionally, they may have actual materials relevant to project objectives—articles, handouts, exercises, games and so forth. And as teams help their students learn, serve and reflect, these subject-area teachers may want to assist personally in some part of a project as a way of becoming familiar with service-learning themselves.

Other Subject-Area Teachers

Teachers in other subject areas can provide invaluable assistance in strengthening aspects of projects that naturally lie outside the subject-area expertise of the team's teacher member. For example, high-school English students who have adapted a short story as a play they will present to raise money for a senior center, must keep records of all expenses and income. The school's accounting teacher can provide them with a brief instructional session that helps them use computerized accounting software to do this. Or sixth-graders extending their study of mammals by writing brochures on the care of dogs and cats for a local humane society can benefit from pointers from an English teacher on how to identify and address the audiences for their pamphlets and from an art teacher on effective pamphlet layout.

Teachers With Service-Learning Experience

As newly formed project teams inquire about resources, they may find that other teachers in other schools have carried out service-learning projects. By inviting these teachers to share their experiences, identify resources they know of, point out aspects of service-learning that need priority emphasis as well as pitfalls to be wary of, teams can develop a knowledge-base that may make a critical difference in the success of their own projects. As teams implement their projects and rough spots arise, they may be able to call upon these more experienced teachers to help them gain a sense of perspective on the dynamics of a problem area and to offer different ways of dealing with problems. This kind of support helps a team take heart when difficulties arise and push through to success rather than abandoning their projects.

School Administrators

While some principals may be able to serve on project teams, many do not have time to do this. Principals can, however, be included as ex officio team members and be counted on for support consistent with their own leadership goals. Frequently principals' leadership goals include supporting a variety of teaching methods, linking their schools to the community, and carrying out action research on what contributes to school success. They often have discretionary funds to carry out initiatives within these goals. When teams frame their projects as explorations of a new teaching method and invite principals to link the projects to their own action research, principals may be able to support their work with released time for planning and perhaps even funding for materials and supplies. When project teams share special needs within their instructional plans, principals can often suggest community contacts that will help them. For example, in the Chapter V dramatic monologue project where students serve in nursing homes then compose and present monologues on aging, their school principal knows two actors in the local community theater and helps the team arrange for these actors to provide students with a special workshop on monologues.

Vice principals, too, can provide special resources to project teams. In many schools these administrators take primary responsibility for scheduling of all types. They understand the relationships of their own transportation services to the overall transportation activities of their school system. As teams work through the intricacies of scheduling students for extended class periods and transporting them to service sites, vice principals may be able to provide pivotal consultant assistance. They can look at logistical plans and troubleshoot them and suggest strategies that will facilitate projects in creating the kind of time blocks that will keep them moving steadily forward. They may also be able to find ways to get students to and from service sites.

School Workers

People work in schools in good part because they commit to youth and want to support education. This holds true for secretaries, cafeteria workers, custodians, teaching aides and others who are not educational professionals but upon whom the educational enterprise depends. Many of these people have ways to support service-learning projects. Secretaries, for example, can suggest which parents are not working outside the home and might be able to help supervise students as they move into the community. Cafeteria workers know about nutrition and cooking for large numbers of people, custodians know where to find materials and tools to construct the booths and signs essential to may projects, and teaching aides know many ways to assist with classroom-based, academic components of service-learning projects. An example of a service-learning approach-design project that calls upon all of these workers for support demonstrates how important they are even though they do not directly serve on the project's team. Sixth-graders are working on a health standard that states, "Explain relationships between nutrition and the prevention of injury, illness and premature death." In response to a request for student in-school service from their superintendent, they decide to launch a "smart eating" campaign in their middle school. They learn about their school system's nutritionally balanced diet plans from their cafeteria director and two cafeteria workers, and reflect with their teacher aide and project team (which consists of their teacher, a guidance counselor and a parent) on the multitude of ways contemporary culture deflects middle-schoolers from smart eating habits. Then with help from a school custodian, they make framed, smart-eating posters for the cafeteria and work with one of the school secretaries to distribute an invitation to all students in their school to enter a "smart snacks" recipe contest.

Parents

Parents care about their children's learning experiences and have a wide variety of skills and abilities. Thus they have great potential as supporters of service-learning projects. Project teams enlist parent support by communicating with parents about service-learning in general and about planned projects in particular. Teams can explain service-learning as a teaching/learning method at meetings of their schools' Parent Teacher Associations and school advisory groups, and share details of projects in letters, e-mail, phone calls or newsletters—strategies that keep teams in direct and continuing contact with parents. Teams communicate with parents well in advance of project implementation, then bring them together in a meeting where students, themselves, show how their projects link academic study to service and identify parts of their projects that need specific parental support. Where such meetings are not feasible, students can send parents explanations of projects and their academic and service links, and include lists of particular project needs such as student transportation and supervision, box lunches, notebooks for journals, loan of video cameras, expertise in fields related to the project and so forth. For example, a high-school civics class working on the standard "Understand ways individuals become citizens" assists a coalition of local civic groups in informing seasonal migrant workers on how to become citizens. They design their project in the fall semester during which they e-mail their parents every two weeks about their plans. Just before Thanksgiving they send parents a request for funding for small holiday gifts for workers. They also ask parents to help them role play their initial meetings with the migrant workers. Finally they ask parents experienced with the workers' culture to help them understand issues these people are confronting in the United States. As parents contribute in various ways, students continue e-mailing information about contributions to all parents.

School and School System Resource Staff

School counselors and system staff who serve as curriculum and instruction supervisors, directors of assessment and evaluation, and directors of special resource programs, public relations and transportation can all provide extra assistance to service-learning project teams. Among these, school counselors are perhaps among the most important human resources that beginning teams can call upon because of their expertise in human interaction and reflective thinking. Counselors can help teams guide students through the maze of new experiences that service-learning entails in ways that integrate those experiences in terms of students' evolving value systems. They can help students make connections between academic and service experiences and vocational exploration, and they can assist project teams in prioritizing their concerns and implementing cooperative processes. Counselors can also help students and teams understand how people thrive by setting personal goals and finding resources to accomplish their goals. Whenever possible service-learning teams benefit from having a counselor as a regular member, but when this is not possible, teams should make every effort to have a counselor "amicus" to whom they can turn when necessary.

Curriculum and instruction supervisors can help teams accurately link genuine service to curriculum goals and objectives and develop reflective learning experiences. These supervisors often know of model service-learning projects that implement the goals and objectives of the disciplines in which they supervise as well as state-level funding for projects related to their discipline areas. Directors of assessment and evaluation can help teams specify appropriate student outcomes of service-learning, identify assessment instruments for measuring indicators of those outcomes, and instruments for carrying out project evaluation. Their expertise in the logistics of measurement and evaluation can be particularly helpful as teams plan for the administration of instruments and collection and interpretation of resulting data and information. Teams may often find that service-learning projects meet the needs of special student populations in uniquely helpful ways and thus warrant special funding support from directors of special programs for students. For example, a park planting project may be particularly helpful to students with basic skills needs and thus merit a support grant from state funding to which the director for basic skills advancement has access. Public relations directors can support project teams from start to finish by helping them disseminate both initial project plans and summary reports and thus gain a full range of support from the community. And in addition to contributing actual transport for students, directors of transportation can help teams lay out safe and efficient routes for student travel to community sites and back.

Higher Education Faculty

Service-learning is increasingly central to the ethos of higher education. Consequently more and more colleges and universities include service-learning in their programs of study and conduct research on all aspects of the method. The Campus Compact, for example, joins 650 public and private, post-secondary school presidents in a nationwide coalition dedicated to the support of students and faculty engaged in service-learning. Thus a middle- or high-school service-learning project team that has a college or university in its local area is likely to have important and extensive resources for service-learning in its own backyard. The faculty and service-learning coordinators in these institutions usually see assistance to elementary and secondary schools as a professional responsibility. They can help teams think through their projects, explore ways to measure student outcomes, and evaluate project impact in terms of principles emerging from research and best practice. They are aware of grants and awards that can support service-learning projects. These faculty may also be willing to connect their own service-learning projects with projects in middle and high schools and find ways that their post-secondary students can help middle- and high-school students as they link academic studies to service action and grow personally and as citizens.

Community Contacts

Project team members, their colleagues, administrators, resource staff and parents are often members of civic and social organizations. Service is usually part of these organizations' missions, and many of them have committees that focus on community service. Team members can contact these organizations and their committees, and may find them willing to donate funds to support service-learning projects consistent with their missions. Civic clubs often offer competitive grants for innovative programs that can be duplicated in other schools. They may also sponsor student service groups in area high schools and these can serve as liaisons to service-learning projects in the schools. Team members may also be members of nonprofit boards that are made up of community business and non-profit agency leaders who can provide funding resources to project teams. A team member or colleague may be a member of the local Chamber of Commerce and come into contact with many local business leaders who may donate time, talent, and other resources to school projects. Local governments may have officials or personnel who are willing to assist with service-learning projects. For example, a county council president may be willing to talk with students about how to testify at public meetings or a judge may be willing to explain the requirements for citizenship. In short, anyone in the community that team members know and any organization to which they team members belong represent potential resources for service-learning projects.

As the preceding discussion makes clear, project teams can connect through personal contacts to individuals and groups with abundant resources for service-learning. The existence of so many potential resources points to a key issue in service-learning project development, and that is that teams will be most effective when they select resources that best support actualization of their particular projects. It is not the number of resources, but the appropriateness of resources with respect to a project that counts. Teams that know what they need—in the classroom and at community-partner sites—facilitate assembly of appropriate resources. This means teams need to develop student outcomes, instruction, evaluation and dissemination plans that clearly indicate resources at hand and resources needed. They can then share these needs selectively with colleagues, school administrators, school workers, parents, school system resource staff, higher education faculty, and community members and through this sharing garner resources to carry out their projects.

Internet Resources for Service-Learning

Use of the Internet by colleges and universities, service agencies and government commissions, research and development foundations and others interested in service-learning creates a vast additional resource for those interested in the method. Project teams can go to World Wide Web addresses of educational and civic organizations and governmental agencies to find information about every aspect of service-learning. This includes but is not limited to rationales for engaging in service-learning, research on its effectiveness, ideas for service-learning projects, examples of successful projects, guidelines for implementing and assessing the method, sources of funding for projects, and awards for students, schools and organizations that use service-learning. Members of project teams have but to go to one or two websites and by using search engines and hyperlinks, they will immediately connect to the ever-growing electronic network of service-learning resources.

Just as with human resources, the abundance of Internet resources can inundate project teams, and selectivity is the key. In order to efficiently select useful Internet resources, teams need to use their student outcomes, instruction, evaluation and dissemination plans to determine what will help them and their students actualize their service-learning projects. Teams can focus their quest for useful Internet resources by using steps such as the following.

1. Teams examine their project planning documents to determine support information needs, then list these as key phrases.
2. Individual team members search service-learning-related websites for information on particular key phrases, obtain information leads to resources, and then share these with the team.
3. Teams agree on resource leads to pursue, then prepare and send request-for-support packets to selected support sources.

For example, a team seeks Internet information about resources to support their project in which eighth-grade students mount a community-wide literacy initiative in cooperation with community public libraries. They examine their core project plans and identify support information needs as shown in Table 12.1

Table 12.1 Search Phrases for Obtaining Internet Information About Resources Available to Support a Service-Learning Project

Plan	Need	Phrase for Internet Search
Student Outcomes	Released time for assessment development Commitment-to-service survey	Service-learning project grants Service-learning assessment
Instruction	Literacy training materials Models of similar projects	National literacy projects Service-learning literacy project models
Evaluation	Paper and postage for client feedback instrument	Service-learning project grants
Dissemination	Funding for literacy newsletter	Service-learning project grants

Team members now use two strategies to gain information about the availability of the three kinds of support they need—time for developing tests, models of similar projects, and funding. They use an Internet browser to identify sites related to reading and literacy, such as the International Reading Association (http//www.reading.org) and the National Education Association (http//www.nea.org) that might support service-learning projects. At these sites they enter their key phrases in search boxes or find underlined hyperlinks that match their key phrases and this leads them to descriptions of resources that may help them. They also go to the websites of service-learning support organizations such as the following and again use search boxes and hyperlinks to find descriptions of resources for their project.

American Association of School Administrators - http://www.aasa.org
America's Promise: The Alliance for Youth - http://www.americaspromise.org
Center for Democracy and Citizenship - http://www.publicwork.org
Center for Youth as Resources - http://www.ysa.org
Constitutional Rights Foundation - http://www.crf.usa.org

Corporation for National and Community Service - http://www.nationalservice.org
Council of Chief State School Officers - http://www.ccsso.org
Education Commission of the States - http://www.ecs.org
Grantmaker Forum on Community and National Service - http://www.gfcns.org
Home of Service Learning on the World Wide Web - http://csf.colorado.edu
National Commission on Service-Learning - http://www.servicelearning.org
National Service-Learning Clearinghouse – http://www.servicelearning.org
National Service-Learning Partnership - http://www.servicelearningpartnership.org
National Society for Experiential Education - http://www.nsee.org
National Youth Leadership Council - http://www.nylc.org
Phi Delta Kappa, International - http://www.pdkintl.org
Points of Light Foundation - http://www.pointsoflight.org
State Education Agency K-12 Service-Learning Network - http://www.seanetonline.org
The USA Freedom Corps - http://www.usafreedomcorps.gov
Youth Service America - http://www.ysa.org

Once team members identify website information about resources they need, they may find material they can immediately download and use, or may find that they will have to request or apply for material and funds according to instructions posted at the sites. In some cases, they will have to become members of the organizations that maintain the sites in order to take advantage of the resources offered. Typically memberships are very low in cost, and teams can usually convince their schools, school systems or service partners to pay for memberships.

An additional benefit of becoming familiar with websites such as those listed above is that many of them provide on-line newsletters on service-learning and related matters that keep project teams in the mainstream of developments in their states and across the country. Some sites also provide opportunities for teachers and students to share and celebrate their service-learning experiences and in this way to become active members of the vast and growing service-learning network.

Conflict Resolution Resources for Service-Learning

Collaborative service-learning project teams bring people together who have much in common through their general service orientation, but have different perspectives about their own work and the work they do as team members. Conflicts arise from time to time as these differences manifest themselves in behaviors and attitudes that cause friction among members. If these conflicts continue, they can damage relationships within teams and in some instances, bring service-learning projects to a halt. Fortunately, teams have built-in resources for conflict resolution and can very frequently resolve conflicts on their own. These resources include team members' shared commitment to serving others who may be their students, children, clients or fellow citizens; human relations skills team members have as a result of parenthood and work in service professions; and formal conflict-resolution training in which team members may have participated. In essence, service-learning team members have more than average capacities to deal productively with conflict by virtue of personal and professional orientation and experience. When team members accept the premise that conflict can occur in even the most collaborative of teams, they can capitalize on their conflict resolution capacities in three ways: by regularly scanning sources of conflict typical within service-learning teams, using problem-solving skills to resolve conflicts that arise, and enlisting the aid of conflict-resolution mediators when that seems appropriate. The following discussion explores these three channels for conflict resolution.

Scanning for Conflict

Project team conflicts usually arise from two sources: the ways in which teams members contribute to team function and the ways team members, students and service clients carry out project activities. Teams can identify conflicts related to these two sources by systematically scanning them each time they meet. Scanning for conflict arising from team function involves analysis of the team's use of cooperative-learning strategies. Scanning for conflict that arises from project implementation involves attending to team members' expectations about how other team members and their affiliates should meet the needs of the students and service clients for whom team members are responsible.

Scanning Cooperative Team Function

Chapter XI asserts that service-learning project teams function most effectively when they organize their efforts in terms of the five principles of cooperative learning: face-to-face promotive interaction, positive interdependence, individual accountability, interpersonal and small group skills, and group process reflection. Failure of one or more team members to contribute to use of these principles can produce conflict. For example, a team member may not interact directly, promotively and interdependently with others, and instead triangulates—gossips about absent members in order to create alliances with members who are present. Another team member fails to complete assignments thoroughly or does not complete them at all. Another presents ideas aggressively and fails to listen to student members' suggestions, and several team members regularly cut group reflection short because of the press of their personal schedules. The first thing teams need to do to reverse these kinds of behaviors and resolve the conflicts they can engender is to use group reflection—the fifth cooperative-learning principle—to identify them. In many instances the teacher who originally assembled the team leads this effort. The teacher asks team members to consider each of the five cooperative-learning principles in turn and to identify which, if any, are being inadequately served by team member attitudes and behaviors. The teacher then asks team members to use "Confrontive I-messages" (Adams, Lenz & Gordon, 1987) to state their concerns about inadequate team function in a way that identifies an attitude or behavior and its problematic effect but does not blame anyone for it. Once team members surface conflict-potential, team-function issues in this way, they record them for use in a problem-solving process described later in this section.

Stating Confrontive I-Messages - Confrontive I-Messages consist of three parts. One reports the attitude or behavior of concern without blame, evaluation or moralizing in a "when" statement. Another part specifies the effect of the attitude or behavior that the reporting person perceives, and a third part reports the feelings that this effect causes in the person who is reporting. Although order of parts is not proscribed, confrontive I-messages usually begin with a when statement that objectively describes the attitude or behavior of concern. The teacher may lead confrontive I-messaging by asking the team to think about, then express their concerns about attitudes of behaviors related to each of the cooperative learning principles. The teacher offers an opening statement about a troubling attitude or behavior that has occurred as a model and points out its three components.

Promotive Interaction – "When I come to a meeting and find that two or three members have already decided on a change in student activities without involving me in the discussion *(identification of behavior – lack of promotive interaction)*, I know students will get confused *(effect on project)*, I get angry and I don't teach as well *(effect on person reporting).*"

Analyzing Confrontive I-Messages for Problem-Solving – Now team members use this model to state their own confrontive I-messages. As each team member makes a statement, the team discusses it to identify its three components. Then the leader asks another team member to record these components in a three-column summary with the headings "attitude/behavior of concern, "effect on project," and "effect on team member." As the team members consider each cooperative-learning principle, I-messages such as the following emerge and their components are recorded.

Positive Interdependence- "When only two team members show up at the orientation session I planned, those who weren't present don't know how to help the students provide service, and I can't do it all on my own."

Accountability – "When no one sends me an outline of the basic material students have covered, I can't show them how their study of marine grasses specifically relates to Bay water quality, and I wonder why I'm even a part of the project."

Group Skills – "When we don't ask each team member for activity suggestions, one or two people decide on all the activities, and I don't feel that any of my ideas count."

Group Process – "When we don't take time as a team to talk about students' concerns about the zoo animals, I can't think through how to use reflection with them, and I don't want to even deal with their concerns."

Table 12.2 shows the analytical record of these statements a team member makes for use in subsequent problem-solving.

Table 12.2 Record of Scanning for Cooperative Learning Team Function

Attitude/Behavior	Effect on Project	Effect on Team Member
Learning activity changes made and not shared	Student confusion	Reduced professional performance
No-shows at orientation	Incomplete training for service	Inability to engage students in planned service
Lack of information about student academic knowledge and competence	Inability to connect learning to service	Isolation from project
Lack of democratic process	Narrowed input to project activities	Poor professional esteem
Insufficient time for team work	Inadequate student reflection on concerns	Desire to withdraw from project responsibilities

It is important to note that when teams scan for cooperative-learning function, it is neither necessary nor expected that each team member will raise an issue for problem-solving. On the other hand, it is vital that each team member is given the opportunity to think about how the team is using cooperative learning and has a chance to express genuine concerns he or she perceives.

Scanning for Unmet Expectations

As service-learning projects go forward and participants interact with each other to accomplish new objectives in new settings, conflict may arise from discrepancies members perceive between the expectations that responsible parties have and the behaviors and attitudes of others. For example, teachers may feel that those who are supervising students on site are not helping the students interact effectively with service clients. Parents may be concerned that site experiences are inappropriate in terms of students' emotional maturity. Service partners may feel that students are unprepared to provide client services in competent ways. Community members may feel that teachers are not taking enough responsibility for students' learning. Again, the team's teacher can lead team identification of conflict-potential issues such as these, this time by asking each team member to express his or her concerns in discrepancy statements using the following frame.

I need _____ to _____ but this isn't happening because _____.

Team members do not use names of individuals to fill in the last blank in the frame, rather they fill it in by describing the situation that is preventing them from meeting the project needs they state in the first part of the frame. For example, team member use the frame to make statements such as the following.

Teacher – "I need students to practice writing letters, but this isn't happening because they're not meeting with the senior citizens they're supposed to be writing letters for."

Parent – "I need students to understand that the handicapped are people like everyone else, but this isn't happening because the kids are frightened by a lot of the disabilities they're seeing."

Service Partner – "I need students to play reading readiness games with the children in the waiting room, but this isn't happening because students don't seem to know any games."

Community Member – "I need students to learn basic math skills but this isn't happening because only four in a class of 25 are involved with laying out the outdoor lunch area."

When team members identify conflicts in this way, they can record them in the two-column format shown in Table 12.3 for use within subsequent problem-solving.

Table 12.3 Record of Scanning for Unmet Expectations

Need	Discrepancy
Letter-writing practice	Lack of meetings with seniors citizens who need letters written
Understanding humanity of handicapped clients	Fear of client's disabilities
Game playing with child service clients	No knowledge of appropriate games
Learning of basic math skills	Lack of student involvement in service-learning activity

Using Problem-Solving to Resolve Conflicts

Coercion, accommodation, compromise and avoidance are strategies for conflict resolution that teacher leaders of project teams may find useful and necessary on some occasions, and the conflict resolution literature discusses these strategies in depth (e.g. Whetten &Cameron, 2002). In the majority of situations, however, teams are best served by using integrative problem-solving to resolve their conflicts. Staff development expert Joan Richardson (1999) offers the following seven-step process that teams can use to address their conflicts with problem-solving.

1. Identify the problem as a group.
2. List interests of the individuals involved in the problem.
3. Define common areas of interest and difference.

4. Generate possible resolutions.
5. Combine obviously overlapping resolutions.
6. Test the acceptability of resolutions.
7. Derive a resolution that can be used on a trial basis.

An example of the use of this process by the team described in the opening scenario of this chapter shows how it can be fruitfully implemented. In the project, twelfth-grade Spanish-class students have linked requests for service from an Hispanic community center with their language-learning standard that states "Use second language to interact substantively with native speakers." Students work with a project team composed of their teacher and guidance counselor, the director of the Hispanic House community center, an Hispanic and non-Hispanic parent and a community social services representative. The team designs a service-learning project in which students help Hispanic agricultural workers and their families learn English and explore similarities and differences in their own and US cultures. The following describes how the team identifies and solves a problem in the course of their work together.

An Example of Resolving a Service-Learning Conflict with Problem-Solving

During systematic scanning of unmet expectations once the project is well underway, Hispanic House director Miguel Ramon says, "I need our nine- and ten-year old children to practice their English, but this isn't happening because they're not participating in the English language sessions."

With teacher Tolly Petranova's guidance, the team identifies those involved in this problem as the Hispanic children, twelfth-grade service-learning students and mothers of the middle-schoolers who sit quietly by during the language sessions. It becomes clear that service-learning students feel uncomfortable about pressing middle schoolers to take part in practicing English when their mothers are present, especially because at the end of the second and third sessions, one of the mothers spoke extensively with much heat and gesture to the three twelfth-grade teachers for the day. They couldn't understand everything she said, but they were sure she didn't like their approach with the children.

Team discussion results in the idea that communication and authority within the language sessions are causing conflict. All agree that middle-schoolers and their mothers need to learn English, but some on the team say mothers will gain by observing their children at work, while other point out that mothers' presence may be encouraging students to be quiet rather than to become involved. Emotions suddenly rise as Miguel insists that families need to work together to feel comfortable with "Anglo" service-learning students and the non-Hispanic parent fiercely defends the devotion and hard work twelfth-graders have invested in the project.

"How can we meet both needs here?" asks Tolly, "the need to get the children involved independently and yet let their mothers know what they're doing? Let's list everything we can think of, even partial solutions."

The team's first response is surprisingly negative. Students suggest that parents not be allowed to attend sessions. Miguel suggests that the twelfth-graders should teach English to adults only then let the adults work with their own children. One parent suggests video-taping sessions for parents to observe later, and the other counters that Miguel should be present at all times to describe to parents in Spanish what twelfth-graders are doing with their children. Tolly lists these suggestions and ask all to study them, then propose possible combinations of ideas that might help resolve the problem. A long silence ensues, then Miguel speaks tentatively.

"If we could turn it around, get the students to teach the parents. You know, when they've finished a page in those little workbooks you made, then they could do the page again with their parents."

"We could video the first independent session with the children using the workbooks, show the video to the parents . . ." says Tolly.

Student Lakisha Robbins joins in. "A double lesson—kids first, then the parents. And you could help us explain how it'll work, Senor Ramon, then leave it to us."

As the plan emerges, Tolly sums it up, then asks, "Can we try this new approach, then take a look at what worked and what didn't—involve some of the mothers in the discussion?"

Analyzing the Example

In addition to demonstrating use of the seven problem-solving steps to resolve service-learning conflicts, the example above shows that teachers who lead project teams in conflict resolution through problem-solving need to be confident as leaders and to use facilitating behaviors such as clarifying and conceptualizing needs and proposing solutions. At their management skills assessment website, http://www.prenhall.com/whetten_dms/chap7.html, Whetten and Cameron (2002) offer two self assessments that teachers who want to become aware of the additional leadership and facilitating skills demonstrated in the example as well as in their own work with project teams will find especially useful.

Involving a Conflict-Resolution Mediator

Conflict resolution through problem-solving is essentially an effort to help people who disagree work together by using a rational framework—a series of steps that focuses their thinking on the nature of a problem and ways to solve it. Sometimes this is not enough. People who are attempting to deal with a conflict are emotionally invested, and sometimes it is not possible for them to manage their emotions in ways that permit the rational steps of problem-solving to go forward. When emotions increasingly dominate a team's interactions and little if any progress is made toward problem identification and clarification, or when members seem unwilling or incapable of offering possible resolutions, conflicts may best be resolved through the assistance of a mediator, someone who can help team members deal with and understand their emotions and eventually set them aside to some degree so that they can engage in problem-solving.

It is wise for teams to agree at the outset of their work together that they will call upon mediators if they find themselves in conflict situations ruled by emotion. If possible, they should then identify at least two individuals—one from the school or school system supporting the project and one from the service partner's organization—who are willing and able to assist them. If emotion-laden conflict does arise, the teacher or another team member can remind the team of these agreements. In the Hispanic House example, for instance, when the director and parent began to engage emotionally, other team members might have joined the fray and cultural antagonism might have ensued. In such a situation, the teacher or another team member could propose that since emotions are running high, the guidance counselor member on the team—who was originally named as a potential mediator—might help the group, or that the team could turn to a clergyman who mediates conflicts between Hispanic House clients and their employers.

In drawing this section to a close, it is important to reiterate that service-learning project teams are not immune to conflict on the one hand, but that they have many skills for conflict resolution on the other. As they work to resolve their conflicts, teams can strengthen and add to these skills by referring to the rich and extensive conflict resolution literature. And when teams find that emotions are deflecting their energies from solving the problems that conflicts represent, they can call upon many individuals in their own situations who can help them work toward mutual problem-solving.

In Conclusion

In addition to the resource networks within which service-learning teams design and develop their projects, there are many additional resources available to them. Among these are the unique resources that infuse project teams' situations, service-learning resources on the Internet and resources for conflict resolution. Teams can identify individuals and organizations in their own settings that subscribe to a service ethos and may support service-learning projects in a variety of ways. They can use the project plans they develop to identify Internet information sources that will help them find expertise, assessment instruments, reflective learning experience models and funding to carry out activities within their plans. They can use their own and others' conflict-resolution skills within a problem-solving framework to address the conflicts that may arise as a natural function of their work together and their implementation of their projects.

A Final Word

Service-learning is a method of teaching and learning that brings together people from different generations with different perspectives and values and calls upon them to share responsibility for the education of young people through service. This shared responsibility is what makes possible the remarkable promise of service-learning for 21st century middle- and high-school students, a promise that Judith Ramaley, assistant director of the National Science Foundation Directorate for Education and Human Resources describes. In the National Commission on Service-Learning's report (2002, Implementing Quality Service-Learning, para. 7) she states, "If we want our students to lead creative, productive, and responsible lives, we must give them opportunities to learn in ways that have consequences for others, as well as for themselves. I know of no better way to invoke the many facets of cognitive development, moral reasoning and social responsibility than to engage students in service-learning. At its best, a service-learning experience can be transformative. Clearly learning within a context of responsibility is powerful."

Shared responsibility holds equal promise for the teachers and parents, schools, service partners and community members who collaboratively design, carry out and evaluate service-learning projects. As they work together, these people have unparalleled opportunities to come to new understandings of education itself and to be transformed by deeper commitment to students, the communities in which they live and work, and to service.

Activities for Increasing Understanding

1. Assemble the planning documents you completed for end-of chapter activities. These include the following.
    a. A service-learning commitment plan for a project you might design with students you teach or plan to teach (Chapter IV, Activity 2)
    b. The student outcomes plan you envisioned for this project (Chapter V, Activity 2)
    c. The instructional plan you envisioned for this project (Chapter X, Activity 2)
    d. The evaluation plan you would use to judge the quality of your project. (Chapter VII, Activity 1 and Chapter XI, Activity 1)
    e. The culminating activity you envisioned for the project and the name of the professional organization to which you plan to disseminate information about the project (Chapter XI, Activity 4)

    Analyze these plans as an outline for your service-learning project to make sure they are coherent and relate to one another in ways that could guide you, a project team and service-learning students from start to finish through the project. Make any modifications or revisions you feel necessary to shape and refine your work as an example of a workable service-

learning curriculum. Write a brief introductory statement for your curriculum and put it in a notebook for sharing with others.
2. List the name of one person you know who might be helpful to your project in each of the categories of human resources for service-learning projects: colleagues, school administrators, school workers, parents, school system resource staff, higher education faculty, and community members. List these as "Human Resources" on a sheet entitled "Resources for the Project."
3. Use your service-learning project outline to identify at least one resource each that you will need to implement your student outcomes, instructional, evaluation and dissemination plans. Use the list of websites in this chapter and other Internet resources you know of to find information about the resources you need. List these as "Internet Resources" on your Resources for the Project sheet and include this sheet at the end of your curriculum.
4. Find the two conflict-resolution self assessment at the Whetten and Cameron website (http://www.prenhall.com/whetten_dms/chap7.html) and use the instruments to determine areas where you need to develop conflict-resolution skills. Make a statement in 100 words or less about what your results suggest about areas in which you need to grow as a resolver of conflicts.
5. Analyze the "Hispanic House" example in this chapter to identify its project teams' use of Richardson's seven-step problem-solving process repeated below:
   a. Identify the problem as a group.
   b. List interests of the individuals involved in the problem.
   c. Define common areas of interest and difference.
   d. Generate possible resolutions.
   e. Combine obviously overlapping resolutions.
   f. Test the acceptability of resolutions.
   g. Derive a resolution that can be used on a trial basis.

References

Adams, L., Lenz, E., & Gordon, T. (1987). *Effectiveness training for women.* New York: Berkley Publishing Group.

Anderson, L. W., & Krathwhol, D. R. (Eds.). (2001). *A taxonomy for learning, teaching and assessing: A revision of Bloom's taxonomy of educational objectives.* New York: Addison Wesley Longman.

Anderson, L. W., & Bourke, S. F. (2000). *Assessing affective characteristics in the schools* (2nd ed.). Mahwah, NJ: Lawrence Erlbaum Associates.

Armstrong, T. (1994). *Multiple intelligences in the classroom.* Alexandria, VA: Association for Supervision and Curriculum Development.

Armstrong, T. (2000). *Multiple intelligences in the classroom.* Alexandria, VA: Association for Supervision and Curriculum Development.

Ausubel, D. P. (2000). *The acquisition and retention of knowledge: A cognitive view.* Boston: Kluwer Academic Publishers.

Bean, C., Drenk, D., & Lee, F. D. (1982). Microtheme strategies for developing cognitive skills. In C. W. Griffin (Ed.). New directions in teaching and learning: Teaching writing in all disciplines. San Francisco: Jossey Bass.

Billig, S. H. (1999). The impacts of service-learning on youth, schools and communities: Research on K-12 school-based service-learning, 1990-1999. Retrieved June 23, 2003 from http://learningindeed.org.research/slresearch/slrsrchsy.html.

Billig, S. H. (2000a). The impacts of service-learning on youth, schools and communities: Research on K-12 school-based service-learning, 1990-1999. *Phi Delta Kappan, 81,* 658-664

Billig, S. H. (2000b). Recent research on service learning: Abstracts (2000). Retrieved June 23, 2003 from http://learningindeed.org.research/slresearch/abstracts.html.

Bloom, B. S. (Ed.). (1956). *Taxonomy of educational objectives. Handbook I: Cognitive domain.* New York: David McKay.

Bringle, R. G., & Hatcher, J. A. (1996). Implementing service learning in higher education. *Journal of Higher Education, 67,* 221-239.

Bruner, J. S. (1962). *On knowing: Essays for the left hand.* Cambridge, MA: Harvard University Press.

Bruner, J. S. (1966). *Toward a theory of instruction.* Cambridge, MA: Harvard University Press.

Campus Compact, (1998). *Findings of the campus compact wingspread conference, April 1998: Benchmarks for campus community partnerships.* Retrieved June 23, 2003, from http//www.compact.org/ccpartnerships/benchmarks-overview.html.

Capote, T. (1996). *A Christmas memory, one Christmas, and a Thanksgiving visitor.* New York: Random House.

Cohen, E. G., Lotan, R. A., Whitcomb, J. A., Balderrama, M.V., Cossey, R. & Swanson, P. E. (1994). Complex instruction: Higher order thinking in heterogeneous classrooms. In S. Sharan, (Ed.), *Handbook of cooperative learning methods* (pp. 82-96). Westport, CT: Greenwood.

Compact for Learning and Citizenship (2001). *Service-learning and standards tool kit: Achieving academic excellence by serving communities.* Denver: Education Commission of the States.

Compendium of Assessment and Research Tools for Measuring Education and Youth Development Outcomes (CART). http://cart.rmcdenver.com.

Cone, D., & Harris, S. (1996). Service-learning practice: Developing a theoretical framework. *Michigan Journal of Community Service Learning, 3,* 31-43.

Cumbo, K. B., & Vadeboncoeur, J. A., (1999). What are students learning?: Assessing cognitive outcomes in K-12 service-learning. *Michigan Journal of Community Service Learning, 6,* 84-96.

Dewey, J. (1933). *How we think.* Boston: Houghton Mifflin Company.

England A., & Spence, J. (2001). *Reflection: A guide to effective service learning.* Clemson, SC: National Dropout Prevention Center.

Eyler, J. (2000). What do we most need to know about the impact of service-learning on student learning? *Michigan Journal of Community Service Learning,* (Special Issue), 11-17.

Eyler, J., Giles, D., & Schmiede, A. (1996). *A practitioner's guide to reflection in service-learning.* Corporation for National Service. Nashville, TN: Vanderbilt University.

Eyler, J., Giles, D., Stenson, C., & Gray, C. (2001). *At a glance: What we know about the effects of service-learning on college students, faculty, Institutions and communities, 1993-2000:* Third edition. Corporation for National Service Learn and Serve America National Service Learning Clearinghouse.

Ferrari, J., & Worrall, L. (2000). Assessments by community agencies: How the "other side" sees service-learning. *Michigan Journal of Community Service Learning, 7,* 35-40.

Fertman, C. I. (1998). Sharing what we learn. In J. Smink & M. Duckenfield (Eds.), *Making the case for service-learning action research & evaluation guidebook for teachers* (pp. 31-33). Columbia, SC: South Carolina State Department of Education.

Frechtling, J., & Sharp, L. (Eds.). (1997). *User-friendly handbook for mixed-method evaluations.* Arlington, VA: Directorate for Education and Human Resources, National Science Foundation.

Freeman, D. (1998). *Doing teacher research: From inquiry to understanding.* Toronto: Heinle and Heinle.

Gagnon, G. W., & Collay, M. (2000). *Designing for learning: Six elements in constructivist classrooms.* Thousand Oaks, CA: Corwin Press.

Gardner, H. (1983, 1993). *Frames of mind: The theory of multiple intelligences.* New York: Basic Books.

Gardner, H. (2000). *Intelligence reframed: Multiple intelligences for the 21st century.* New York: Basic Books.

Gelmon, S., Holland, B., Driscoll, A., Spring, A., & Kerrigan, S. (2001). *Assessing service-learning and civic engagement: Principles and techniques.* Providence, RI: Campus Compact.

Gent, P. J., & Guercka, L. E. (2001). Service-Learning: A disservice to people with disabilities? *Michigan Journal of Community Service Learning, 8,* 36-43.

Gilligan, C. (1982). *In a different voice: Psychological theory and women's development.* Cambridge, MA: Harvard University Press.

Harvey, W. (1996). Reflection leads to real learning. In G. Gulati-Partee & W. R. Finger (Eds.), *Critical issues in K-12 service-learning: Case studies and reflections* (pp. 127-131). Raleigh, NC: National Society for Experiential Education.

Irizarry, J. (1996). Designing meaningful projects that meet community needs. In G. Gulati-Partee & W. R. Finger (Eds.), *Critical issues in K-12 service-learning: Case studies and reflections* (pp. 225-230). Raleigh, NC: National Society for Experiential Education.

Johnson, B. (1996). *Performance assessment handbook volume 1: Portfolios and Socratic seminars.* Princeton, NJ: Eye on Education.

Johnson, B. (1996). *Performance assessment handbook volume 2: Performances and exhibitions.* Princeton, NJ: Eye on Education.

Johnson, D. W., Johnson, R. T., & Smith, K. A. (1995). Cooperative learning and individual student achievement in secondary schools. In D. Pederson & A. Digby (Eds.), *Secondary schools and cooperative learning: Theories and methods* (pp. 3-54). New York: Garland.

Joyce, B. & Weil, M. with Calhoun, C. (2000). *Models of teaching* (6th ed.) Boston: Allyn and Bacon.

Kolb, D. A. (1984). *Experiential learning: Experience as the source of learning and development.* Englewood Cliffs, NJ: Prentice Hall.

Krathwhol, D. R., Bloom, B. S., & Masia, B. B. (1999). *Taxonomy of educational objectives: The classification of educational goals. Handbook II: Affective domain.* New York: Longman Publishing Group

League of Professional Schools. (2003). Definition of democratic learning. Retrieved June 23, 2003 from http://www.coe.uga.edu/lps/democratic.html.

Lewin, K. (1947a). Frontiers in group dynamics: concept, method and reality in social science, social equilibria and social change. *Human Relations, 1,* 5-42.

Lewin, K. (1947b). Group decision and social change. In E. Maccoby, T. Newcomb & E. Hartley (Eds.), *Readings in social psychology* (pp. 197-219). New York: Holt, Rinehart and Winston.

Liddell, D. L., Halpin G., & Halpin, W. G. (1992). The measure of moral orientation: Measuring the ethics of care and justice. *Journal of College Student Development, 33,* 325-330.

Melchoir, A., & Bailis, L. N. (2002). Impact of service-learning on civic attitudes and behaviors of middle and high school youth: Findings from three national evaluations. In A. Furco & S. Billig (Eds.), *Advances in Service-Learning Research: Volume 1: The Essence of Pedagogy* (pp. 201-222). Greenwich, CT: Information Age Publishing.

Mezirow, J. (1994). Understanding transformation theory. *Adult Education Quarterly, 44,* 222-232.

Mitchell, J. (1992). *Adolescent struggle for selfhood and identity.* Calgary: Detselig Enterprises.

Morgan, W. (1998). *Evaluation of school-based learning in Indiana, 1997-98.* Report prepared for the Indiana Department of Education

Morton, K. (1995). The irony of service: Charity, project and social change in service-learning. *Michigan Journal of Community Service Learning, 2,* 19-32.

National Commission on Service Learning. (2002). *Executive summary: Learning in deed: The power of service-learning for American schools.* Newton, MA: National Commission on Service-learning. Funded by the W. K. Kellogg Foundation in partnership with the John Glenn Institute for Public Service and Public Policy. Retrieved June 23, 2003 from http://www.learningindeed.org.

National Occupational Information Coordinating Committee. (1986). Career development competencies by area and level. Retrieved from National Career Development Guidelines web page http://icdl.uncg.edu/ncdg.html.

National Service-learning Clearinghouse. http://www.servicelearning.org.

National Youth Leadership Council. http://www.nylc.org.

Pearson, S. S. (2002). *Finding common ground: Service-learning and educational reform: A survey of 28 leading school reform models.* Washington DC.: American Youth Policy Forum. Retrieved June 23, 2003 from http://aypf.org/publications/findingcommonground.pdf.

Piaget, J. (1936). The origins of intelligence in children. In H. E. Gruber, & J. J. Voneche (Eds.), *The essential Piaget* (pp. 215-249). New York: Basic Books.

Piaget, J. (1955). The stages of intellectual development in childhood and adolescence. In H. E. Gruber, & J. J. Voneche (Eds.), *The essential Piaget* (pp. 814-819). New York: Basic Books.

Piaget, J. (1975). Phenocopy in biology and the psychological development of knowledge. In H. E. Gruber, & J. J. Voneche (Eds.), *The essential Piaget* (pp. 803-813). New York: Basic Books.

Popham, W. J. (1993). *Educational evaluation* (3rd ed.). Needham Heights, MA: Allyn and Bacon.

Purdy, A. (1996). How do you assess service-learning? In G. Gulati-Partee & . R. Finger (Eds.), *Critical issues in K-12 service-learning: Case studies and reflections* (pp. 190-195). Raleigh, NC: National Society for Experiential Education.

Putnam, J. W. (1998). *Cooperative learning and strategies for inclusion: Celebrating diversity in the classroom.* Baltimore: Brookes.

Ramaley, J. A. (2002). In *Executive summary : Learning in deed: The power of service-learning for American schools.* Newton, Mass: National Commission on Service-learning. Funded by the W. K Kellogg Foundation in partnership with the John Glenn Institute for Public Service and Public Policy. Retrieved June 23, 2003 from http://www.learningindeed.org.

Richardson, J. (1999). Common goals override individual interests. *Tools for schools.* National Staff Development Council. (http//www.nsdc.org/library/tools/tools12-98rich.html).

RMC Research Corporation. (2003). Citizenship and service-learning in K-12 Schools. Retrieved June 23, 2003, from National Service Learning Clearinghouse Fact Sheet. http://www.servicelearning.org/static/article/121.html.

Root, S. (1998). Data analysis is fun and easy. In Smink J., & Duckenfield, M. (Eds.). *Making the case for service learning action research and evaluation guidebook for teachers* (pp. 31-33). Columbia, SC: South Carolina State Department of Education.

Saltmarsh, J. (1996). Education for critical citizenship: John Dewey's contribution to the pedagogy of community service learning. *Michigan Journal of Community Service Learning,* 3, 13-21.

Santmire, T., Giraud, G., & Grosskopf, K. (1999, April) *Furthering attainment of academic standards through service-learning.* Presented at the National Service-learning Conference, San Jose, CA.

Schine, J. (1997). Looking ahead: Issues and challenges. In K. J. Rehage (Series Ed.) & J. Schine (Vol. Ed.), *Ninety-sixth yearbook of the National Society for the Study of Education, Part 1. Service-learning* (pp. 186-199). Chicago: The University of Chicago Press.

Sharan, S. (Ed.). (1994). *Handbook of cooperative learning methods.* Westport, CT: Greenwood.

Sharan, Y. & Sharan, S. (1992). *Expanding cooperative learning through group investigation.* New York: Teachers College Press.

Sigmon, R. L. (1996). Community partnerships in service-based experiential learning. In G. Gulati-Partee & W. R. Finger (Eds.), *Critical issues in K-12 service-learning: Case studies and reflections.* (pp. 225-230). Raleigh, NC: National Society for Experiential Education.

Slavin, R. E. (1995). *Cooperative learning: Theory, research and practice.* Boston: Allyn and Bacon.

Steinke, P. & Buresh, S. (2002). Cognitive outcomes of service-learning: Reviewing the past and glimpsing the future. *Michigan Journal of Community Service Learning, 8,* 5-14.

Thelen, H. A. (1972). *Education and the human quest.* Chicago: University of Chicago Press.

Thelen, H. A. (1981). *The classroom society.* London: John Wiley & Sons.

Torrance, E. P. (1962). *Guiding creative talent.* Englewood Cliffs, NJ: Prentice Hall.

Vygotsky, L. S. (1987a). The development of scientific concepts in childhood. In R. W. Rieber & A. S. Carton (Eds.), *The collected works of L. S. Vygotsky: Volume 1: Problems of general psychology* (pp. 167-241). New York: Plenum Press.

Vygotsky, L. S. (1987b). The problem of speech and thinking in Piaget's theory. In R. W. Rieber & A. S. Carton (Eds.), *The collected works of L. S. Vygotsky: Volume 1: Problems of general psychology* (pp. 53-91). New York: Plenum Press.

Wells, A. (1996). The grand reflection: How to bring closure to an open-ended service-learning course. In G. Gulati-Partee & W. R. Finger (Eds.), *Critical issues in K-12 service-learning: Case studies and reflections* (pp. 132-136). Raleigh, NC: National Society for Experiential Education.

Whetten, D. A., & Cameron, K. S. (2002). *Developing management skills* (5th ed.). Upper Saddle River, NJ: Prentice Hall.

Whitfield, T. S. (1999). Connecting service- and classroom-based learning: The use of problem-based learning. *Michigan Journal of Community Service Learning, 6,* 106-111.

Wolfson, L., & Willinsky, J. (1998). What service-learning can learn from situated learning. *Michigan Journal of Community Service Learning, 5,* 22-31.

Author Index

Adams, L., 254, 263
Anderson, L.W., 77, 158, 175, 176, 177, 179, 263
Armstrong, T., 102, 195, 196, 263
Ausubel, D. P., 206, 263
Bailis, L. N., 8, 266
Balderrama, M. V., 40, 264
Bean, C., 210, 263
Billig, S. H., 7, 10, 18, 77, 80, 263
Bloom, B. S., 77, 186, 263, 265
Bourke, S.F., 158, 175, 176, 177, 179, 263
Bringle, R. G., 51, 52, 263
Bruner, J. S. 5, 6, 7, 13, 111, 263
Buresh, S., 79, 268
Calhoun, C., 12, 49, 205, 206, 265
Cameron, K.S., 39, 45, 256, 258, 268
Capote, T., 198, 264
Cohen, E. G., 40, 264
Collay, M., 111, 265
Cone, D., 13, 264
Cossey, R., 40, 264
Cumbo, K. B., 72, 159, 264
Dewey, J., 10, 11, 203, 264
Drenk, D., 210, 263
Driscoll, A., 75, 77, 80, 83, 84, 85, 86, 116, 265
England, A., 193, 264
Eyler, J. S., 75, 76, 77, 107, 264
Ferrari, J. R., 77, 78, 124, 171, 264
Fertman, C. I., 240, 264
Frechtling, J., 185, 264
Freeman, D., 126, 265
Gagnon, G.W., 111, 265
Gardner, H., 41, 102, 103, 153, 265
Gelmon, S.B., 75, 77, 80, 83, 84, 85, 86, 116, 265
Gent, P. J., 174, 265
Giles, D.E., Jr., 77, 107, 108, 264
Gilligan, C., 77, 265
Giraud, G., 8, 267

Gordon, T., 254, 263
Gray, C.J., 77, 264
Grosskopf, K., 8, 267
Guerecka, L. E., 174, 265
Halpin, G., 77, 79, 266
Halpin, W. G., 77, 79, 266
Harris, S., 13, 264
Harvey, W., 203, 265
Hatcher, J. A., 51, 52, 263
Holland, B.A., 75, 77, 80, 83, 84, 85, 86, 116, 265
Irizarry, J., 70, 265
Johnson, B., 169, 265
Johnson, D. W., 75, 77, 80, 83, 84, 85, 86, 116, 265
Johnson, R. T., 75, 77, 80, 83, 84, 85, 86, 116, 265
Joyce, B., 12, 49, 205, 206, 265
Kerrigan, S., 75, 77, 80, 83, 84, 85, 86, 116, 265
Kolb, D. A., 10, 11, 111, 265
Krathwhol, D. R., 77, 186, 263, 265
Lee, F. D., 210, 263
Lenz, E., 254, 263
Lewin, K., 10, 11, 266
Liddel, D. L., 77, 79, 266
Lotan, R. A., 40, 264
Masia, B. B., 186, 265
Melchoir, A., 8, 266
Mezirow, J., 205, 266
Mitchell, J., 79, 266
Morgan, W., 8, 266
Morton, K., 66, 266
Pearson, S. S., 9, 10, 266
Piaget, J., 5, 6, 7, 10, 111, 266, 267
Popham, W. J., 120. 132, 145, 158, 161, 182, 183, 189, 267
Purdy, A., 169, 267
Putnam, J. W., 48, 267
Ramaley, J.A., 260. 267
Richardson, J., 256. 267

Root, S., 185, 267
Saltmarsh, J., 107, 203, 267
Santmire, T., 8, 267
Schine, J., 2, 267
Schmiede, A., 107, 108, 264
Sharan, S., 11, 12, 58, 202, 267, 268
Sharan, Y., 11, 12, 268
Sharp, L., 185, 264
Sigmon, R. L., 65, 268
Slavin, R. E.,, 48, 268
Smith, K. A., 75, 77, 80, 83, 84, 85, 86, 116, 265
Spence, J., 193, 264
Spring, A., 75, 77, 80, 83, 84, 85, 86, 116, 265
Steinke, P., 79, 268

Stenson, C., 77, 264
Swanson, P. E., 40, 264
Thelen, H. A., 11, 268
Torrance, E. P., 48. 268
Vadeboncoeur, J. A., 72. 159. 264
Vygotsky, L. S., 5, 6, 7, 13, 111, 268
Weil, M., 12, 49, 205, 206, 265,
Wells, A., 234, 268
Whetten, D. A., 39, 45, 256, 258, 268
Whitcomb, J. A., 40, 264
Whitfield, T. S., 13, 18, 268
Willinsky, J., 13, 268
Wolfson, L., 13, 268
Worrall, L., 77, 78, 171, 264

Subject Index

Academic study and service, 61-64
   examples, 33, 63
   linking, 32, 61
   via curriculum development, 62-64
Anecdotal observations, 82, 173
   critical features, 83
Assessment, *see* Student outcomes measurement
Celebration, 133, 233
   dimensions of, 233
Cognitive Structures, 5, 6
   for service, 47
Collaborative Service-Learning Model, 12
   experiential learning sources of, 10
      Kolb's Experiential Learning Model, 11
   social-process learning sources of, 11
      Thelen's Group Investigation Model, 11
   use, 13
Community analysis, 142-145
   fact sheets, 143
   mapping, 143
   needs assessment, 149-151
   service-needs exploration, 14
   success story use, 146-148
   umbrella agency contacts, 148
Community partner motivation, 151-154
   class directories, 154
   class introductions, 152
   resource group descriptions, 153
   strategy selection, 154
Compendium of Assessment and Research Tools (CART), 219
Complex instruction, 40, 45
Comprehensive School Reform, 9
Conceptualizing Activities, 110, 207-211
   characteristics, 110, 207
   types, 111, 208-211
   use of, 112-113, 207
Conflict resolution, 252-259
   example, 257
   mediators, 258
   problem solving, 256-258
   resources, 252
   scanning for 253-256
Constituent outcomes measurement, 94
   examples, 94-96
Constructivist learning, 5, 110
Cooperative Learning, 105
   in complex instruction, 41
   elements of, 105
   in focusing activities, 197
      example, 198
   research, 105
   student problem solving and, 42
   student readiness and, 48
   student roles, 197
   team conflict resolution and, 253
   team member roles, 199-203
      example, 200-201
   team process evaluation and, 124, 221
Criterion-referenced tests, 82, 159-170
   State standards tests, 159-161
   Teacher-developed tests, 82, 161-170
      paper-pencil, 161-166
      performance, 166-169
      problem-solving, 169, 170

Culminating activities, 133, 234
  benefits of, 135
  example, 134
  steps for developing and
    implementing, 135
  types of, 231-236
Dissemination plans, 138-9
  example, 134
Dissemination strategies, 133, 236
  benefits of, 136
  example, 134
  steps for developing and
    implementing 136-140
  types of, 237-240
Evaluation plans, 120
  example, 125-128
  implementing, 129
  project impact component, 123
  project team self-evaluation
    component, 124
  resources for creating
    instruments, 223
  student outcomes component,
    121
Experience analysis essays, 82,
186-189
  judging, 188
  prompt templates, 187
Focus groups, 82, 182-186
  analyzing results, 185
  implementing, 184
  planning, 182
  setting up, 183
Focusing activities, 100, 194-202
  and cooperative learning, 105,
    197
  design of, 101
  examples, 106, 198
  material for, 194
  and multiple intelligences, 102-
    105, 195

Forms of Service, 64-67
  advocacy, 66
  direct, 65
  examples, 67
  indirect. 65
Human resources, 244-245
  community contacts, 249
  higher education faculty, 249
  parents, 247
  resource staff, 248
  school administrators, 246
  school workers, 247
  teachers, 245
Inductive thinking, 227, 229
  with evaluation information,
    129, 227
  expressing results of, 130-132,
    231-233
  practicing, 230
  in reflection activities, 206
  use with partners, 130
Instructional management skills,
30, 38-46
  analytical and creative
    problem solving, 42
  indicators and profiling, 45
  motivating others, 39
  supportive communication, 41
  team building, 40
  time-management skills, 43
Instructional planning, 98, 192
  as reflective-learning
    sequences, 99
  examples, 99, 193, 200-203
  goals and objectives for, 98, 192
  process, 114, 211
Internet resources, 250-252
  addresses, 251
  search phrases, 251
  steps for using, 250

Interviews, 82, 179-182
   analyzing results, 182
   blueprints, 179
   directions, 180
   pilot testing, 182
   reviewing 181
Motivations for service, 1
Multiple Intelligences, 102
   component intelligences, 196
   in culminating activities, 234-236
   defined, 102
   in dissemination strategies, 236-240
   in focusing activities 102-105, 195
   helping project teams use, 195
   in resource group description, 153
National Service-Learning Clearinghouse, 29, 219
Needs and issues information gathering, 58
   awareness support networks, 61
   example, 148
   strategies, 61, 145-151
   planning support networks, 60
   resource support networks, 59
No Child Left Behind Act of 2002, 9
Outcomes measurement coordinator, 84
Participants in student outcomes planning, 72-75
   clients to be served, 72
   community members, 73
   formally inviting, 74
   parents, 73
   school administrators, 73
Problem-solving for conflict resolution, 256-258
   example, 257
   steps in, 256

Project designs, 18-29
   cross-disciplinary, 28-30
   in-class approach, 18-21
   one-day event, 21-23
   prototype project, 23-25
   recurring curriculum component, 25-27
   selection variables, 30-34
   summary of, 34-36
Project commitment, 58
   example, 68-70
   preparing for, 53
   process, 67
   summary of strategies, 155
Project teams, 14
   composition, 72, 58
   sharing responsibilities,
      evaluation, 216-218
      instruction, 115-117, 212
      outcomes measurement, 85, 96, 122
Rating scales, 82, 171-173
   constructing, , 172
   format, 171
   using existing, 172
Reflection activities, 107, 203-207
   characteristics, 107-109
   interrogative, 109, 205
   emotion-based, 109, 205
   critical-thinking, 110, 206
   metaphoric, 110, 206
   symbolic, 110, 207
   use of, 204
Reflective learning experiences, 99-114
   components of, 100
   content and process of, 211
   integrating with journals, 212
Self-report outcomes measurement, 83, 174
   strategies, 175-189

Service-learning benefits, 4
  academic achievement, , 7
  citizenship education, 8
  impact research, 7, 8,
  intellectual development, 5-7
  school reform, 9
Service-learning definition, 4
  Compact for Learning and
Citizenship, 2-3
  National and Community
Service Trust Act, 2
  National Commission on
Service-Learning, 3
Service-learning readiness factors, 38-51
State standards tests, 82, 159-161
  using results of, 160
Student outcomes measurement, 158
  strategies, 158-190
    content validity, 158, 161,166,172,178,180
Student outcomes planning, 75
  and support networks, 89
  assigning responsibilities, 84-88
  as backward mapping, 75
  examples, 89-93
    outcome expectation indicators, 78-81
  outcome expectations, 76-78
  multi-constituency approach, 75
  resources for, 88
  selecting measurement strategies, 82-83, 94
    time and value considerations, 84
    steps, 88-89
Student service-learning competencies, 46
  ability to work with authority figures, 49
  ability to work with people from diverse cultures, 50
  conceptual readiness, 47
  cooperative-learning skills, 48
  information-gathering skills, 48
  self-management skills, 47
  profiling, 50, 51
Support networks, 51-53
  types, 52, 59
Surveys, 82, 175-179
  blueprints, 176
  directions, 177
  items, 176
  pilot testing, 178
  preparing, 179
  reviewing, 178
Zone of proximal development, 6